THE GREAT SPANISH FILMS: 1950-1990

by

Ronald Schwartz

The Scarecrow Press, Inc.
Metuchen, N.J., & London
1991

All stills and photographs are courtesy of the Ministry of Culture and the Filmoteca Nacional (Madrid) and, where noted, courtesy of the Museum of Modern Art (New York).

British Library Cataloguing-in-Publication data available

Library of Congress Cataloging-in-Publication Data

Schwartz, Ronald, 1937–
The great Spanish films, 1950–1990 / by Ronald Schwartz.
p. cm.
Includes bibliographical references and index.
ISBN 0-8108-2488-4 (alk. paper)
1. Motion pictures—Spain. I. Title.
PN1993.5.S7S29 1991
791.43′0946′09045—dc20 91-38947

Manufactured in the United States of America

Printed on acid-free paper

For my wonderful son,

Jonathan Fletcher

CONTENTS

ACKNOWLEDGMENTS

The writing of another film book on Spain involved viewing of hundreds of Spanish films on both sides of the Atlantic. For this, I am especially grateful once again to the following institutions and individuals here and abroad:

In New York City: (1) The Museum of Modern Art Film & Library Center, especially Charles Silver and Ron Magliozzi; (2) the third-floor staff of librarians of the Lincoln Center Library for the Performing Arts and (3) The American Film Institute in Washington, D.C.

In Madrid: (1) The Ministry of Culture under the leadership of Fernando Menendez-Leite and Carmelo Romero who helped me to secure pressbooks and the majority of stills that appear in this book with their permission; (2) Peter Besas, the *Variety* critic, who became my best personal critic and friend over the past several years in the pursuit of Spanish cinema; (3) Jose Luis Borau, film director *extraordinaire,* who gave me my first lesson in cutting a film and introduced me to *La movida;* (4) Fernando Colomo, who let me wander on to his latest set, introducing me to filmmaking at midnight in a mental ward in Madrid with Antonio Banderas and Chus Lampreave; (5) Placido Saenz Plaza and Ramon, who worked with me in the *sotano* (basement) of the Ministry, watching old films on the movieola and providing press books and stills, and (6) Dolores Devesa, Chief Librarian of the Filmoteca Nacional, who provided me with much critical material from periodicals while the Filmoteca was undergoing renovation and repairs under the leadership of critic Miguel Marias.

I am also indebted once again to the PSC-CUNY Research Foundation for travel grants which made this "sequel" to *Spanish Film Directors (1950–1985): 21 Profiles* a reality. At City University of New York (Kingsborough), I am once again appreciative of my chairperson, Dr. Julio Hernandez-Miyares, and all the staff of the Department of Foreign Languages, Professors Alba, Fine, Gersh, Kibbee, Miller, Soto (retired) and Mr. Luis Tirado, College Laboratory Technician, who have continued their dialogues with me about the direction of Spanish cinema and who have encouraged me to teach a survey course in Spanish film as well as a new monograph course dedicated exclusively to the films of Luis Buñuel.

Many resource people should also be mentioned as this book

goes to press: Ernest Burns of the now defunct but sorely needed film bookstore Cinemabilia, who provided encouragement and stills; Mark, Kevin, Matthew and Lucas at the Applause Cinema Bookstore at Lincoln Center, who continue to send materials and keep me informed about the latest events in international cinema, and Jack Gaudioso at Kingsborough Community College of City University of New York, my video resource person who has added many dimensions to my thoughts about Spanish cinema through his appreciation of and dedication to American films. Also, much appreciation is given to Professors Klune, Tripicchio, Schneider, Houser, Orr, and Kharkanis at Kingsborough's Library, and Michael Rosson and Susan Stonehill and her aides in the Media Centre.

Finally, I must thank my wonderful wife, Amelia Fletcher, once again for enduring yet another period of research, writing and editing of another volume of movie criticism about the country we both love, Spain. Also my son, Jonathan Fletcher, having been to Santiago de Compostela and Madrid, can now visualize some of the difficulties and pleasures of doing research in a foreign country. My blessings and love to you both for having faith in the completion of this project.

Imperio Argentino and Miguel Ligero in *Morena clara*. Courtesy of The Museum of Modern Art/Film Stills Archive.

PREFACE

The idea for this book began in the early eighties as a sequel to my last volume, *Spanish Film Directors (1950–1985): 21 Profiles.* Various publishers brought out tomes in their "great films series," but not a single volume appeared about the great Spanish films. Spanish cinema is perhaps one of the national cinemas most neglected by critics over the past fifty years. Recently, a spate of histories of Spanish cinema has appeared in English, notably Peter Besas' *Behind the Spanish Lens,* Virginia Higginbotham's *Spanish Cinema after Franco* and John Hopewell's *Out of the Past,* all published in the mid-eighties. Fernando Menendez-Leite's *Historia del cine espanol en cien peliculas* in Spanish and Emmanuel Larraz' *Le cinéma espagnol des origines à nos jours* in French complete the bibliographical prerequisites for published histories of modern Spanish cinema to date. All of these critics trace the history of Spanish film from the silent days to the present. However, if one delves carefully into their criticism, all critics would agree that the truly significant films which we designate as "modern" were produced in 1950 and thereafter: 1950 is the watershed year for Spanish cinema. That is the reason I have divided this volume into four sections, beginning with the fifties and ending with the late eighties.

Most Spanish films pre-1950 belonged to the stagnating "white telephone" school of the 1930s and 1940s, which essentially copied their Hollywood models. It was in the 1950s that the real, authentic Spanish cinema was born, with directors like Juan Bardem and Luis Garcia Berlanga. Although they used somewhat traditional filmmaking methods, they examined essentially Spanish themes, comically and dramatically, utilizing a neo-realist style borrowed from the late forties' Italian cinema, the style of Rossellini, Visconti and De Sica. Realism became the modus operandi for most new directors of the era. It is in this epoch that Spanish cinema began to flourish.

This volume then, is a personal selection of significant Spanish films, beginning with the fifties and ending with the late eighties. It seeks to present the films in chronological order. My hope is that the reader will consider these films as a reflection of Spanish society and elicit the important thematic concerns of the numerous directors presented in this book. Some of these films are not masterpieces; others may even be considered mediocre. But all reflect in some way the mentality of Spanish society during the Franco era. Some of the selections are masterpieces and have been shown internationally. Others have never been seen beyond the Iberian peninsula. This volume also contains a treasure trove of stills and art work, all reproduced with the permission of Spain's Ministry of Culture under the direction of Fernandez Menendez-Leite.

After perusal of these pages, readers still may note the absence of some films and wonder at the inclusion of others. It is impossible to write a complete tome on forty years of Spanish cinema. What I have sought to do is document, through a thorough examination of styles and genres, the most representative films of the periods. Although there may be fewer films under examination in certain sections of this work, 1975 is also considered a seminal year for Spanish cinema, the year of the *apertura* and the death of Spain's dictator, General Francisco Franco. There was literally an "explosion" on the Spanish screens, formerly taboo subjects, diverse directorial styles, elitist, camp, documentary and fantasy features being presented in Spanish cinemas for the first time.

This book then, should be regarded as a companion to my earlier work on Spanish film directors. As you read through four decades of my personal selection of Spanish films, you may familiarize yourself with representative films of the fifties, sixties, seventies and eighties, through a film-by-film chronological analysis. You will be able to grasp the main thematic concerns of the directors, their films, in some cases, being reflections of their society. Rather than write another "history" of Spanish cinema, I shall let the films and the film stills speak for themselves—ranging from the neo-realistic school of the fifties to the crassly commercial sexual comedies of the late eighties and early nineties. I hope the reader will gain insights into the more artistic films that truly reflect the glorious heritage of Spain and the Spanish people.

Ronald Schwartz
Professor of Romance Languages
City University of New York

INTRODUCTION

The Great Spanish Films (1950–1990) is the first book in English to explore chronologically and cinematically the emergence of a heretofore internationally unrecognized national cinema. Since its beginnings, modern Spanish cinema was under strict censorship by the church and the state, during and after the Spanish Civil War (1936–1939), because it had to conform to the ideological demands of the Nationalist regime. In 1950 the New Spanish Cinema was born as a protest over General Francisco Franco's policies. The imitative Hollywood "white telephone" school of Spanish cinema was over. A new series of directors and films began to move away from the conformist line and to offer a bold new look at Spain through its own brand of Spanish realism.

In the early 1950s, Bardem, Berlanga, Buñuel and Nieves-Conde appeared, expressing a liberal image of Spain to the world in such films as *Muerte de un ciclista* (*Death of a Cyclist*), *Bienvenido Senor Marshall* (*Welcome Mr. Marshall*), *Viridiana,* and *Surcos* (*Furrows*). The emergence of a new Spanish cinema and new directors continued into the sixties and seventies with Saura and *Los golfos* (*The Hooligans*), Patino and *Nueve cartas a Berta* (*Nine Letters to Berta*) and Picazo and *La tia Tula* (*Aunt Tula*). Other directors of the seventies, such as Borau with *Furtivos* (*Poachers*), Chavarri and *El desencanto* (*The Disenchanted Ones*), Erice and *El espiritu de la colmena* (*The Spirit of the Beehive*), Gutierrez-Aragon and *Camada negra* (*Black Brood*) and Olea and *Tormento* (*Torment*), also contributed to the new movement.

When Franco died in 1975, censorship was abolished and with this development was born the new and exciting Spanish cinema of the mid-seventies and early eighties. Formerly taboo subjects—sexuality, the church, the army, the Civil War, drugs, AIDS—were openly explored. The Spanish cinema was no longer escapist and entertaining but, at long last, realistically mirrored the society it depicted in its films. New directors such as Aranda in *Cambio de sexo* (*Sex Change*), Camino in *Las largas vaccaciones del '36* (*The Long Vacation of 1936*), Franco in *Pascual Duarte* and Garci in *Asignatura pendiente* (*Unfinished Assignment*) emerged during the "boom" of the late seventies.

After Franco's death there was a reawakening. Censorship was held to a maximum of tolerance and films of substantial interest were produced. Spanish cinema began to express itself within its newly-found freedom in the late seventies and early eighties. Almodovar in *Que he hecho para merecer esto?* (*What Have I Done to Deserve This?*), Armendariz in *Tasio,* Colomo in *La linea del cielo* (*Skyline*), Garcia-Sanchez in *La corte de Faraon* (*The Court of the Pharaoh*), Martinez-Lazaro in *Las palabras de Max* (*Max's Words*), Minon & Trujillo in *Kargus,* Salgot in *Mater amatisima* (*Beloved Mother*), Trueba in *Opera prima* (*First Work*), Uribe in *La muerte de Mikel* (*The Death of Mikel*) and Zulueta in *Arrebato* (*Rapture*) all represent the "new wave" of Spanish cinema of the early eighties, while other directors of the fifties and sixties such as Berlanga and Bardem still make commercial films that continue to earn huge grosses at the Spanish box office.

Spanish filmmakers and filmmaking have successfully gone through a period of recovery since the mid-seventies and are now giving preference to themes that are more intimate and personal. Aranda in *Fanny Pelopaja* (*Towhaired Fanny*), Berlanga in *La vaquilla* (*The Little Calf*), Borau in *Rio abajo* (*On the Line*), Camus in *Los santos inocentes* (*The Holy Innocents*), Gutierrez-Aragon in *Demonios en el jardin* (*Demons in the Garden*), Patino in *Los paraisos perdidos* (*Lost Paradise*) and Saura in *El amor brujo* (*Bewitched Love*) are major directors whose films represent a variety of themes and styles that continue to set the standards in contemporary Spanish filmmaking.

In addition to films that reflect the problems of Spanish society,

Martxelo Rubio, Maribel Verdu, and Jon San Sebastian in *27 horas.*

the fantasy film has finally emerged in Spain. Colomo's *El caballero del dragon* (*The Knight of the Dragon*) has an abundance of special effects that respond to the Spaniard's need for pure entertainment. Spanish filmmakers now have total freedom of expression and some financial independence. Spanish Film Festivals, under the direction of Fernando Menendez-Leite and the newly-appointed Minister of Culture, novelist Jorge Semprun, travel around the world in an effort to display the great variety, creativity and virtuosity within the world of Spanish cinema.

American audiences have been indeed fortunate, since there have been no less than *four* Spanish Film Festivals in New York City since 1983. The American Film Institute recently sponsored a truly comprehensive retrospective of nearly one hundred Spanish films entitled *Images in the Shadows: A History of Spanish Cinema from the Silents to the Eighties,* which began its two-month showing in Washington, D.C. and ended its run at New York's Museum of Modern Art in early 1989.

The late eighties were a truly prolific period for Spanish cinema. Not only was the most expensive film ever produced in Spain at this time, Carlos Saura's two-and-one-half-hour historical epic, *El Dorado,* but the Ministry of Culture experienced a significant change in leadership with the appointment of Jorge Semprun. The almost totally government-financed film industry is still feeling the repercussions of this change in leadership. It was said that Saura's film was Spain's *Heaven's Gate,* and as the Spanish film industry moves into the nineties, financing from governmental and other sources is its biggest problem.

The most exciting director of the moment is Pedro Almodovar, whose comedy, *Women on the Edge of a Nervous Breakdown,* has been nominated for the Foreign Film Academy Award for 1989. Almodovar is Spain's most commercially "hot" director and has a "gay" sensibility. His past films, *Matador* and *La ley del deseo* (*Law of Desire*) among others, have been Spain's best commercial hits of the late eighties.

Other filmmakers continue their interest in expanding the horizons of Spanish cinema. Gonzalo Suarez and Ricardo Franco have made their last films in English! *Remando al viento* (*Rowing with the Wind*) treated the lives and loves of Byron and Shelley (the film was made in England and Norway) while *Berlin Blues* (1988) was shot on location in Berlin with American actress-singer Teresa Migenes. Like Saura's, both films were shot on fairly high budgets, and gave an "international" dimension to Spanish cinema. Apart from the Almodovar international success story, nationally the most successful commercial films were *El Lute: Camina o revienta* (*Run for Your Life*) and its sequel, *Manana sere libre* (*Tomorrow I'll Be Free*), based upon the exploits of a real-life criminal, Elueterio Sanchez.

The Spanish crime film abounds with Gutierrez-Aragon's *Malaventura* (*Misadventure*), Rotateta's *El placer de matar* (*The Pleasure of Killing*) and Moleon's color-noirish *Baton Rouge.* The Spanish comedy of "black humor" continues in its heyday with Arminan's

Mi general (*My General*), Mercero's *Esperame en el cielo* (*Wait for Me in Heaven*) and Berlanga's visceral and sarcastic attack called *Moros y cristianos* (*Moors and Christians*).

Films of farce and fantasy continue to be made, such as Cuerda's *El bosque animado* (*The Animated Forest*), a recent box-office champion of the late eighties. Directors such as Camus and Garcia-Sanchez continue to film the great Spanish literary classics such as Lorca's play, *La casa de Bernarda Alba* (*The House of Bernarda Alba*), and Valle-Inclan's novel, *Divinas palabras* (*Divine Words*). Garci, winner of the Foreign Film Academy Oscar for *Volver a empezar* (*To Begin Again*) in 1983, has just completed his "asignatura" series of films with *Asignatura aprobada* (*Assignment Completed*), which is Spain's first feature about AIDS, the current sexual revolution and its effect upon a family in Gijon.

Experimental cinema abundance includes Reguiero's strange film, *Diario de invierno* (*Winter Diary*), and the Catalan film industry contributes features in its own language, historical works such as Gerardo Gomezano's *El vent de l'illa* (*The Island Wind*).

As this book goes to press in the early nineties, it is clear that modern Spanish cinema is certainly not succumbing to the trap of violent nationalism or its past abulic state, but seeks international exposure in its maturity. My selection of the best films Spanish cinema has to offer will, I hope, document this progressive trajectory.

CHRONOLOGY

Part One: 1896–1949

[The following chronology outlines a series of major events and films in the evolution of Spanish cinema from 1896 to the present and should serve only as a reference guide to the reader. Film title is listed first, then the director's name.]

Vida en sombras, starring a very youthful Fernando Fernan Gomez. Courtesy of The Museum of Modern Art/Film Stills Archive.

1896

First film shown in Madrid, May 15 at the San Isidro Festival.

First Spanish film made by Eduardo Jimeno, entitled *Salida de la misa de doce en la iglesia del Pilar de Zaragoza* (*Leaving High Mass at the Pilar of Zaragoza Cathedral*).

1897

Rina en un cafe (*Cafe Brawl*), first Catalan film by Fructuoso Gelabert.

1905

El hotel electrico (*The Electric Hotel*), silent film by Segundo de Chomon.

1907

El ciego de la aldea (*Blind Man of the Village*) by Jose Maria Codina.

Theater adaptations appear on film for the first time, such as Fructuoso Gelabert's *Terra baixa* (*Lowland*), based on the work of Angel Guimera.

1908

The silent version of Zorilla's *Don Juan Tenorio* by Ricardo Banos appears, another play on film.

A version of Cervantes' novel *Don Quixote* is filmed by Narciso Cuyas.

1915

Debut of the "serials": *Los misterios de Barcelona* (*The Mysteries of Barcelona*) in 8 episodes by Alberto Marro.

La gitanilla (*The Little Gypsy*) of Cervantes and *El Alcalde de Zalamea* (*The Mayor of Zalamea*) of Calderon, both Golden Age plays, are adapted for the silent screen by Adria Gual.

1916

The first silent Spanish version of *Sangre y arena* (*Blood and Sand*) by the novelist Vicente Blasco Ibañez is filmed.

1917

The famous social drama, *Juan Jose* by Ricardo Banos, is filmed.

1918

Jacinto de Benavente adapts his own social drama, *Los intereses creados* (*Vested Interests*), for the silent screen.

1921

The zarzuela, or Spanish operetta, is first adapted for the silent screen by Jose Buchs with his presentation of *La verbena de la paloma* (*Paloma Fair*).

1923

The famous drama, *La Dolores* by Feliu y Codina, is adapted for the screen by Maximiliano Thous.

1925

The director Florian Rey makes his silent debut, adapting two literary works for the screen: *La revoltosa* (*The Mischievous Girl*) and the picaresque novel, *Lazarillo de Tormes*.

1926

The director Benito Perojo makes his debut, adapting *Boy*, the novel by Father Coloma.

Eusebio Fernandez Ardavin films *La Bejarana* (*The Woman from Bejar*). Francisco Gomez Hidalgo films *La malcasada* (*The Unhappy Bride*).

1927

Benito Perojo achieves fame with his silent film, *El negro que tenia el alma blanca* (*The Black Who Had a White Soul*).

Jose Buchs films *El dos de mayo* (*The Second of May*), about the Spanish Revolution.

1928

The most scandalous silent feature and first Surrealist film, by Luis Bunuel, Salvador Dali and Man Ray, is shown in Paris: *Un chien andalou* (*El perro andaluz*) (*The Andalusian Dog*).

Florian Rey films *La hermana de San Sulpicio* (*Sister Saint Sulpicio*) and introduces the great Spanish musical comedy star, Imperio Argentina.

1929

The end of the silent film era in Spain. American films with Spanish soundtracks are produced in the United States and in France at Joinville.

Florian Rey directs his last silent, *La aldea maldita* (*The Cursed Village*), the most famous silent film of the era. Sound was added the following year.

1930

El misterio de la Puerta de Sol (*The Puerta del Sol Mystery*) by Francisco Elias is the first sound film made in the Iberian peninsula.

1931

Jose Buchs films *Prim,* the biography of a liberal general, a few years before the outbreak of the Spanish Civil War.

1932

Pax by Francisco Elias.

Las Hurdes, a famous documentary by Luis Buñuel.

1933

Susana tiene un secreto (*Susan Has a Secret*) by Benito Perojo.

Sierra de Ronda by Florian Rey.

Boliche by Francisco Elias.

La traviesa molinera (*The Mischievous Miller Girl*) by Harry d'Abbadie d'Arrast.

1934

El negro que tenia el alma blanca, sound version by Benito Perojo.

Sor Angelica (*Sister Angelica*) by Francisco Gargallo.

La hermana San Sulpicio, sound version by Florian Rey.

Patricio miro una estrella (*Patricio Looked at a Star*) by J. L. Saenz de Heredia, his debut film.

Una de miedo (*One about Fear*) and *Una de fieras* (*One about Wild Beasts*), and *Y ahora, una de ladrones* (*And Now, One about Crooks*), all satires by Eduardo Garcia Maroto.

1935

El malvado Carabel (*The Wicked Carabel*) by Edgar Neville.

Nobleza baturra (*Nobility of Brute Action*) by Florian Rey.

La verbena de la paloma (*Paloma Fair*), sound version by Benito Perojo.

1936

Morena clara (*Clara the Brunette*) by Florian Rey, the biggest box-office musical of the thirties, with Imperio Argentina.

La senorita de Trevelez (*The Young Lady from Trevelez*) by Edgar Neville.

Note: During the period of the Civil War, from 1936 to 1939, several documentaries (short features) were produced, as well as feature films of "social" significance. They are:

1936–1937

Aurora de esperanza (*Dawn of Hope*) by Anthony Sau.

Nosotros somos asi (*We're Like That*) by Valentin R. Gonzalez.

Asi venceremos (*We Shall Overcome*) by Fernando Roldan.

Barrios bajos (*Lower-class Districts*) by Pedro Puche.

Nuestro culpable (*Our Culprit*) by Fernando Mignoni.

1938

Paquete, el fotografo publico numero uno (*Paquete, the Number One Public Photographer*) by Ignacio Farres Iquino, a documentary.

Other Spanish films produced this year in Berlin were:

Carmen de la Triana by Florian Rey.

El Barbero de Sevilla, *Mariquilla Terremoto* and *Suspiros de Espana* (*Sighs from Spain*), all by Benito Perojo.

1939

Two foreign documentaries were shot in Spain detailing the action of the Civil War: they were Joris Ivens' *Tierra de Espana* (*The Spanish Earth*), begun in 1937, and Andre Malraux' *Sierra de Teruel*, alternately titled *L'espoir* (*Hope*), both released this year.

La cancion de Aixa (*Aixa's Song*) by Florian Rey.

Frente de madrid (*Frontline: Madrid*) by Edgar Neville

1940

Filming begins again in Franco's Spain and recognized artists return from abroad. The best films of the decade are the following:

Marianela (based upon the Perez Galdos novel) by Benito Perojo.

La Dolores by Florian Rey.

1941

Raza (*Race*) by Saenz de Heredia, scripted by General Franco under the pseudonym Jaime de Andrade.

Harka by Carlos Arevalo.

Pepe Conde by Jose Lopez Rubio.

1942

A mi la legion! (*The Legion for Me!*) by Juan de Orduna.

Malavoca (*Hollyhock*) by Luis Marquina.

Huella de luz (*A Sign of Light*) by Rafael Gil.

Boda en el infierno (*Wedding in Hell*) by Antonio Roman.

1943

Intriga (*Intrigue*) by Antonio Roman.

El escandalo (*The Scandal*) by Jose Luis Saenz de Heredia.

Eloisa esta debajo de un almendro (*Eloise Is Underneath an Almond Tree*) by W. Fernandez Flores.

1944

Ella, el y sus milliones (*Hers, His and the Millions*) by Juan de Orduna.

El clavo (*The Nail*) by Rafael Gil.

La torre de los siete jorobados (*The Tower of the Seven Hunchbacks*) by Edgar Neville.

Lola Montes by Antonio Roman.

1945

La vida en un hilo (*Life by a Thread*) by Edgar Neville.

Los ultimos de Filipinas (*The Last from the Philippines*) by Antonio Roman.

El destino se disculpa (*Destiny Says It's Sorry*) by Jose Luis Saenz de Heredia.

1946

Abel Sanchez (based upon Miguel de Unamuno's novel) by Carlos Serrano de Osma.

El crimen de la calle de Bordadores (*Crime on Bordadores Street*) by Edgar Neville.

Embrujo (*Bewitched*) by Carlos Serrano de Osma.

1947

La fe (*Faith*) by Rafael Gil.

Don Quijote de la Mancha by Rafael Gil.

Mariona Rebull by Jose Luis Saenz de Heredia.

1948

Locura de amor (*Love Crazy*) by Juan de Orduna.

Vida en sombras (*Life in the Shadows*) by L. Llobet Gracia.

La duquesa de Benameji (*Duchess Benameji*) by Luis Lucia.

La calle sin sol (*Sunless Street*) by Rafael Gil.

Brindis a Manolete (*Toast to Manolete*) by Florian Rey.

1949

El santuario no se rinde (*The Sanctuary Refuses to Surrender*) by Arturo Ruiz Castillo.

Un hombre va por el camino (*A Man Goes Down the Street*) by Manuel Mur-Oti.

Part Two: 1950–1959

1950

Balarrasa (*Hot Head*) by Jose Antonio Nieves Conde.

Apartado de correos 1001 (*P.O. Box 1001*) by Julio Salvador.

Debla, la virgen gitana (*Debla, the Gypsy Virgin*) by Ramon Torrado.

Don Juan by Saenz de Heredia.

Agustina de Aragon by Juan de Orduna.

1951

The neo-realistic style of filming in Spanish cinema begins.

Surcos (*Furrows*) by Jose Antonio Nieves-Conde.

Esa pareja feliz (*That Happy Couple*) by Luis Garcia Berlanga.

La senora de Fatima (*The Lady of Fatima*) by Rafael Gil.

Alba de America (*Dawn of America*) by Juan de Orduna.

Dia tras dia (*Day After Day*) by Antonio del Amo.

1952

Bienvenido Senor Marshall (*Welcome Mr. Marshall*) by Luis Garcia Berlanga.

Ronda espanola (*Spanish "Ronda"*) by Ladislao Vadja.

Cerca de la ciudad (*Near the City*) by Luis Lucia.

El judas (*Judas*) by Farres Iquino.

1953

Novio a la vista (*Boyfriend in Sight*) by Luis Garcia Berlanga.

La guerra de Dios (*God's War*) by Rafael Gil.

1954

Sierra maldita (*Cursed Land*) by Antonio del Amo.

El beso de Judas (*Judas' Kiss*) by Rafael Gil.

La patrulla (*The Patrol*) by Pedro Lazaga.

Comicos (*Comics*) by Juan Antonio Bardem.

Felices Pascuas (*Happy Easter*) by Juan Antonio Bardem.

1955

Marcelino pan y vino (*Marcelino, Bread & Wine*) by Ladislao Vadja.

Murio hace quince anos (*Dead Fifteen Years Ago*) by Rafael Gil.

Historias de la radio (*Radio Stories*) by Saenz de Heredia.

Muerte de un ciclista (*Death of a Cyclist*) by J. A. Bardem.

1956

Calle Mayor (*Main Street*) by Juan Antonio Bardem.

Calabuch by Luis Garcia Berlanga.

El pequeno ruisenor (*The Small Nightingale*) by Antonio del Amo.

Tarde de toros (*Afternoon of Bulls*) by Ladislao Vadja.

El tigre de Chamberi (*Tiger from Chamberi*) by Pedro L. Ramirez.

Embajadores en el infierno (*Ambassadors in Hell*) by J. M. Forque.

1957

La venganza (*Revenge*) by Juan Antonio Bardem.

El ultimo cuple (*The Last Song*) by Juan de Orduna, beginning the heyday of Sarita Montiel musicals.

Donde vas, Alfonso XII? (*Where Are You Going, Alfonso?*) by Luis C. Amadori.

Amanecer en Puerta Oscura (*Dawn in Puerta Oscura*) by Jose Maria Forque.

1958

El pisito (*The Little Flat*) by Marco Ferreri.

La vida por delante (*The Life Ahead*) by Fernando Fernan Gomez.

1959

La vida alrededor (*The Life Around*) by Fernando Fernan Gomez.

Los golfos (*The Hooligans*) by Carlos Saura.

Sonatas by Juan Antonio Bardem.

Las chicas de la Cruz Roja (*Girls of the Red Cross*) by R. J. Salvia.

La fiel infanteria (*The Faithful Infantry*) by Pedro Lazaga.

Part Three: 1960–1969

1960

El Lazarillo de Tormes by Cesar Fernandez Ardavin, filming of the famous picaresque novel.

El cochecito (*The Little Car*) by Marco Ferreri.

Un rayo de luz (*A Ray of Light*) by Luis Lucia.

Los tramposos (*The Swindlers*) by Pedro Lazaga.

A las cinco de la tarde (*At Five in the Afternoon*) by J. A. Bardem.

1961

Viridiana by Luis Bunuel, censored by the Spanish government, wins the Cannes Film Festival Prize and is not shown in Spain until 1977.

Placido by Luis Garcia Berlanga.

1962

Los inocentes (*Innocents*) by Juan Antonio Bardem.

La gran familia (*The Great Family*) by Fernando Palacios.

Gritos en la noche (*Cries in the Night*) by Jesus Franco.

Cuerda de presos (*Chain Gang*) by Pedro Lazaga.

Noche de verano (*Summer Night*) by Jorge Grau.

La venganza de Don Mendo (*Don Mendo's Revenge*) by F. F. Gomez.

1963

El verdugo (*Not on Your Life*) by Luis Garcia Berlanga, his first comedy of "black humor."

Del rosa . . . al amarillo (*From Rose to Yellow*) by Manuel Summers.

Nunca pasa nada (*Nothing Ever Happens*) by Juan Antonio Bardem, the first Franco-Spanish co-production in CinemaScope.

Los tarantos by Francisco Rovira Beleta, one of the first flamenco films starring Carmen Amaya and Antonio Gades.

Brandy by Jose Luis Borau.

Llanto por un bandido (*Lament for a Bandit*) by Carlos Saura, beginning the age of the "spaghetti westerns."

El buen amor (*Good Love*) by Francisco Reguiero.

El mundo sigue (*The World Goes By*) by F. F. Gomez.

1964

La tia Tula (*Aunt Tula*) by Miguel Picazo.

El extrano viaje (*Strange Journey*) by F. F. Gomez.

Los felices sesenta (*The Happy Sixties*) by Jaime Camino.

Tiempo de amor (*Time for Love*) by Julio Diamante.

Espana insolita (*Unusual Spain*) by Javier Aguirre.

Franco, ese hombre (*Franco, That Man*) by Saenz de Heredia.

1965

Estambul-65 (*Istambul-1965*) by Antonio Isasi.

La caza (*The Hunt*) by Carlos Saura.

Nueve cartas a Berta (*Nine Letters to Bertha*) by B. M. Patino.

Con el viento solano (*With the East Wind*) by Mario Camus.

Los pianos mecanicos (*Player Pianos*) by J. A. Bardem.

Morir en Espana (*Dying in Spain*) by Mariano Ozores.

Amador (*Lover*) by Francisco Reguiero.

1966

Fata morgana by Vicente Aranda.

Juguetes rotos (*Broken Toys*) by Manuel Summers.

La piel quemada (*Burnt Skin*) by Jose Maria Forn.

La ciudad no es para mi (*The City Isn't the Place for Me*) by Pedro Lazaga.

La busca (*The Search*) by Angelino Fons.

El precio de un hombre (*A Man's Price*) by Eugenio Martin.

1967

La boutique by Luis Garcia Berlanga.

Peppermint frappe by Carlos Saura.

Ditirambo (*Dithyramb*) by Gonzalo Suarez.

1968

Stress es tres, tres (*Stress in Three*) by Carlos Saura.

Nocturno 29 (*Nocturnal 29*) by Pedro Portabella.

Despues del diluvio (*After the Storm*) by J. E. Grewe.

1969

Vivan los novios! (*Long Live the Bride & Groom!*) by Luis Garcia Berlanga.

La madriguera (*The Den*) by Carlos Saura.

Los desafios (*The Challenges*) by Victor Erice, Claudio Guerin and Jose Luis Egea.

Tristana by Luis Buñuel, marking his return to Spain and a softening of the Franco regime towards his films.

Part Four: 1970–1979

1970

El jardin de las delicias (*The Garden of Delights*) by Carlos Saura.

Espanolas en Paris (*Spanish Women in Paris*) by Roberto Bodegas.

El bosque del lobo (*The Wolf's Forest*) by Pedro Olea.

El hombre oculto (*The Hidden Man*) by Alfonso Ungria.

Goya, historia de una soledad (*Goya, A Story of Loneliness*) by Nino Quevedo.

Varietes by Juan Antonio Bardem.

1971

Adios, ciguena, adios (*Goodbye, Stork, Goodbye*) by Manuel Summers.

Canciones para despues de una guerra (*Songs After a War*) by Basilio Martin Patino.

Mi querida senorita (*My Dear Young Miss*) by Jaime de Arminan.

1972

Ana y los lobos (*Ana and the Wolves*) by Carlos Saura.

El love feroz (*The Fierce "Love"/Wolf*) by J. L. Garcia Sanchez.

Corazon solitario (*Lonely Heart*) by Francisco Betriu.

Experiencia prematrimonial (*Premarital Experience*) by Pedro Maso.

1973

Tamano natural (*Life Size*) by Luis Garcia Berlanga.

La prima Angelica (*My Cousin Angelica*) by Carlos Saura.

El espiritu de la colmena (*Spirit of the Beehive*) by Victor Erice.

Habla, mudita (*Speak, Mute Girl*) by Gutierrez-Aragon.

1974

Tormento (*Torment*) by Pedro Olea.

Duerme, duerme, mi amor (*Sleep, Sleep My Love*) by Francisco Reguiero.

Los nuevos espanoles (*The New Spaniards*) by Robert Bodegas.

El amor del capitan Brando (*The Love of Captain Brando*) by Jaime de Arminan.

Furia espanola (*Spanish Fury*) by Francisco Betriu.

Hay que matar a B (*B Must Die*) by Jose Luis Borau.

Queridisimos verdugos (*Dearest Executioners*) by B. M. Patino.

1975

With General Francisco Franco's death on November 20, censorship restrictions were considerably eased on most filmmakers.

Furtivos (*Poachers*) by Jose Luis Borau is the seminal film that signals the new freedoms for Spanish directors.

Pim, pam, pum . . . fuego (*Ready, Aim . . . Fire!*) by Pedro Olea.

Pascual Duarte by Ricardo Franco.

Cria cuervos (*Raise Ravens*) by Carlos Saura.

1976

Films of the post-Franco era:

Las largas vaccaciones del 36 (*The Long Vacations of 1936*) by Jaime Camino.

Retrato de familia (*Family Portrait*) by Gimenez-Rico.

La ciudad cremada (*Burnt City*) by Antoni Ribas.

El perro (*Dog*) y Antonio Isasi.

1977

El puente (*The Long Weekend*) by J. A. Bardem.

Tigres de papel (*Paper Tigers*) by Fernando Colomo.

A un Dios desconocido (*To an Unknown God*) by Jaime Chavarri.

Asignatura pendiente (*Pending Exam*) by Jose Luis Garci.

Camada negra (*Black Brood*) by Gutierrez-Aragon.

La guerra de papa (*Daddy's War*) by Antonio Mercero.

Caudillo (*Leader*) by B. M. Patino.

Elisa, vida mia (*Elisa, My Love*) by Carlos Saura.

Raza, el espiritu de Franco (*Race, the Spirit of Franco*) by Gonzalo Herralde.

La vieja memoria (*The Old Memory*) by Jaime Camino.

[The preceding films of Camino, Herralde and Patino revive the documentary as feature film.]

Los claros motivos del deseo (*Clear Motives of Desire*) by Miguel Picazo.

Las palabras de Max (*Max's Words*) by Martinez-Lazaro.

Un hombre llamado 'Flor de Otono' (*A Man Named 'Flower of Autumn'*) by Pedro Olea.

1978

Escopeta nacional (*National Shotgun*) by Luis G. Berlanga.

Bilbao by Bigas-Luna.

Los dias del pasado (*Days Gone By*) by Mario Camus.

Sonambulos (*Sleep Walkers*) by Gutierrez-Aragon.

Los ojos vendados (*Blindfolded*) by Carlos Saura.

Arriba Hazana by Jose Maria Gutierrez.

El corazon del bosque (*Heart of the Forest*) by Gutierrez-Aragon.

La verdad sobre el caso Savolta (*The Truth About the Savolta Case*) by Antonio Drove.

Las truchas (*The Trout*) by Jose Luis Garcia Sanchez.

1979

El diputado (*The Deputy*) by Eloy de la Iglesia, one of the first films about homosexuality and politics.

La Sabina by Jose Luis Borau.

Siete dias de enero (*Seven Days in January*) by J. A. Bardem.

Mama cumple cien anos (*Mama Turns 100*) by Carlos Saura.

Dos (*Two*) by Alvaro del Amo.

El crimen de Cuenca (*The Cuenca Crime*) by Pilar Miro, the box-office champion of the decade.

Part Five: 1980–1990

1980

Arrebato (*Rapture*) by Ivan Zulueta, one of the first films to deal with drug addiction.

El nido (*The Nest*) by Jaime de Arminan.

La mano negra (*The Black Hand*) by Fernando Colomo.

Gary Cooper, que estas en los cielos (*Gary Cooper, Who Art in Heaven*) by Pilar Miro.

Mater amatisima (*Beloved Mother*) by Jose A. Salgot.

Opera prima (*First Work*) by Fernando Trueba.

El proceso de Burgos (*The Burgos Trial*) by Imanol Uribe.

Funcion de noche (*Evening Performance*) by Josefina Molina.

Pepi, Lucy, Bom y otras chicas del monton (*Pepi, Lucy, Bom and a Whole Lot of Other Girls*) by Pedro Almodovar; Spain's first "camp" feature.

Sus anos dorados (*Golden Years*) by Martinez-Lazaro.

1981

Deprisa, deprisa (*Hurry, Hurry*) by Carlos Saura.

Bodas de sangre (*Blood Wedding*) by Carlos Saura, first of a trilogy of his "dance" films.

Kargus by Juan Minon & Miguel Angel Trujillo.

La quinta del porro (*The Pot Generation*) by F. Bellmunt.

Vecinos (*Neighbors*) by Alberto Bermejo.

El Crack (*The Crash*) by Jose Luis Garci; a homage to "film noir."

Maravillas by Gutierrez-Aragon.

Angeles gordos (*Fat Angels*) by Manuel Summers.

La fuga de Segovia (*The Segovia Escape*) by Imanol Uribe.

Patrimonio nacional (*National Patrimony*) by Luis Garcia Berlanga.

1982

La muchacha con las bragas de oro (*The Girl With the Golden Panties*) by Vicente Aranda.

Dulces horas (*Sweet Hours*) by Carlos Saura.

Reborn by Bigas-Luna; shot on location in Texas.

Asesinato en el comite central (*Murder in the Central Committee*) by Vicente Aranda.

Volver a empezar (*To Begin Again,* or aka *Begin the Beguine*) by Jose Luis Garci; Foreign Language Film Oscar.

Laberinto de pasiones (*Labyrinth of Passions*) by Pedro Almodovar.

Valentina by Antonio Betancour.

Colegas (*Pals*) by Eloy de la Iglesia.

La plaza del diamante (*Diamond Plaza*) by Francisco Betriu; a production filmed and spoken in Catalonian.

La colmena (*The Hive*) by Mario Camus, based upon Cela's famous novel of the fifties.

Demonios en el jardin (*Demons in the Garden*) by Gutierrez-Aragon.

Nacional III by Luis Garcia Berlanga.

Vida perra (*Dog's Life*) by Javier Aguirre.

Antonieta by Carlos Saura; shot on location in Mexico.

1983

El sur (*The South*) by Victor Erice.

Las biclicetas son para el verano (*Bicycles Are for Summer*) by Jaime Chavarri.

La linea del cielo (*Skyline*) by Fernando Colomo; filmed entirely in New York.

Vestida de azul (*Dressed in Blue*) by A. Gimenez-Rico; a moving documentary about the problems of transvestites.

Soldados de plomo (*Lead Soldiers*) by Jose Sacristan.

Pares y nones (*Odds & Evens*) by Jose Luis Cuerda.

Carmen by Carlos Saura.

Victoria (*Victory*) by Antoni Ribas; a Catalan historical film.

Rio abajo (*On the Line*) by Jose Luis Borau; shot on location in Texas.

Entre tinieblas (*In the Dark*) by Pedro Almodovar.

Akelarre (*Witches Sabbath*) by Pedro Olea.

1984

La muerte de Mikel (*Mikel's Death*) by Imanol Uribe.

Tasio by Montxo Armendariz; filmed in Basque country.

Los santos inocentes (*The Holy Innocents*) by Mario Camus.

Los zancos (*Stilts*) by Carlos Saura.

Que he hecho para merecer esto? (*What Have I Done to Deserve This?*) by Pedro Almodovar.

La noche mas hermosa (*The Most Beautiful Night*) by Gutierrez-Aragon.

Fanny Pelopaja (*Towhaired Fanny*) by Vicente Aranda; a noirish crimer shot on location in France.

Sal gorda (*Get Lost, Fatso*) by Fernando Trueba.

Tu solo (*You Alone*) by Teo Escamilla; cameraman's first directorial effort.

Sesion continua (*Double Feature*) by Jose Luis Garci; his homage to the movies.

1985

La vaquilla (*The Little Calf*) by Luis Garcia Berlanga.

Padre nuestro (*Our Father*) by Francisco Reguiero.

La corte de Faraon (*Court of the Pharaoh*) by J. L. Garcia Sanchez; fascinating transition of the famous *zarzuela* to the screen.

Los paraisos perdidos (*Lost Paradises*) by B. M. Patino.

La hora bruja (*The Witching Hour*) by Jaime de Arminan.

Stico by Jaime de Arminan.

El caballero del dragon (*The Knight of the Dragon*) by Fernando Colomo; a science fiction epic complete with special effects, shot originally in English.

Requiem para un campesino espanol (*Requiem for a Spanish Peasant*) by Francisco Betriu; based upon the famous novel of Ramon Sender.

Los motivos de Berta (*Bertha's Motives*) by J. L. Guerin.

Se infiel y no mires con quien (*Be Unfaithful But Don't Let Me See You with Whom*) by Fernando Trueba.

Werther by Pilar Miro; a modern version of Goethe's work.

Banderas negras (*Black Flags*) by Pedro Olea.

El ano en que murio Franco (*The Year Franco Died*) by Gonzalo Suarez.

Lola by Bigas-Luna.

La vieja musica (*The Old Music*) by Mario Camus.

Extramuros (*Outside the Walls*) by Miguel Picazo.

Luna de agosto (*August Moon*) by Juan Minon; filmed in North Africa.

Tras el cristal (*In a Glass Cage*) by Agustin Villaronga, a stylish Catalan thriller.

1986

El amor brujo (*Bewitched Love*) by Carlos Saura; last in a trilogy of flamenco dance films with Antonio Gades.

Tata mia (*Nanny, Dear*) by Jose Luis Borau; the triumphant return of thirties actress Imperio Argentina to the screen.

Tiempo de silencio (*Time of Silence*) by Vicente Aranda; based upon the novel by Luis Martin-Santos.

Dragon Rapide by Jaime Camino; a historical semi-fictional film depicting the arrival of General Franco from the Canary Islands.

La mitad del cielo (*Half of Heaven*) by Gutierrez-Aragon.

Madrid by Basilio Martin Patino.

Matador by Pedro Almodovar; a "camp" send-up about bullfighting.

Rio de oro (*Golden River*) by Jaime Chavarri.

Mambru se fue a la guerra (*Mambru Went to War*) by Fernando Fernan Gomez.

27 Horas (*27 Hours*) by Montxo Armendariz; teenagers and narcotics in the Basque country.

Viaje a ninguna parte (*Trip to Nowhere*) by Fernando Fernan Gomez; a modern picaresque story.

La guerra de los locos (*War of the Loonies*) by Manuel Matji.

Delirios de amor (*Love Frenzies*) by Felix Rotateta.

1987

El Dorado by Carlos Saura; possibly the most expensive film in Spanish film history shot on location in Costa Rica.

Mi general (*My General*) by Jaime de Arminan.

El ano de las luces (*The Year of Awakening*) by Fernando Trueba.

Cara de acelga (*Turnip Top*) by Jose Sacristan.

Lulu de noche (*Lulu by Night*) by E. Martinez-Lazaro.

La ley del deseo (*Law of Desire*) by Pedro Almodovar; fascinating story of a homosexual *ménage à trois*.

Angustia (*Anguish*) by Bigas-Luna; a horror film made in California in English.

El Lute: Camina o revienta (*Run for Your Life*) by Vicente Aranda; most successful film in Spain.

Manana sere libre (*Tomorrow I'll Be Free*) by Vicente Aranda; sequel to *El Lute*.

La casa de Bernarda Alba (*The House of Bernarda Alba*) by Mario Camus; based upon the famous play of Garcia Lorca.

El bosque animado (*The Animated Forest*) by Jose Luis Cuerda.

Asignatura aprobada (*Course Completed*) by Jose Luis Garci; Spain's first film about AIDS.

Divinas palabras (*Divine Words*) by Jose Luis Garcia Sanchez; based on the famous novel of Valle-Inclan.

Malaventura (*Misadventure*) by Gutierrez-Aragon.

Esperame en el cielo (*Wait for Me in Heaven*) by Antonio Mercero.

Baton Rouge by Rafael Moleon; a color noirish thriller.

El placer de matar (*The Pleasure of Killing*) by Felix Rotateta.

Moros y cristianos (Moors & Christians) by L. G. Berlanga.

Pasos largos: El ultimo bandido andaluz (*Long Strider*) by Rafael Moreno.

Sufre Mamon (*Suffer Mammon*) by Manuel Summers.

Asi como habian sido (*The Way They Were*) by Andres Linares.

La radio folla (*Radio Speed*) by Francesco Bellmunt.

Hay que deshacer la casa (*We Must Undo the House*) by Jose Luis Garcia Sanchez.

1988

Berlin Blues by Ricardo Franco; shot on location in English.

Pasodoble (*Two-step*) by Jose Luis Garcia Sanchez.

El viento de la isla (*The Island Wind*) by Gerardo Gormezano; a Catalan historical film shot in English and Spanish.

El tesoro (*The Treasure*) by Antonio Mercero.

Diario de invierno (*Winter Diary*) by Francisco Reguiero.

Remando al viento (*Rowing with the Wind*) by Gonzalo Suarez; filmed on location in English.

La rusa (*Code Name: Russian*) by Mario Camus.

El tunel (*The Tunnel*) by Antonio Drove.

El juego mas divertido (*The Most Amusing Game*) by E. Martinez-Lazaro.

Jarapellejos by Antonio Gimenez-Rico.

Luna de lobos (*Wolves Moon*) by Julio Sanchez Valdez.

Laura (*From Heaven to Hell*) by Gonzalo Herralde.

El aire de un crimen (*The Hint of a Crime*) by Antonio Isasi.

Esa cosa con plumas (*With Feathers*) by Oscar Ladoire.

Danya, Jardin del harem (*Danya, Garden of the Harem*) by Carlos Mira.

Slugs by Jose Piquer Simon.

Sueltate el pelo (*Let Down Your Hair*) by Manuel Summers.

1989

El vuelo de la paloma (*The Flight of the Dove*) by Jose Luis Garcia Sanchez.

Esquilache by Josefina Molina.

La noche mas oscura (*The Dark Night*) by Carlos Saura.

L'home de neo (*Man of Neon*) by Albert Abril.

El nino de la luna (*The Boy From the Moon*, aka *Moon Child*) by Augustin Villaronga.

Barroco (*Baroque*) by Paul Leduc.

Estacion Central (*Central Station*) by Jose A. Salgot.

Si Te Dicen Que Cai (*If They Tell You I Fell*) by Vicente Aranda.

El mono loco (*The Mad Monkey*), shot in English by Fernando Trueba.

Blood and Sand by Javier Elorrieta.

Soldadito Espanol (*The Little Spanish Soldier*) by Antonio Gimenez Rico.

Bajarse al Moro by Fernando Colomo.

El rio que nos lleva (*The River Takes Us*) by Antonio Leal.

Las cosas del querer (*Wanting Things*) by Jaime Chavarri.

Lorca, Muerte de un Poeta (*Lorca, Death of a Poet*), filmed as a six-episode television seriese for RTVE by Juan Antonio Bardem.

Llumes i ombres (*Luces y sombras*) (*Lights & Shadows*) by Jaime Camino.

Matar al Nani (To *Kill* "el *Nani*") by Roberto Bodegas.

Miss Caribe by Fernando Colomo.

Sinatra by Francesc Betriu.

Sueltate el pelo (*Let Your Hair Down*) by Manuel Summers.

Un Negro Con Un Saxo (*A Black with a Saxophone*) by Francesc Bellmunt.

Pasion de hombre (*A Man of Passion*) by Jose Arturo de la Loma.

Al filo del hacha (*The Axe's Blade*) by Jose Frade.

El amor es extrano (*Love is Strange*) by Carlos Balague.

El complot de los anillos (*The Ring Conspiracy*) by Francesc Bellmunt.

Gallego (*Gallician*) by Manuel Octavio Gomez.

Lluvia de otono (*Autumn Rain*) by Jose Angel Rebolledo.

Gaudi by Manuel Huerga.

Dali by Antoni Ribas.

El bosque animado (*The Animated Forest*) by Jose Luis Cuerda.

La senyora (*The Senora*) by Jordi Cadena.

1990

Atame (*Tie Me Up, Tie Me Down*) by Pedro Almodovar.

El baile del pato (*Dance of the Duck*) by Manuel Iborra.

La leyenda del cura Bargota (*The Legend of the Priest of Bargota*) by Pedro Olea.

Ay, Carmela (*Ho! Carmela!*) by Carlos Saura.

Pont de Varsovia (*Warsaw Bridge*) by Pere Portabella.

Dias de humo (*Days of Smoke*) by Antonio Ezcisa.

Montoyas y Tarantos (remake of *Los Tarantos*) by Vicente Escriva.

El rey del Mambo (*King of the Mambo*) by Carlos Mira.

El vuelo de la paloma (*Flight of the Dove*) by Jose Luis Garcia Sanchez.

Los negros tambien comen (*Blacks Also Eat*) by Marco Ferreri.

Las cosas del querer (*Things About Love*) by Jaime Chavarri.

Proceso a E.T.A. (*Basque Trial*) by Manuel Macia.

Pareja enloquecida busca madre de alquiler (*Desirable Couple Wants Mother for Rent*) by Mariano Ozores.

La grieta (*The Rift*), an underwater sci-fi film by Juan Piquer Simon.

El mar y el tiempo (*Weather & the Sea*) by F. Fernan Gomez.

Don Quijote by Manuel Gutierrez Aragon.

Las cartas de Alou (*Letters to Alou*) by Montxo Armendariz.

Las edades de Lulu (*The Ages of Lulu*) by Bigas Luna.

La noche mas larga (*The Longest Night*) by J. M. Garcia Sanchez.

Lo mas natural (*The Most Natural*) by Josefina Molina.

A Solas Contigo (*Alone With You*) by Eduardo Campoy.

Solo o en la compania de otros (*Alone or in the Company of Others*) by Santiago San Miguel.

Latino Bar by Paul Leduc.

El invierno en Lisboa (*The Winter in Lisbon*), a French-Portugese co-production featuring Dizzy Gillespie by Jose Zorilla.

El cura Santa Cruz (*The Priest Santa Cruz*) by Jose M. Tuduri.

Macao, a Portugese co-production by Luis Felipe Rocha.

Retrato de Familia (*Family Portrait*) a Portugese co-production by Luis Galvao Tellez.

N.B. At times the actual release date of a film may differ from its date of initial production, which may account for some of the discrepancies in this chronology and within the pages that follow.

A classic case is Carlos Saura's historical epic, *El Dorado*. Its production began in 1987 but actual release took place in January of 1988. In Spain, as well as in other countries, the film has been listed in chronologies under both dates.

PROLEGOMENON

My earliest memories of the movies date back to 1944, when my mother took me to our local movie house, the Surf Theatre in Coney Island, where I saw Jon Hall and Maria Montez emote in the Universal technicolor epic, *Ali Baba and the Forty Thieves.* I was seven years old then and have been hooked on the movies ever since. It was a double feature, complete with newsreels, cartoons and trailers of future films.

My earliest recollection of a foreign film was delayed by some ten years; then I saw a revival of the French film, *Devil in the Flesh,* starring Gerard Phillipe and Micheline Presle, in one of the two theatres that dared to show foreign films in the fifties. It was not until 1953, when I first began studying Spanish in junior high school, that I saw my first Spanish film with subtitles, the 1947 rendition by Rafael Gil of Miguel de Cervantes' classic novel, *Don Quixote de la Mancha.* It was in glorious black and white, spoken in a Castilian I could barely understand, and so poorly titled that one could hardly read the words on the screen. (An inauspicious beginning for a writer and critic of Spanish cinema!) Undaunted by this poor experience, I was yet to marvel at the glories of the Spanish technicolor musical in 1958 when Juan de Orduna's *El ultimo cuple* (*The Last Song*) starring the Mexican song bird, Sarita Montiel arrived in New York. Just as I was a rapt fan of Jane Powell in the M-G-M musicals of the forties, *la Sarita* won me over as a teenager. However, there were so few Spanish films presented in America in the fifties. It was not until the early sixties, when the films of Bardem and Berlanga crossed the Atlantic, that my interest in Spanish cinema really took hold.

When I look back over my filmgoing experiences over the past half-century, I take great pleasure in having mastered several languages, notably French and Spanish, and in having had some stake in proselytizing for one of the most neglected of world cinemas to date, the Spanish film.

Before getting to the meat of this book, Spanish cinema of the fifties to the present, in hindsight, after having watched many hundreds of Spanish films from the silent era to the present, I can discern several "peaks" that deserve mention.

The misery of the peasants in Florian Rey's silent epic, *La aldea maldita* (*The Cursed Village*) (1929), fleeing from drought to the cities in search of a better life, stays profoundly in my memory, especially the "mad scene" of the unfaithful wife and her eventual return to her husband.

Of the 1930s, two films are extraordinary: Florian Rey's rendition of the famous *zarzuela, La verbena de la paloma* (*Paloma Fair*) (1935), starring his wife, the talented Imperio Argentina, and in 1936, his film *Morena clara* (*Clara the Brunette*), once again with his wife as a mischievous Gypsy servant to a young judge who chooses *her* as his wife. Both musicals are memorable because of their unique rendition of the popular folklore of the Spanish people and the portrayals of both upper and lower social classes of the period.

In the forties, *Raza* (1941), scripted by General Franco himself, directed by Juan de Orduna and starring Alfredo Maya in the title role of Jose Churruca, is the epitome of "patriotic cinema." The director and screenwriter have fashioned a melodrama, churned out somewhat fictitiously, treating the rise of the Nationalists and the glory of their victory in the civil war. It is thrilling, heroic, pulsating, memorable and totally enthralling, although somewhat banal.

Another fascinating experience of forties Spanish cinema is Carlos Serrano de Osma's expert film version of Miguel de Unamuno's modern classic psychological-philosophical novel, *Abel Sanchez* (1945), based loosely on the Biblical Cain and Abel story from Genesis. Treating the theme of "envidia" (envy), Serrano de Osma utilizes his actors, Manuel Larra and Roberto Rey, to fine effect (in penetrating black and white images) as they vie for the love of Alicia Romay, only to suffer the pain of their frustrated longings.

The year 1950 is the moment when Spanish cinema begins to cease imitating Hollywood models and turns the camera eye onto its own society, explicating Spain's particular societal problems. The first film I shall deal with in this book, *Balarrasa* (*Hot Head*) represents the first transitional film between the forties and the new Spanish cinema of social conscience of the fifties. Another watershed year is 1975, when Spanish cinema makes a further transition from dictatorship to democracy, probing the country's past and current problems occurring with the death of General Francisco Franco.

The following explications of forty years of Spanish cinema will take the reader on a journey, through times of repression, censorship and finally freedom and the beginnings of international recognition for Spain and its prolific film industry. I have spent fifteen of those years living and working in Spain and with the Spanish film industry. I sincerely hope that my critiques of the best Spanish cinema has to offer over the period covered by this volume will enlighten and reveal the greatness of this most overlooked area of world cinema.

I. THE FIFTIES

Although some six hundred and thirteen feature films were made in the decade of the fifties, only seven are worthy of classic status.

1950

BALARRASA (HOT HEAD)

DIRECTOR: JOSE ANTONIO NIEVES-CONDE

CREDITS: Screenplay: Vicente Escriva; Photography: Manuel Berenger and Jose M. Aguayo; Producer: Aspa Films for CIFESA; Music: Jesus Garcia Leoz.

CAST: Fernando Fernan Gomez (Javier Mendoza alias "Balarrasa"), Luis Prendes (Fernando Mendoza), Maria Rosa Salgado (Maite), Eduardo Fajardo (Mario Santos).

BACKGROUND: *Balarrasa* is the first transitional neo-realist film of the fifties, utilizing forties melodrama to propagandize outrageously for the Catholic church in a backlash against the cold war and the growth of European communism in the late forties and early fifties. Besides its heavily religious bent, the film also proselytizes for somewhat naive psychological revelations and social conformity—and this while a sea of social protest and university strikes was engulfing Spain in this era. The film takes a moral position against the materialism of the fifties as well as modern technology, insisting, somewhat retrogressively, on a return to faith as the single, most reliable solution for the wavering Spaniard.

PLOT: Balarrasa is a renowned soldier in the Nationalist army, decorated many times for bravery but with a penchant for gambling, loose living and *machismo.* After gambling one night, he feels tremendously guilty and responsible for the death of his best friend, a fellow soldier who replaced him on guard duty during the Civil War. (The bullet could have been meant for him!)

Unable to continue in the military, he

Maria Rosa Salgado and Fernando Fernan Gomez in *Balarrasa*.

joins a seminary in Salamanca and becomes a missionary (a soldier for Christ) to expiate his guilt. However, Balarrasa is now beset by family problems. He makes sure his youngest sister marries a young professional instead of a hot-shot tennis champ. He bails another brother out of an illegal scheme involving passing hot money from the United States into Spain. But he has bad luck with his eldest sister, who dies in a car crash with a gangster whom she blindly loves.

Balarrasa himself tells the whole story of his past in flashback. The last scene of the film shows him ordained as a priest, then quickly shifts to the top of a high, isolated mountain somewhere in Alaska where he is seeking communion with God and probably perishes in the snow. Balarrasa dies as a missionary-soldier-legionnaire in the service of both God and country.

COMMENTARY: *Balarrasa* is the culmination of the "missionary film," colored by Catholicism which served the morality of the Franco regime, providing the very keystone of Francoism. It is easy to see the influence of A. J. Cronin's *The Keys of the Kingdom* (1945) (both novel and film version) on its director, Nieves-Conde. This film, like *Keys,* is vulgar and authoritarian, preachy and contradictory, moralistic and redundant. Yet it is pure melodrama, sublime, highly principled, hyperbolic. It is the best example of "religious" cinema, emphasizing the military conduct of priests who fought in favor of the insurrectionists. (The film also resembles John Ford's film *The Fugitive* [1947], with Henry Fonda as the soldier hero turned priest.)

Fernando Fernan Gomez, who magnificently incarnates the role of Balarrasa, serves as an example of lawfulness and virtue, leading his dissipated brothers and sisters out of the black market onto the road of respectability. He is willing to die, and does, to defend the moral values espoused by the Catholic Franco regime.

1951

ESA PAREJA FELIZ (THAT HAPPY COUPLE)

DIRECTORS: JUAN ANTONIO BARDEM & LUIS GARCIA BERLANGA

CREDITS: Screenplay: J. A. Bardem & L. G. Berlanga; Photography: Guillermo Goldberger; Producer: Miguel Angel, Martin Proharam & Jose Maria Ramos for Altamira Films; Music: Ramon Ferres

CAST: Fernando Fernan Gomez (Juan), Elvira Quintilla (Carmen), Jose Luis Ozores (Luis), Felix Fernandez (Rafa).

BACKGROUND: Parody and satire are the keys to this first work of the director-screenwriting team of Bardem and Berlanga. Resembling very much the plot of the Preston Sturges film of 1940, *Christmas in July,* and filmed in a neo-realist style imitative of the Italian cinema of the mid-forties, *Esa pareja feliz* is a film about the "reality" of everyday Madrillian society of the fifties, full of sharp observations

Fernando Fernan Gomez and Elvira Quintilla in *Esa pareja feliz.*

of human nature and critical of radio and sports broadcasts, radio contests, correspondence courses, the making of historical films and the military.

PLOT: Juan works as an electrician in a major movie studio and his wife Carmen works as a dressmaker. They live poorly in a small furnished room and have different ideas of happiness. Carmen loves gambling and entering contests. Juan prefers to succeed through his own efforts, and takes a correspondence course to become a radio engineer. Unknown to Juan, Carmen enters a contest for the soap manufacturer "Florit," whose prize is "One Happy Day in Madrid for One Happy Couple." Before the results are announced, Juan loses his job at the studio, experiences failure as a prospective radio engineer when experiments with a loud-speaker he has designed fall through, and loses money in a scheme with Rafa to open a photography business. Just as Carmen reproaches him for all of the aforementioned, they win the Florit soap contest.

Using a car put at their disposal, they capture Rafa, who has absconded with their money, and then go on with the contest prize, first visiting a classy restaurant, then a night club. They are stared at as curiosities and Juan realizes that he cannot endure this false notion of happiness, even for one single day. He provokes a fight with the nightclub singer, who was mocking him and his wife in song.

Gathering up all the gifts they won in the contest, he and Carmen return to their small furnished apartment, on the way dropping gifts in the streets among beggars so that they can embrace each other and recapture their love as the dawn of a new day breaks. They realize that their true happiness rests in their simple life with each other. They will continue to strive for it.

COMMENTARY: From the outset of their careers, Bardem and Berlanga developed a sharply critical and satiric style. In fact, *That Happy Couple* was an extremely personal film, dealing with the themes of poverty and the Spanish economic crises of the 1950s, in significant contrast with the traditional Spanish films of the era that only treated patriotic, religious or "folkloric" subjects. Bardem and Berlanga's true genius manifested itself in their lampooning of certain aspects of Spain's political and social worlds, and their hysterical satirizing of certain Spanish foibles did not endear them to the Franco regime.

Like the Italian neo-realists, Bardem and Berlanga had captured the pulse of everyday life in this particular film. Somewhat downbeat, they portrayed the futility of the "Spanish dream" to rise in society and escape a drab, everyday existence, retreating to a world of escapist cinema, soap operas and pulp fiction. The directors emphasize the humiliation, naiveté and implicit faith of the young marrieds, as well as their disenchantment with the Cinderella dream, their resignation to hard work, their disillusion with society, their resolution to continue the struggle for elusive and sometimes inaccessible material benefits. It was clearly an unflattering picture of Madrillian society and the Franco regime held up the film's release until 1953, after the release of Berlanga's more successful and cheerful satire, *Bienvenido Senor Marshall* (*Welcome Mr. Marshall*).

When viewed today, *Esa pareja feliz* is quite charming and sentimental. Bardem & Berlanga make wonderful use of the flashback device, especially when the young marrieds remember their initial bliss, and they also shoot a film within a film, since Fernando Fernan Gomez works in a movie studio. They are quite critical of materialism and the use of advertising within movie houses and films themselves, and do not pander to this practice which has become obsessive in American cinema. In its critical posture the film is certainly ahead of its time and forecasts more successful and incisive films from its director-screenwriting team.

1951

SURCOS (FURROWS)

DIRECTOR: JOSE-ANTONIO NIEVES-CONDE

CREDITS: Screenplay: Gonzalo Torrente Ballester & Natividad Zaro; Photography: Sebestian Perera; Producer: Felipe Gerely for Sevilla Films; Music: Jesus Garcia Leoz.

CAST: Maruja Asquerino (Pili), Luis Pena (Mellao), Marisa de Leza (Tonia), Felix Dafuce (don Roque "El Chamberlain"), Francisco Arenzana (Pepe) and Jose Prada (el padre).

BACKGROUND: *Surcos* (*Furrows*) was the first Spanish film of its era that had international appeal. It dealt with immigrants and their problems in moving from the countryside to the big city. Unable to make the adjustment, one of the daughters, an intending singer, resorts to prostitution and the entire family is forced to return to their former meager life after encounters with the black market, bad housing and treacherous people.

Surcos contains the melodramatic, populist and social elements that make it the sole Spanish film to embrace totally the Italian neo-realist style. It is the forerunner of Luchino Visconti's epic *Rocco and His Brothers* (1961).

Franciso Arenzana (*left*) in *Surcos.*

PLOT: A provincial family decides to come to Madrid in search of a better life. However, once they are there, events do not turn to their advantage. The eldest son becomes involved with a gang of petty thieves. The eldest daughter becomes the mistress of "El Chamberlain," an unscrupulous and ruthless businessman who is involved in the death of the family's youngest son, Pepe. One daughter, Pili, becomes a prostitute, succumbing to the immorality of the big city.

Realizing that their adjustment to the urban milieu has been a disaster, the family is routed back to the country. However, the prostitute-daughter jumps off the train in the last scene, a train that would have carried her back to respectable poverty and ennui. She joins the ranks of the downtrodden, those corrupted by Madrid city life.

COMMENTARY: On its initial release, *Surcos* was not well received by the Franco government because of its graphic settings, its critiques of the black market and prostitution, and realistic scenes depicting poverty in both urban and suburban milieus. (It reminded this critic of William Wyler's trenchant film about tenements versus high society in New York City circa 1937, *Dead End,* based upon the Sidney Kingsley play.)

Two of the most flagrant scenes depicted in *Surcos* were: first, a girl lying on a bed in a slip, smoking a cigarette while another girl was undressing off screen, and second, the concluding scene (cut from the original print but later restored) showing the prostitute Pili jumping from the train to return to the corrupt life of Madrid. The Spanish government could not help but condemn Pili's scandalous choice of urban deprivation over suburban starvation.

Surcos is, to my mind, a continuation and update of Florian Rey's *La aldea maldita* (*The Cursed Village*), but with a far more depressing denouement. Even its brilliant music score adds to our emotional stress as we witness the collapse of an entire village family on screen. The score is reminiscent of all the great music written for films in which the protagonist is really the city. (Compare Max Steiner's *Symphony for Six Million* and Alfred Newman's particularly marvelous creation entitled *Street Scene*.)

Brilliantly photographed, excellently scored, stunningly acted, *Surcos* is strikingly candid as melodrama and a worthy successor to *Balarrasa*, which is still considered the crowning achievement in Nieves-Conde's career although *Surcos* is a vastly superior and more courageous film. Although it was the director's intention to use the film as a critique of the government's uncontrolled emigration to the cities, *Surcos* became instead a combination city symphony, gangster thriller and social melodrama. It certainly belongs to and enhances the Spanish neo-realistic school of cinema.

1952

BIENVENIDO SENOR MARSHALL (WELCOME MR. MARSHALL)

DIRECTOR: LUIS GARCIA BERLANGA

CREDITS: Screenplay: J. A. Bardem, L. G. Berlanga & M. Mihura; Photography: Manuel Berenger; Producer: UNINCI Films; Music: Jesus Garcia Leoz.

Manolo Moran (*center*) in *Bienvenido Sr. Marshall*.

CAST: Jose Isbert (Don Pablo, the mayor ["el alcalde"]); Manolo Moran (Manolo); Lolita Sevilla (Carmen Vargas); Alberto Romea (Don Luis, the gentleman ["el hidalgo"]); Elvira Quintilla (Eloisa, the schoolteacher).

BACKGROUND: Beginning with its title, *Welcome Mr. Marshall* is a gentle, humorous and sometimes caustic satire with "picaresque" tendencies about a local Castilian village's reaction to Marshall Plan aid. The film abounds with flashes of malicious humor and finely observed satirical touches about the United States. When the film was first shown in Cannes, Edward G. Robinson (an American actor and jury member) denounced it for its anti-American bias and managed to have it censored. During these years of the Cold War, the film was obviously misunderstood. Rather than an anti-American satire, it was a burlesque of a small village eager to ingratiate and disfigure itself in order to get the promised benefits of Marshall Plan aid.

PLOT: The film is set in the small Castilian town of Villar del Rio, a local village which has the usual quiet church, serene plaza and simple people you would find in any Northern Spanish town. A surprise visit from the local governor disturbs the town's customary tranquillity as all the farmers rush off to hide their harvest produce, fearing the governor has come to take stock of it and tax them. The latter, however, has come to tell them of the impending visit of the Marshall Plan Commission to Villar del Rio. The entire village must get ready to meet the Commission because the amount of monetary aid given will depend upon what the official delegation views as necessary in each town and what "kindnesses" these Americans receive from the local farmers. Nevertheless, the townspeople cannot foresee what actually happens.

Their mayor (Isbert), together with a local impresario (Moran), organizes a special "folkloric" reception, an Andalusian fiesta setting—women with shawls, mantillas and castanets, bullfighters, all designed to seduce Mr. Marshall. The villagers invest all their spare *pesetas* in creating this stereotype, dream-like vision of a town in Southern Spain (resembling Cordoba), masking their own misery and poverty, and dreaming of future wealth and riches because of Mr. Marshall. Their dreams are soon shattered when the official convoy sweeps through the town in three autos that do not stop even for an instant, leaving the townspeople in a great cloud of dust. They are desolate: all their hopes and dreams of future wealth vanish.

COMMENTARY: What elevates the plot above the ordinary are Berlanga's political critiques of American life. In three finely honed dream sequences, Berlanga satirizes the American Western film, replete with saloon, gambling wheels, gunfights, womanizing sheriffs and bar girls; the Ku Klux Klan hanging a local priest, and victims giving testimony at the House Un-American Activities Committee hearings. Such elements led to the film being censored in the United States.

Berlanga also took this film out of the studio and actually used local townspeople in the village of Guadalix de la Sierra, giving the film the kind of neo-realistic authenticity of a De Sica or Rossellini film. Some of the images are fascinating, such as a tractor being parachuted down to a waiting farmer by an American plane, very reminiscent of the fulfillment of the peasants' dreams in Russian films of the 1930s.

The film also pokes fun at the Spanish *conquistadores,* eaten alive by Indians, pointing to an ignominious rather than a noble national past. The prissy school teacher also dreams of American football players struggling to get at her, to end her sexual repression. This latter scene was cut by the censors and has never been shown in the U.S. to date.

The film is still popular today and remains a breath of fresh air in the stuffy, priggish world of Spanish cinema. Another scene cut from the original shows an

American flag floating downstream in a local river, demonstrating the Spaniard's dissatisfaction with "Yank fever" after the townspeople's dreams have been scuttled. The film retains a kind of freshness and naiveté that is remarkable in light of the bold critical posturings and unconventional attitudes expressed by Bardem and Berlanga in the early fifties. It was the key film that sealed the success of Berlanga and Bardem's future collaborative and individual efforts.

1955

MUERTE DE UN CICLISTA (DEATH OF A CYCLIST)

DIRECTOR: JUAN ANTONIO BARDEM

CREDITS: Screenplay: J. A. Bardem; Photography: Alfredo Fraile; Producer: Manuel J. Goyanes; Music: Isidro B. Maizetegui.

CAST: Lucia Bose (Maria Jose), Alberto Closas (Juan), Bruna Corra (Matilde), Otelo Toso (Miguel), Carlos Casaravilla (Rafa), Manuel Alexandre (cyclist).

BACKGROUND: Bardem's first film production outside of his partnership with Luis Garcia Berlanga was *Death of a Cyclist*, probably still considered his best-known film outside of Spain. With this film, Bardem hoped to create (in his own words) "a national cinema with love, sincerity and honor. . . . A filmmaker cannot hope to change the world . . . he must make a contribution . . . donate all his efforts to a positive, useful cinema that will reveal the reality of things so they will change." The emergence of committed, realistic films from Franco's Spain aroused international interest in Bardem's work. When university strikes broke out all over the country, Bardem was accused of fomenting many of them, since the script of *Cyclist* contains a student strike scene, a genuine parallel and model for some students who were seeking university reforms. Bardem is interested in films that contain some note of political criticism and *Cyclist* is the forerunner, his most famous film. It usually appears on critics' lists of the ten or fifteen best films from Spain.

PLOT: *Death of a Cyclist* tells the story of Juan, a university professor who, while driving back from a rendezvous with his mistress, Maria Jose, accidentally knocks down and kills an unknown cyclist. Panicking, the couple leave the scene, afraid that their clandestine affair will be discovered. When they read about the cyclist's death in a local newspaper article, Juan tries to convince Maria Jose to confess to the crime. She, unable to give up her husband Miguel, her wealth and social position, decides to run down her lover, Juan, instead. While leaving the scene, she swerves her car to avoid hitting yet another cyclist, but goes to her own death, crashing into a ravine.

COMMENTARY: Although the denouement of this film is a bit melodramatic, Bardem was obliged to punish the adulterous woman, beautifully played by Lucia Bose. The film's moral, social and political implications offered a scathing commentary on contemporary Spanish society of the mid-fifties.

Cyclist conveys its social anger through the medium of a popularly acceptable thriller, although the story of adultery is still quite conventional. The sub-plots of the film, however, are more interesting. We learn that Juan holds his university position through the patronage of influential rich friends. It is he who triggers the student reform movement for better university conditions and equality in testing

Lucia Bose and Alberto Closas in *Muerte de un ciclista.*

procedures because he can no longer accept the vulgarity and greed of his own social set. He tries to identify himself with simpler values, and envisages his own guilt as part of a wider guilt of the privileged towards the rest of society. His decision to surrender to the police suggests self-expiation, a purgation of his own association with a society and class system he cannot ever hope to change.

Bardem asserts the power of the individual and the preservation of his dignity in the face of a decadent society as the principal message of the film. The "message" is somewhat obfuscated, however, by Bardem's own lack of continuity and editing style. Sometimes we feel we do not get close enough to the characters and sometimes we are confused because the husband and the lover look so much alike physically.

The two levels of society—the rich upper classes and the poor student population of the middle and lower strata—are presented as extreme opposites. Bardem contrasts the ruthless character of the rich decadents and the banal, thin motivations of the "good" people who supposedly embody the real values of the film.

Nevertheless, *Death of a Cyclist* is a superior effort, in which Bardem reveals in depth the social implications of the plot, even though his individual characters are cold and bloodless and are sacrificed to the trajectory of the narrative. *Muerte de un ciclista* modernizes Spanish cinema, restoring Spanish film to an international level of discourse, unmasking social conformity and indicting the comfortable but socially corrupt upper-middle class. It is one of the most perceptive social portraits of Madrillian life of the fifties.

1957

CALLE MAYOR (MAIN STREET)

DIRECTOR: JUAN ANTONIO BARDEM

CREDITS: Screenplay: Juan Antonio Bardem, based upon Carlos Arniches' 1916 play, *La senorita de Trevelez;* Photography: Michel Kelber; Producer: Manuel J. Goyanes for Chamartin Studios (Madrid); Music: Joseph Kosma & Isidro Maizetegui.

CAST: Betsy Blair (Isabel); Jose Suarez (Juan); Yves Massard (Federico); Matilde Munoz Sampedro (La chacha); Maria Gamez (the mother).

BACKGROUND: While filming *Calle Mayor* in 1957, Juan Antonio Bardem, its director and screenwriter, was imprisoned on unjust "political" charges. He was released two weeks later because of a huge international outcry.

Calle Mayor is another early Bardem film containing ambiguous or oblique critiques of social injustice, if not profound penetration into the psyches of its protagonists. It was filmed in two versions: Spanish and French. At this point in his career, Bardem began searching for an audience beyond the frontiers of Iberia and found one in France. The film uses the alternate title of *The Lovemaker* in other English-speaking countries. Bardem's essential theme is that of the individual who suffers as a consequence of small-town gossip.

PLOT: *Calle Mayor* stars the plain-looking American actress Betsy Blair, previously seen in the 1956 Academy Award Winner, *Marty,* authored by Paddy Chayefsky and co-starring Ernest Borgnine as a bland but robust butcher searching for love and marriage. Here Blair plays Isabel, a "wallflower" who is the butt of a practical joke. In the role of a thirty-five-year-old spinster, living in a small provincial town, with little means and no dowry, she is falsely made love to by one of the town's local gigolos, Juan, and then jilted by him.

Juan is a handsome weakling who obliges the love-smitten spinster only to find that he has a conscience and is stricken by the enormity and cruelty of the practical "joke" played on her by the townsmen. (It

Jose Suarez and Betsy Blair in *Calle mayor.*

would have been wonderful if Bardem had let the emotions the two characters discovered within each other reach a conclusion other than the expected one of the pessimistic screenplay.) But in this tender but brutal film, Bardem's spinster becomes a symbol of all the homely, unloved women in the world who wait but never fulfill their dreams. Isabel's friend Federico, the nonconformist intellectual outsider, warns her about the scheme and advises her to leave town. But she prefers to stroll with the ladies of the town and be seen rather than be driven out of her home. So Juan runs off to Madrid at the film's conclusion and Isabel, still desperately in love, is left to her lonely destiny.

COMMENTARY: *Calle Mayor* is a perceptive portrait of small-town life in contemporary Spain of the fifties. It shows the *senoritos,* the rich, bored young men searching for their dreary pleasures among the *senoritas,* the women trapped by their religion and traditions in a male-dominated society. If Isabel had a dream of a profession (becoming a stewardess), her provincial upbringing works against its fulfillment.

Bardem's critique of the males is even more strident. They drink themselves to oblivion out of boredom because of the stultifying, *macho* life style they lead. Their only social contact with the women of the town occurs during the evening strolls on the Calle Mayor or Main Street, which serve to isolate rather than bring together the lonely men and women of the town. In this film about the social injustices taking place in a provincial setting, Betsy Blair's Isabel is left alone at the conclusion, looking out a rain-stained window pane, left to her solitude, resignation and sexual frustration as was Olivia De Havilland in William Wyler's film of Henry James' *Washington Square,* entitled *The Heiress.* But there is one important difference: De Havilland's Catherine locked out her suitor; Blair's Isabel waits forever, always depressed and in vain.

Once again, in the quest for an international cinema, Bardem had conceived a plot which could be set in any country and at any time. He realized the universality of his theme. In fact, the behavior of the men is reminiscent of Fellini's 1953 Italian film, *I Vitelloni. Calle Mayor* is also a remake of Edgar Neville's *La senorita de Trevelez,* filmed in Spain and released in 1936, which also exposed the repression, pettiness and cruelty of provincial society. Despite his own pro-Communist sympathies, Bardem had once again put himself at odds with the Franco regime, presenting another unflattering critique to the world of an isolationist Spain.

1957

EL ULTIMO CUPLE (THE LAST SONG)

DIRECTOR: JUAN DE ORDUNA

CREDITS: Screenplay: Antonio Mas-Guindal & Jesus Maria de Arozamena; Photography: Jose Fernandez Aguayo; Producer: Juan de Orduna for CIFESA Films; Music: Maestro Solano. In color.

CAST: Sarita Montiel (Maria Lujan); Armando Calvo (Juan Contreras); Matilde Munoz Sampedro (Maria's aunt); Jose Moreno (Candido); Enrique Vera (Pepe); Julita Martinez (Trini); Alfredo Mayo (The Grand Duke Vladimir of Russia).

BACKGROUND: Apart from the propaganda and religious films made in Spain during this period, there were also films produced for the sheer joy and happiness they generated. They were the Spanish "musicals" of the period, which served as escapist cinema. In the early fifties, "flamenco" musicals were produced such as *Duende y misterio del flamenco* (*'Duende' and the Mystery of the Flamenco*) (1953) and *Esa voz es una mina* (*That Voice Is a Gold Mine*) (1956), the story of flamenco singer Antonio Molina. Joselito, the child singer, captured the hearts of the Spanish nation in the Antonio del Amo musical, *El pequeno ruisenor* (*The Little Nightingale*), which was released early in 1957, just before the mid-May premiere of *El ultimo cuple*. There were also some "folkloric" stars of the fifties such as Luis Mariano, Lola Flores, Carmen Sevilla and Paquita Rico. But all were eclipsed by the appearance of Sarita Montiel in *El ultimo cuple*.

PLOT: The film begins in the present but proceeds with a series of flashbacks, first to the youth of Maria Lujan (Sarita Montiel) singing *cuples* (music hall songs) at the turn of the century, and then following her success and her relations with a series of lovers, leading us to her triumph, her loneliness and her on-stage death while singing her last *cuple* in the present.

It is the old, old story of a singing star who sacrifices love for ambition and her career. She gives up her first lover, Candido, in favor of her impresario, Juan Contreras. However, Maria has many other love interests, including an Archduke and a young bullfighter. She is fought over by the former and gives up the latter, who reconciles with his girlfriend, Trini. Distraught, Maria turns to alcohol to soothe her sorrow over her poor love life. She is redeemed at the conclusion, when, during a homage to her as the great music hall actress, she performs one last time for Juan Contreras, only to die on stage from the excess of emotional stress she has suffered over the years. She dies in the arms of Contreras, who was her most faithful lover. He announces to the audience Maria's departure, that she has sung

Sarita Montiel and Enrique Vera in *El ultimo cuple*. Courtesy of The Museum of Modern Art/Film Stills Archive.

her last music hall song. The luxurious, plush, red felt curtain with gold trim that was raised at the beginning of Maria Lujan's story now falls at the conclusion of the film.

COMMENTARY: *El ultimo cuple* is still a champion at the box office, for several reasons: the songs themselves, *Nena, Balance, Ven y ven, Clavelitos* and many others tell about love stories with ingenious double meanings with which everyone in the audience can identify; Sarita Montiel projected a kind of steamy sexuality which led to affairs from which there was always some sort of redemption, yet at a cost to her health and her happiness; and finally, although the film is pure melodrama, it shows that sex was still possible despite a repressive tendency towards joy or fulfillment.

Montiel's songs excite the imagination with piquant and erotic illusions which are dashed to smithereens in the name of respectability at their conclusion. Yet, while singing them, Montiel projected a brilliant eroticism that stayed with her viewers.

El ultimo cuple was considered the Spanish film industry's most successful musical, and with it the cult for nostalgia reached its acme. In its initial run in Madrid the film lasted one year, and it is revived continually. Its success was beyond the expectations of both director and star and made Sarita Montiel the rival of Imperio Argentina, who was then the reigning "queen" of Spanish musicals. Once more, escapist cinema or the evasion of reality proved to be most successful at the box office. In contrast to the reception of other films examined in this section, its overwhelming success in Spain (and later, in Latin America) indicates an industry manipulated by the government to the detriment of its people, reflecting an untrue picture of Spanish society as we knew it to be in the late nineteen-fifties.

II. THE SIXTIES

During the decade of the sixties, one thousand one hundred and seventy-three Spanish feature films were produced, only five of which deserve to be recognized as classics.

1961

VIRIDIANA

DIRECTOR: LUIS BUNUEL

CREDITS: Screenplay: Luis Buñuel & Julio Alejandro; Photography: Jose Fernandez Aguayo; Producer: Pedro Portabella for Films 59; Music: Gustavo Pitaluga.

CAST: Silvia Pinal (Viridiana), Francisco Rabal (Jorge), Fernando Rey (Don Jaime), Margarita Lozano (Ramona), Victoria Zinny (Lucia), Teresa Rabal (Rita).

BACKGROUND: No book on Spanish cinema would be complete without the mention of the prolific career of Luis Buñuel. He has always been considered the "bad boy" of Spanish cinema. And yet, every film director mentioned in this volume owes something to Buñuel.

Buñuel has had much critical exposure internationally because of the great variety of his films, beginning in the late 1920s with the silent *Le chien andalou* (*The Andalusian Dog*, 1929) and ending with his last "French" film, *Cet obscur objet du desir* (*That Obscure Object of Desire*) in 1977.

Living and working in France, Spain and Mexico, Buñuel has produced a body of film works that are outstanding and astounding. Before *L'age d'or* (*The Golden Age*) was made in Paris in 1930 according to the doctrines of the Surrealist Movement, Buñuel returned to Spain in the late twenties to film a documentary entitled *Las Hurdes: Tierra sin pan* (*Las Hurdes: Land Without Bread*) in 1928. An unrelenting film about the poverty of provincial Spaniards, it did not find favor with the government and so, Buñuel began to work in the United States, Mexico and France, returning periodically to Spain for an occasional film, always under great scrutiny of the Spanish censors.

Although Buñuel directed and wrote some twenty-six films, my personal favor-

Fernando Rey, Silvia Pinal, and Margarita Lozano in *Viridiana*.

ites include two made in Spain during his "revolutionary period," two films which will be discussed at length in this section: *Viridiana* (1961) and *Tristana* (1969). Although I must include *Le chien andalou, Los olvidados* (*The Young & the Damned*) (Mexico, 1950) and *Le charme discret de la bourgeoisie* (*The Discreet Charm of the Bourgeoisie*) (France, 1972) among my personal favorites, *Viridiana* (1961) and *Tristana* (1969) are his most authentic, interesting and powerful Spanish films of the decade.

One of Luis Buñuel's chief targets is the Catholic church and *Viridiana* is extremely critical of the church, the clergy, their practices and their hypocrisy, their life-style being out of touch with modern Spain of the sixties. Buñuel uses his sometimes "surreal" style to shock his Spanish viewers into disbelief and revisionist thinking regarding the church in relation to their own life styles. He continually counterpoints religious elements with profane ones and seeks to shock his audiences with music and imagery that are both violent and thought-provoking. No wonder the film was banned by the Spanish government in Spain and was almost withdrawn from the Cannes Film Festival in 1961, although it won the Palme d'Or that year, the first Spanish film ever to do so. It was only shown in Spain after Franco's death in 1975 but has gained an "underground" reputation among cinephiles for its courage and daring since it was released internationally in 1961.

PLOT: *Viridiana* is a young novice, visiting her uncle, Don Jaime, at his large but neglected estate before she takes her final vows. When Jaime first sees her, he is obsessed by her beauty and how much she resembles his wife who died on their wedding night many years ago. Knowing nothing of this, Viridiana is ready to return after several days of paying homage to her uncle to complete her vows. Jaime asks his niece one favor: to have a final supper with him and dress in his wife's wedding dress. Since Jaime has supported Viridiana's quest to be a nun, she cannot deny him this request.

At one point after dinner, Ramona, Jaime's faithful servant, tells Viridiana that her master would like to marry her. Viridiana is revolted by the thought, but drinks her drugged coffee anyway, since Jaime intends to possess her sexually that very evening, with or without her consent. After carrying Viridiana to the bridal chamber and beginning to undress her, Jaime changes his mind and cannot go through with the seduction. However, on the following morning, he deliberately lies to Viridiana, saying that she was his while she slept. Viridiana, with hatred in her eyes, is more determined to leave than ever. Jaime claims he lied to her so that she would still marry him. Viridiana cannot forgive him for the attempted seduction or the lie and proceeds by carriage to the local bus station. As she begins to board the bus, a civil guard stops her, begging her to return to Jaime's estate. Viridiana looks up to see that Jaime has hung himself from a tree, committing suicide but leaving a last will and testament. So ends the first part of the film.

Part Two begins with Jorge's arrival with his mistress, Lucia. Jorge is Jaime's illegitimate son and the heir to the latter's estate. Jorge meets the cold-hearted Viridiana who has not returned as yet to the convent because of the guilt she feels for not having pardoned her Uncle Jaime. As Jaime seeks to modernize the estate, bringing electricity and new farming methods to turn a profit, Viridiana embarks on a program of good works to cleanse her soul. She takes in a large group of beggars, misfits, thieves, Gypsies, *picaros* all, and seeks to reform them, providing food, living quarters at the bottom of the house, work and prayer. One day, while Jorge, Viridiana and the maid are on a visit to the dentist in the local town, the rabble takes over the house, invades the wine cellar and the food stores and begins one of the best remembered orgies ever filmed. Jorge is knocked unconscious and Viridiana is almost raped before Jorge, awakening to the event, bribes a beggar to kill Viridiana's potential violator.

The last part of the film begins a few

days later. Viridiana has recovered from the shock of the orgy scene, Lucia had left a few days earlier and Jorge is playing cards with Ramona, Jaime's former maid who is now a sexual playmate of his illegitimate son. Viridiana realizes she has embarked on a futile road of purgation, accepts her attraction to Jorge (which she had been repressing throughout the major part of the film) and joins a *ménage à trois* to the degenerate rock and roll song, "Shake, Shimmy, Shimmy and Shake," a far cry from Handel's "Messiah" and other religious music that has dominated the soundtrack until this very last scene.

COMMENTARY: Knowing Buñuel's penchant for subversive subjects, it remains a mystery to this day why General Franco permitted the exiled director's return to Spain to make *Viridiana,* which he originally thought would be a "religious" film proselytizing for the Catholic church. It was thought that Franco wanted to project a new and liberal image for Spain, in an effort to cash in on foreign tourism and make a bid for membership in the European Common Market. Rumor has it, however, that Buñuel turned the tables on Franco, submitting false versions of a script he vowed he was filming, while surreptitiously he made his personal version and vision of the story of the novitiate, Viridiana.

Buñuel had even agreed to change the film's ending, from the *ménage à trois* to Viridiana's return to the convent. But his troubles grew larger. The film was also condemned by the Vatican paper *L'Osservatore Romano* as anti-Christian, containing many offensive scenes, including the vituperative orgy scene which finds parallels with da Vinci's sacred painting, "The Last Supper." With a degenerate blind man standing in for the Christ figure, and all sorts of assorted blasphemies taking place at the supper table as the *Messiah* is blasting on the soundtrack and the rabble eat a lamb slaughtered by them, the worst insult is the freeze frame of this event, resembling the da Vinci painting, taken by the "natural" camera of a drunken Gypsy as she raises her skirts in drunken abandon to capture the moment. It is one of Buñuel's most trenchant commentaries on Christian charity, which he continued to believe useless and ineffective until his death in 1983.

Viridiana is a great film, loaded with religious and profane symbolism. From the lethal knife in the shape of a crucifix, to the cat jumping upon the defenseless rat (paralleling Jorge's seduction of his servant Ramona in the attic), to the use of the child's jump rope, which served as an instrument for self-destruction for the suicidal Jaime, a belt for Viridiana's would-be rapist, and a restraint to tie Viridiana to the bed to ensure her submission.

Many of the characters in the film share fetishistic behavior: Jaime's insistence on wearing his dead wife's corset and trying on her shoes; the leper's wearing of the wife's bridal veil and his feminine dancing routine as he tosses in the air a recently killed dove's feathers during the orgy scene; Viridiana's sleep-walking scene, in which she scatters the ashes from the fireplace onto Don Jaime's bed, indicating death and a lack of issue; Buñuel's insistence on photographing Viridiana's beautiful legs, and many other characters' feet are seen, pumping organ bellows, moving in a variety of provocative and sensual patterns.

Jorge, the illegitimate son, is the most "modern" and pragmatic character in the film. A descendant of the heroes of Perez Galdos' nineteenth-century Spanish novels, he is the prime mover and the recipient of the benefits of the estate. Jorge believes, not in the charity of the middle ages but in the principles of work, progress and success. No loner he, Jorge will redeem the barren estate of his "father" and find success in his relationships with a multitude of women. Life goes on, and although Viridiana quickly gets over her degradation, it is Jorge who rescues the situation, providing Buñuel with a mouthpiece for his own universal attitudes.

What makes *Viridiana* one of the masterpieces of Spanish cinema is its insistence on seeking something new, going against the tide, revisionist thinking, flying by the nets, transcending its own screenplay, provoking new thoughts, fomenting drastic changes, seeking progress and enlightenment, expanding attitudes towards new horizons. Buñuel had surmounted the Spanish censors who were ridiculed internationally when *Viridiana* triumphed at Cannes. Buñuel was always a courageous screenwriter and director. All the Spanish film directors mentioned in this book owe him a debt. Although he died in 1983 his revisionist spirit lives on for them, within their work and in the country of his birth, Spain.

1963

EL VERDUGO (THE EXECUTIONER)

DIRECTOR: LUIS GARCIA BERLANGA

CREDITS: Screenplay: L. G. Berlanga, Rafael Azcona, Ennio Flaiano; Photography: Tonino Delli Coli; Producer: Naga Films and Zebra Films (Italy); Music: Miguel Asins Arbo & Adolfo Waitzman.

CAST: Nino Manfredi (Jose Luis), Emma Penella (Carmen), Amadeo (Jose Isbert), Jose Luis Lopez Vasquez (Antonio).

BACKGROUND: One of the best films ever to come from Spain, *El verdugo* (aka *Not on Your Life*) is a bitter, black comedy about a reluctant hangman. It won prizes at the Venice, Cannes and Moscow film festivals because it is a truly vitriolic satire on capital punishment, replete with caustic satirical observations that caused the Franco government to censor it cruelly. Nevertheless, Berlanga's mordant humor comes through and presents an unflattering picture of the Spanish government under General Franco.

PLOT: *El verdugo* tells the story of Jose Luis (masterfully played by the Italian actor Nino Manfredi), an undertaker's assistant who wishes to marry the daughter (Penella) of the local hangman (Isbert). He agrees to become her father's apprentice and successor in order to qualify for the municipal apartment that goes along with the job. Besides, prisoners are usually pardoned in Spain long before they are to be hanged.

Forced to marry Carmen because of her pregnancy (and giving up ideas of becoming a mechanic and emigrating to Germany), Jose Luis (Manfredi) begins to enjoy life until his father-in-law (Isbert) unexpectedly retires and Jose Luis has to take over as hangman. Here the film shifts from comedy to real drama as Jose Luis is dragged in at one point to perform his duty on a calm, dignified political prisoner (Antonio).

Earlier in the film, there are several false starts: Jose Luis and his family travel to Palma de Mallorca to hang a prisoner, but he receives a pardon just before the fatal hour and Jose Luis and his family become simply tourists. After several such dramatic "eleventh hour" reprieves, Jose Luis is finally called upon to execute a prisoner. After the event, he vows never to do it again, but his father-in-law wisely says, "That's what I said the first time. . . ."

Nino Manfredi and Jose Isbert in *El verdugo*.

COMMENTARY: Because of Berlanga's severe attack on capital punishment, especially the use of the garrote, the film was severely cut. Most critics still felt it was a bitter, highly amusing film, "a curious blending of the merry and the macabre . . . a frothy domestic farce on the surface, it is actually a bitter indictment of capital punishment." (Salmaggi, *New York Times*, 3/30/65.)

Transcending his neo-realist style, Berlanga is at his best here because he uses his morbid sense of humor to crystallize, comment upon and perhaps help change one of the most ghastly punishments in Spanish society. Berlanga had gone farther than any other director to criticize the Franco regime, undermining its myths of duty, honor and patriotism. He was labeled a "communist," a "bad Spaniard" because of the astounding balance of farce and horror in *El verdugo*. Because of this film, Spain suffered great anxiety and loss of face internationally. Berlanga withdrew from directing and waited four years, until 1969, to direct his worst film ever, *Long Live the Lovers!* in exile in Argentina.

What makes this film a true classic is Berlanga's theme: the protagonist's conflict between his personal liberty and his need to carry out his responsibilities. Scenes of pleasure (eating) are juxtaposed with scenes of pain and mental anguish. There is no relief in our laughter at the "humorless situations" which appear on the screen. We witness Jose Luis' loss of innocence, his corruption by society, his complicity with and struggle against the "system" which finally overwhelms him. Berlanga succeeds in disarming his international audience with shots of modern-day Spain placed in apposition to the revelation of the garrote as a medieval form of torture. Pre-dating Basilio Martin Patino's great documentary, *Queridisimos verdugos (Dearest Executioners)* by several years, *El verdugo*, spiked with black, gallows humor, remains the seminal critical film on capital punishment.

1964

LA TIA TULA (AUNT TULA)

DIRECTOR: MIGUEL PICAZO

CREDITS: Screenplay: M. Picazo, Luis Sanchez Enciso, Manuel Lopez Yubero & Jose Miguel Hernandez; Photography: Juan Julio Baena; Producer: Eco Films-Surco Films; Music: Antonio Perez Olea.

CAST: Aurora Batista (Tula), Carlos Estrada (Ramiro), Jose Maria Prada (the priest), Maria Enriqueta Carballeira (Juanita), Laly Soldevila (Amalita), Mari Loli Cobo (Tulita) Irene Gutierrez Caba (Herminia).

BACKGROUND: Miguel Picazo's reputation as one of Spain's finest directors is based upon his filming of Miguel de Unamuno's outstanding novella, *La tia Tula*, his single, film masterpiece, always cited by critics as one of the best ten or fifteen Spanish films ever made.

Tula is a splendid recreation of provincial Spanish life at the turn of the century and an implacable and rigorous psychological analysis of an old maid dominated by sexual, religious and ideological frustrations.

PLOT: Freely adapted from Miguel de Unamuno's 1921 novella, *Tula* deals with a thirty-one-year-old unmarried woman whose sister had just passed away. She decides to bring her brother-in-law (a bank employee) and his two children into her home. As she takes over the management of their lives, she gradually usurps the privileges of her brother-in-law (remarkably well-played by Carlos Estrada) and his children. She acts as a wife-mother figure, but does not accept the sexual commitments or maternal responsibilities of her new role.

Her brother-in-law, Ramiro, is attracted to Tula as she dotes on his children, but she spurns his affections. She is also critical of his interest in other women. As Ramiro's

Jose Maria Prada and Aurora Batista in *La tia Tula.*

sexual frustration grows, he attempts to rape Tula. Tula's priest advises her to marry Ramiro. When she is ready to agree, we discover Ramiro is paying court to another woman (Tula's nubile teenage cousin, Juanita) and obtaining sexual favors elsewhere. Juanita becomes pregnant and Ramiro is forced to marry her, taking his children and new wife (not more than a child herself) to a new life, out of the provinces and into the city.

The closing scene shows Tula waving good-bye to the menage as the train departs, resigned to her spinster status.

COMMENTARY: *La tia Tula* is an excellent film which demonstrates the sexual hypocrisy and middle-class bigotry in Spain in the early twentieth century. Tula will remain one of the eternal "aunts" Spanish society seems to mass-produce, women devoted to "virtue" and "duty" and afraid to live their own lives to the fullest. Tula has indeed been robbed of her love, her husband, her children, everything.

This inspired first feature film is sensitively played by all its actors, including the children. Miguel Picazo gives us such rich details that they transcend the plot and heighten it with marvelous moments of revelation. For example, the bantering of Ramiro's children with their aunt, or Tula's tender care for Ramiro when the latter is ill are scenes expressed in such detail that they give credibility and naturalness to the fictional work.

Although some critics felt that Aurora Batista was too attractive and vivacious to be completely believable, her performance is the centerpiece of the film. Picazo remarked in an interview with me in 1980 that her performance was one of the best he ever got from any actor in the past thirty-five years.

Tia Tula is another of those films made since the 1950s that are critical of mental narrowness, sexual repression and social hypocrisy in provincial Spain. It is yet another indictment of *machismo* (male chauvinism) and feminine retreat to prescribed respectable society roles as either wife or nun, and is filmed with great discretion and elegant cinematic technique.

1966

LA CAZA (THE HUNT)

DIRECTOR: CARLOS SAURA

CREDITS: Screenplay: Angelino Fons & C. Saura; Photography: Luis Cuadrado; Producer: Primitivo Alvaro for Elias Querejeta Productions; Music: Luis de Pablo.

CAST: Ismael Merlo (Jose), Alfredo Mayo (Paco), Jose Maria Prada (Luis), Emilio Gutierrez Caba (Enrique).

BACKGROUND: *The Hunt,* Carlos Saura's most important film of the sixties, is his early allegorical masterpiece about three veterans of the Spanish Civil war who meet to go rabbit hunting.

Presented as a taut, spare psychological thriller, the film is a finely wrought metaphor for its time, a powerful indictment of the war, its participants, and the contemporary society, emphasizing the sexual frustrations, boredom, anxieties and trenchant materialism of the mid-sixties *nouveaux riches*. Saura and the film deservedly won top honors at the Berlin Film Festival of 1966.

PLOT: Three middle-aged men, veteran Falangists, reunite in a provincial village of Castile, spending a hot summer's day drinking, reminiscing and hunting rabbits (and perhaps, each other). Jose instigates the hunt. He is in debt because of an impending divorce and is living beyond his means with a younger woman whom we never actually see in the film, although we look at her photo. His main objective at the reunion is to secure a loan from Paco, a shrewd businessman, also unhappily in love and looking for younger women. Paco brings with him Luis, now employed at his factory. Luis is a weak, forlorn individual, an alcoholic addicted to wine, women and science fiction rather than social conviviality or male camaraderie. A fourth member of the group, Enrique, a teenage relative of Paco's, comes along for the thrill of the rabbit hunt.

Meeting at the local bar, the men proceed to a rundown farm house and hire Juan and his young daughter Nina as well as several ferrets to rout the rabbits from their holes. As the hunters prepare their guns, they reminisce about the Civil War and the excitement of hunting men instead of animals. After a few drinks, Jose asks Paco for a loan; it will cement their relationship, says he. Paco refuses but offers Jose a job instead. Saura is underlining here the conflict between Jose's aristocratic pose and Paco's post-war *nouveau riche* attitude.

During the hunt, Paco kills a ferret; he claims he shot it accidentally but Jose feels he did it maliciously. As the hunt gains in intensity, the gunfire becomes more rapid. The smoldering hatreds and frustrations of the three men are triggered when Paco is hit by a blast from Jose's shotgun and falls, mortally wounded, into a stream. Luis, enraged by the killing, tries to kill Jose by running him down with a Land Rover. Jose retaliates, shooting at Luis, but the latter, an expert sniper, fires a single shot at Jose and kills him instantly. Enrique, unhurt, is left alone in the midst of this carnage, trying to fathom the inexplicable behavior of the three wartime comrades.

COMMENTARY: *The Hunt* is Saura's best film of the 1960s, a strong work with excellent performances. Not one inch of the footage is wasted on superfluous details. Each of the four leading characters is fully developed in the powerful screenplay. The film's action builds steadily to an overwhelming conclusion. We are repelled and

Fernando S. Polack, Emilio Gutierrez Caba, and Violeta Garcia in *La caza*.

yet held by the violence we see on the screen.

Saura worked very well within the constraints of Franco's censorship policies, using his story of four men out on a rabbit hunt as a metaphor for the Fascists hunting down rebels during the Spanish Civil War.

The Hunt's grim theme leads to a shocking conclusion. The film ends with a freeze frame, showing Enrique, the most youthful character, fleeing the horror of the scene, obviously out of touch with the past (the Civil War) and perhaps seeking to push out of memory for all time those grim reminders of the thirties. Saura tells the story simply, brutally, realistically. He is also critical of the lack of individual initiative to develop Spain's natural resources and raise the Spanish nation to the equal of other European powers.

The Hunt is often considered a cruel allegory because of its brilliant detailing of killing, violence, sadism, and the ugliness of these particular human beings. It is, though, a flawless film, exhilarating, tense, ruthless, brilliant, shocking, tough, fascinating, and superbly written, edited and directed by Saura—his first indisputable masterpiece.

1969–1970

TRISTANA

DIRECTOR: LUIS BUNUEL

CREDITS: Screenplay: Luis Buñuel & Julio Alejandro; Photography: Jose F. Aguayo; Producer: Manuel Torres for Epoca Films-

Talia Films (Madrid), Selenia Films (Rome) and Les Films Corona (Paris).

CAST: Catherine Deneuve (Tristana), Fernando Rey (Don Lope), Franco Nero (Horacio), Lola Gaos (Saturna), Jesus Fernandez (Saturno), Antonio Casas (Don Cosme), Sergio Mendizabal (Professor).

BACKGROUND: After the scandal associated with the filming of *Viridiana* in 1961, it was thought that Franco would not permit Buñuel back into Spain to film again, even for the reworking of the classic nineteenth-century Benito Perez Galdos novel upon which Buñuel based his screenplay.

Moving the action from the original locale of Madrid to Toledo of the 1920s, the Francoist authorities provided abundant assistance for the making of this sensational color film which deals with Buñuel's familiar obsessions with sexuality, stifling provincial attitudes and agnosticism.

PLOT: The story begins in Toledo in 1923. Tristana, a teenage pianist, has just arrived there to live with Don Lope, a relative, because of her mother's untimely death. Don Lope takes the orphan in as a stepdaughter.

Lope is a bachelor, a free-thinker who believes neither in God nor in the morality of his gossiping neighbors. When Lope first greets Tristana in his home as she arrives with her maid, Saturna and the maid's retarded son, Saturno, he asks her to love him as a father. Alone and disillusioned, Tristana has no other choice.

Catherine Deneuve in *Tristana*.

As the years pass, Lope finds himself in financial straits and his neighbors are gossiping about his relationship to Tristana, who has now become a lovely young woman. Lope starts to sell the objets d'art in his home to finance a wardrobe for Tristana after she comes out of mourning for her departed mother.

Lope's role begins to change from father to husband as he and Tristana start to be seen in public. Lope denies Tristana her freedom to stroll through the streets of Toledo, even accompanied by her maid, afraid that he might lose her to someone else. It is precisely on one of her sojourns that Tristana meets Horacio, a young and handsome painter. They fall in love and Tristana runs off with him to Madrid in defiance of Lope's jealous rages.

At this time, Lope's sister, who has always repudiated her brother because of his godless attitudes and womanizing, dies, leaving him her fortune. Lope believes that with his new found riches he will able to win back Tristana from her poor painter.

One day, Horacio returns from Madrid with Tristana because she is gravely ill and needs the care of her maid Saturna and Lope's financial support. Don Lope becomes her father figure, vowing never to let Tristana go again. As Tristana becomes more gravely ill, she is forced to suffer the loss of a leg as the result of a bone tumor. Recovering from the loss and using crutches, Tristana becomes Lope's unwilling prisoner. Horacio, having returned to Madrid earlier, is lost to Tristana forever. Realizing the gossips' condemnation of her for living with Lope under the same roof without the sanctity of the marriage vows, Tristana agrees to be his wife. She does not love Lope, however, and becomes even colder to his passionate advances.

As the years pass, Lope ages and becomes desperately ill. Tristana agrees to telephone the doctor in his presence on one snowy evening, but holds the receiver down as she feigns a conversation soliciting help. When Lope is at the height of his fever and delirium, Tristana throws open the windows of their bedroom, hastening his death. Having murdered her husband, Tristana remains aloof, frigid, unperturbed, alone, bitter, resigned to her loneliness and mourning for the love she had experienced and lost.

COMMENTARY: If *Viridiana* (1961) is considered Buñuel's most explosive feature film in black and white, *Tristana* is his most controlled work in color. The Spanish government, fearful of international repercussions if it denied its most famous film director entry into his homeland to film one of the nation's most well-known Galdosian classics, obviously decided it would be easier to cooperate with Buñuel than resist him. Despite Buñuel's continual insistence on filming his obsessions with sexuality and religion, the film is surprisingly tame if compared to *Viridiana,* made just nine years earlier. Nevertheless, there are some scenes which remain imprinted in our memories: Tristana showing her nude and mutilated body to the retarded boy Saturno; Don Lope, an avowed free thinker and atheist, drinking chocolate with a group of priests; Lope's dream of his head as a bell, struck by the clapper, foretelling his agonizing death; Tristana's opening of the balcony doors at the film's conclusion, precipitating Don Lope's death.

Although *Tristana* may be one of the least complicated and symbolic of his films, Buñuel's ironies pierce the heart. The cold eroticism, twisted sexuality, anti-clericalism and vengeful acts of his characters come to startling life in the performances of Catherine Deneuve, the ideal personification of Tristana, and Fernando Rey, the perfect actor to incarnate the lustful and volcanic Don Lope. It is their triumph as well as the director's.

III. THE SEVENTIES

During this decade, over one thousand feature films were produced in Spain, on the average about one hundred per year. When General Francisco Franco died in 1975, there was a sustained increase in the number of *largometrajes* (feature films over an hour in length), and they dealt with many formerly censored themes such as drugs, explicit sexuality, critiques of the church, the army, the Civil War. Here is a sampling of the best films of the bold new Spanish cinema of the seventies.

1971

MI QUERIDA SENORITA (MY DEAREST SENORITA)

DIRECTOR: JAIME DE ARMINAN

CREDITS: Screenplay: Jaime de Arminan & Jose Luis Borau; Color Photography: Luis Cuadrado; Producer: El Iman Films; Music: Rafael Ferro.

CAST: Jose Luis Lopez Vasquez (Adela/Juan), Julieta Serrano (Isabel), Lola Gaos (Chus'aunt), Antonio Ferrandis (Santiago), Monique Randall (Feli, the maid), Enrique Avila (Father Jose Maria), Jose Luis Borau (psychiatrist).

BACKGROUND: The easing up of censorship restrictions is evidenced by the fact that *Mi querida senorita* was virtually untouched by the Spanish censors—a minor miracle, since the theme is bisexuality. That it was produced at all is a major breakthrough.

In fact, Jose Luis Lopez Vasquez gives the bravura performance of his lifetime, with delicacy, discretion and taste, and the film never degenerates into a cheap, sensational comedy but is full of humor, pathos and an extraordinary sense of humility.

PLOT: Jose Luis Lopez Vasquez first plays Adela, a spinster who lives quietly alone in an isolated northern provincial Spanish village. With no other accomplishments of a "lady of rank" and a small annuity, she spends her days sewing and doing charity work. Never feeling particularly attracted to men, she is waited upon in her home by a faithful lady's maid who adores her.

One day, the local manager of a bank starts to court Adela and sets his sights on marriage. Adela, repelled by the physical contact of her suitor, resolves, after an argument with her faithful servant over the situation, to consult a doctor. (The gynecologist is played by another actor-director, Jose Luis Borau, who is also the producer of this film.) Adela discovers after consultation that, after all, she is *not* a woman.

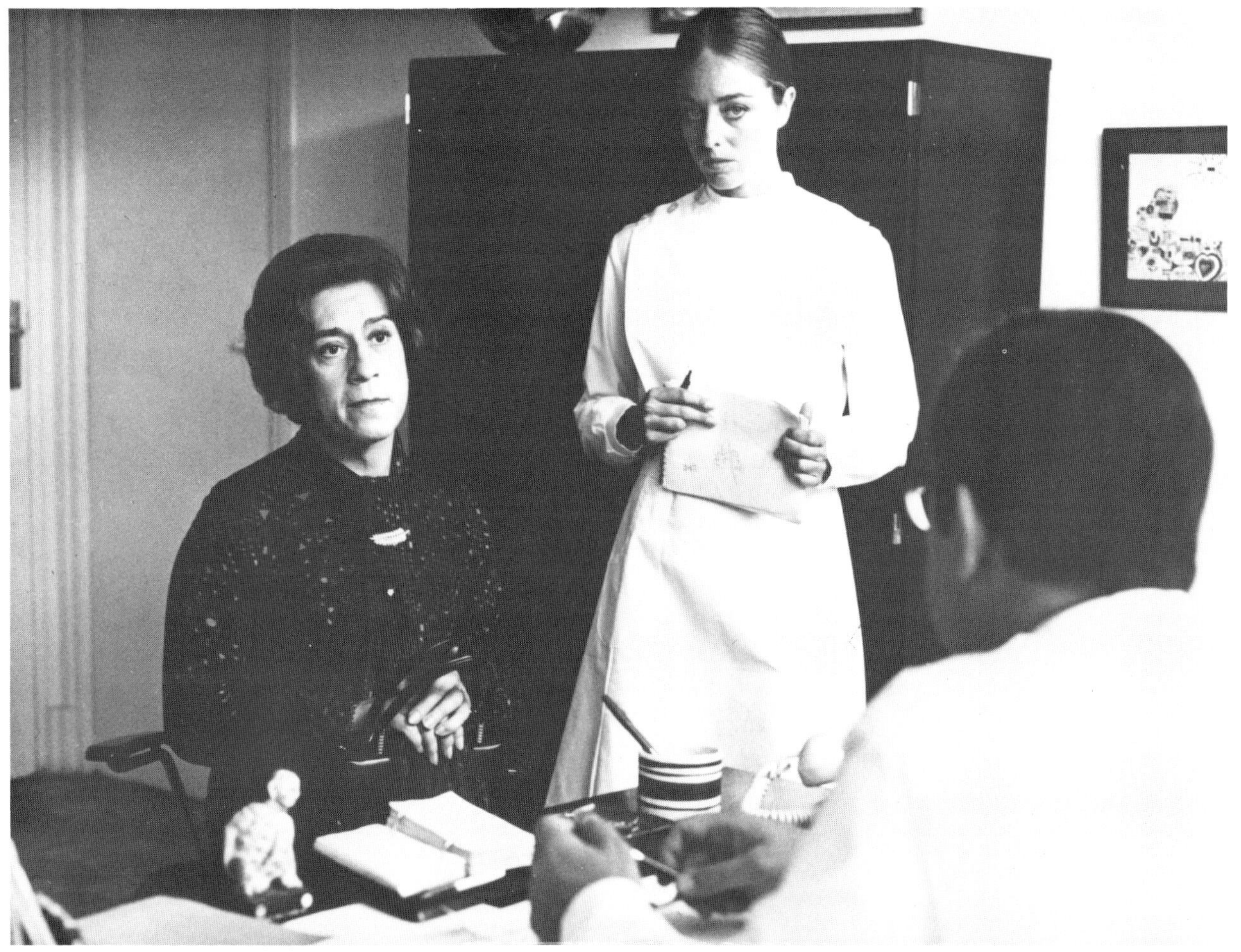

Jose Luis Lopez Vasquez in *Mi querida senorita.*

After several therapy sessions, "Juan" arrives in Madrid and meets the servant girl he fired when he was "Adela." Juan searches for work and a new purpose in life with his new identity. Life is very hard in Madrid and Juan uses his sewing skills to bring him a small income and enable him to obtain a work permit. However, he has problems securing an identity card.

As Juan prospers, he falls in love with Isabelita (the servant girl) but denies himself consummation of their affair for fear of a poor sexual response. The film proceeds to its predictable conclusion: Juan is able to fulfill his duties as a man and is marvelously successful with Isabelita. While making love to her, he warns that one day he will tell her a "secret." In their intimacy, Isabelita sometimes calls her lover "Juan" and sometimes "Adelita." The implication is that Isabelita had known for some time about Juan's "bisexuality."

COMMENTARY: *My Dearest Senorita* is an extremely witty film, played with high style and directed with careful, exquisite taste. It can be considered a "black comedy" on the taboo subject of "sex change" but it also has a whole range of Buñuelesque resonances because of the bizarre initial premise. Nevertheless, it is a fascinating love story, sympathetic, humorous, told with restraint, subtlety and pathos, while also a bit absurd.

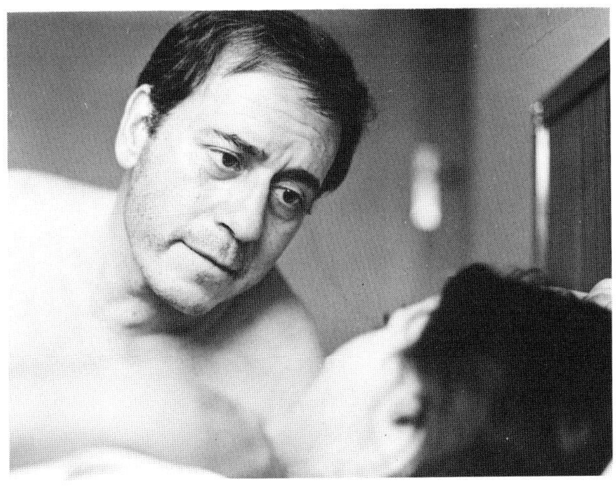

Jose Luis Lopez Vasquez and Julieta Serrano in *Mi querida senorita.*

Although the only scene cut by the censors was of a prostitute who appeared semi-nude, the film is a forerunner in the seemingly endless battle for a free Spanish cinema. That it was nominated in the Best Foreign Film category for an Academy Award in the United States in 1973 is testimony to the international attention it attracted.

De Arminan shows us his own strong literary and theatrical influences which have shaped this film, leading to the emergence of a kind of originality not seen before in Spanish cinema. One hopes that it will precipitate greater commercial success beyond Iberia's frontiers.

1973

EL ESPIRITU DE LA COLMENA (THE SPIRIT OF THE BEEHIVE)

DIRECTOR: VICTOR ERICE

CREDITS: Screenplay: Victor Erice and Angel Fernandez Santos; Color photography: Luis Cuadrado; Producer: Elias Querejeta; Music: Luis de Pablo.

CAST: Ana Torrent (Ana), Isabel Telleria (Isabel), Fernando Fernan Gomez (Fernando), Teresa Gimpera (Teresa).

BACKGROUND: Winner of the First Prize at the San Sebastian Film Festival in 1973 and also awarded the Silver Hugo at the Ninth Chicago Film Festival that year, *Spirit of the Beehive* is the most lyrical, elliptically-styled, intellectually profound film made in Spain in the decade. Because of its vivid and unsentimental evocation of the world of childhood and its masterly direction of child performers, *Spirit* is considered by most critics the ultimate vision of childhood combined with a gently poetic visualization of a dream world.

PLOT: It is difficult to summarize the complex plot of *Beehive,* since the film may be read (and decoded) on several levels.

The action is set in a remote Castilian village in 1940 shortly after the Spanish Civil War. Reminders of the war are seen everywhere, although the village itself was left unscathed. Every Sunday, a traveling movie exhibitor arrives with a new Hollywood film; this week it is James Whale's *Frankenstein,* the 1932 black-and-white Universal production starring Boris Karloff. When the film is shown at a local meeting hall on a small screen, the entire town attends; the streets are entirely deserted. The audience consists mostly of old women and children. Among them is Isabel, age ten, and her sister Ana, age seven.

During the film Ana asks Isabel why the monster kills the little girl and why he dies at the end. Isabel answers, somewhat elaborately, that the monster is a spirit which she can summon anytime just by saying the right words. (What begins as a figment of Isabel's imagination becomes a reality for Ana. Isabel had made up the convoluted story for Ana out of boredom

Isabel Telleria and Ana Torrent in *El espiritu de la colmena.*

more than maliciousness, and boredom with provincial life is one of the film's essential themes.)

We become acquainted with Isabel and Ana's parents very quickly. They are an upper-middle-class family who fled from a larger estate (never identified) and brought a few treasured possessions with them, especially a charming timepiece which the father, Fernando, fondles throughout the film until it disappears.

The mother, Teresa, spends her days writing long letters to her young lover, now in the army, perhaps a prisoner or escapee in France, or probably dead. Fernando's only occupation of sorts is tending his bees and keeping a journal in which he tries to sort out the "unsortable" facts of man's existence. He ponders at length a quotation from Maeterlinck's *Life of the Bee* and makes occasional mysterious early morning trips to the nearest big city.

Clearly, Fernando and Teresa are clandestine hermits, living in a beautiful, austere but now rundown farmhouse that once they may have come to for vacations with their two young daughters. Their sense of isolation from their own daughters and from each other is heart-rending. Along with the geographical devastation of war all around them, there is the physical shabbiness and scarcity of post-Civil War Spain, a country of widows and burnt-out survivors. Ana and Isabel are growing up in this milieu and live among these shadows and dreams.

Frankenstein monster and Ana Torrent in *El espiritu de la colmena*.

The rest of the film deals with Ana's search for her own imagination, her own mystery, her own spirit. Initially looking for the Frankenstein monster, she discovers at one point an army deserter in an abandoned house way out in the country. She brings him food, bandages (he hurt his ankle jumping from the train) and her father's coat for warmth, with his favorite chiming pocket watch still in the coat. When the deserter is shot one evening and the father is called by the local Civil Guard to reclaim his possessions, he interrogates his daughters. Ana cannot bring herself to tell the truth, decides to run away, and many hours later, after an all-night search by the townspeople, she is found sleeping, silent and withdrawn.

According to the town's local doctor, Ana had experienced some sort of nervous breakdown, but with rest, love and medication she will soon be in good health once more. Her sister Isabel feels guilty for scaring Ana with tales about the Frankenstein monster. However, as Ana seems to recuperate, she realizes that she can summon the monster as she did once before, on the night of her fateful breakdown.

In the film's closing scene, Ana looks up sadly at the moon and remembers she has the power to summon Frankenstein as she exorcises the spirits haunting her.

COMMENTARY: When *Spirit of the Beehive* was released in 1973, it created a sensation among Spanish audiences and intellectuals. Erice was highly touted as a leader among Spain's newer, younger intellectual filmmakers, because *Spirit* demonstrated such overwhelming maturity and great narrative control.

Erice's film is a work of such great poetic force and visual beauty, full of allusions and unresolved mysteries, that even the censors could not extricate the director's subtle way of delineating his negative criticism of post-war Francoism, showing the degeneration and decay of the war's aftermath.

Utilizing the myth of the Frankenstein monster, Erice strikes a metaphorical parallel between Mary Shelley's creation and Franco—their shared lack of memory, their willingness to kill, their immoral natures.

Ana Torrent as Ana gives probably the most extraordinary performance by a child actress ever seen in international cinema. The film's comparison with Rene Clement's *Jeux interdits* (*Forbidden Games*) is entirely natural since *Spirit* is also an ambiguous and elliptical film. But unlike Clement's film, *Spirit's* atmospheric quality and blending of the macabre with the gentle, and its unforgettable images, as beautiful and dark as a Goya painting, transform this film into a work of art that could only come from Spain.

The genius displayed in the photography by the late Luis Cuadrado, the carefully underlit scenes that give even sunny days a darkening quality, are touches of genius attributable to both Cuadrado (his use of dark yellow filters) and Erice (his screenplay and direction.) Erice suggests more than he ever tells us about his own past and his post-Civil War childhood experiences in the Basque country. (He was born in Carranza in 1940.)

On occasion, the film's symbolism may be confusing, but *Spirit* is a complex film and possesses its viewers completely. Erice has reconstructed a magical world of childhood, of murmured words and whispers, of beautiful imagery, stark emotions, haunting dreams, of isolation and loneliness, dramatic intensity and spiritual emptiness and decay that may be the pervasive symbol of the entire Spanish nation for 1973.

Offering a truthful view of the loser's side of post-war Spain, Erice said himself in a personal interview I had with him that *Spirit* is a fundamentally lyrical film, with a musical structure, whose images lie deep in the very heart of mythical experience. *Spirit* indeed profits from the ambiguity within its scenario, the elliptical nature of its style and the obliquity of its commentaries.

Erice is a man of great sensitivity and it would have seemed rude to him to spell out literally his "political" intentions. That is why *Spirit of the Beehive* succeeds as a work of art, working within the constraints of Spanish censorship, but transcending both geographical and intellectual boundaries.

1974

TORMENTO (TORMENT)

DIRECTOR: PEDRO OLEA

CREDITS: Screenplay: Ricardo Lopez Aranda, Jose Frade, Pedro Olea & Angel Maria de Lera; Color Photography: Jose Antonio Rojo; Producer: Jose Frade; Music: Carmelo Bernaola.

CAST: Francisco Rabal (Don Agustin), Ana Belen (Amparo), Conchita Velasco (Don Agustin's cousin, Rosario), Javier Escriva (Pedro, the priest).

BACKGROUND: *Tormento,* based upon the famous nineteenth-century novel by Benito Perez Galdos, remains Pedro Olea's biggest commercial success to date.

The film reveals the director's talent at adapting great Spanish novels, reconstructing in minute detail the social and political backgrounds against which the protagonists move in the scenario. It is an extraordinarily beautiful film to look at, especially because of Olea's use of color. The film is limned with good taste, beautifully captures the chapters of Galdos' novel, and expertly probes into the lives and problems of its characters.

PLOT: *Tormento* stars Ana Belen as Amparo, a pretty servant girl, and Francisco Rabal as an *indiano* (a Spaniard who struck it rich in the New World) who returns to visit his relatives in Spain and is also looking for a wife.

At his cousin's home, he meets Amparo, who is having an amorous but inconclusive affair with a "wavering" priest. The latter's family wants him to commit suicide. Amparo meanwhile, is impressed by the attentions paid to her by Don Agustin (Francisco Rabal), who is deeply in love with her. Never admitting Amparo's liaison with him to Don Agustin himself, the priest informs on the affair to Pedro's cousin. When Agustin reveals that he knows about Amparo's affair she takes an overdose of laudanum. At first it seems she will die, but later we find that she is on the road to recovery.

As Agustin says goodbye to her before returning to Latin America, Olea cuts for his next scene to the train station. Pedro's family, who have always profited from his generosity, are all bidding him farewell as he shouts through the train's compartment window, "I guess I'll never marry anyone." Amparo, seated next to Agustin, comes to the compartment window and waves to the family as the train slowly

Francisco Rabal and Ana Belen in *Tormento.*

chugs out of the station. Pedro's cousin Rosario repeats under her breath, "Puta, puta, puta!" (Whore, whore, whore!).

COMMENTARY: Galdos' philosophy comes through at the end of the film. Pedro is the incarnation of Galdos' vision—that truth, not hypocrisy, love, not hate, are the real codes to live by in the modern world. Laws should be tempered with humanity. One should not live according to societal conventions alone or according to the superficial codes of an aristocratic society.

Pedro represents the new American spirit of freedom, which is totally unacceptable in the decadent society of late nineteenth-century Madrid.

Tormento boasts excellent performances by all members of the cast. Francisco Rabal is especially fine as Agustin, but Ana Belen steals the film from him as Amparo, displaying a cool charm that masks her burning sexuality. Javier Escriva as the tormented priest delivers a splendid but thankless performance. Only Conchita Velasco, as the vicious, gossipy cousin Rosario, who seeks to destroy Agustin's love affair for her own selfish motives and financial gain, rivals Belen's performance.

Although there is nothing new to be seen in *Tormento*—its plot is typical of the nineteenth-century Spanish novels then in vogue—Olea has still very capably retold Galdos' story with fine production values in the fashion of traditional realist cinema. Although some critics may have felt the use of color detracted from the narrative strength of the film and resulted in a sumptuous visual spectacle, I maintain that the harsh realities of Spanish bourgeois society, with all of its attention to materialism and harsh cruelties, are enhanced by the use of color. Evil can be even more formidable in color and daylight than in shadow or black and white. Olea captures Goya's harsh and critical spirit as the beginning titles unfold and sustains his mood until the conclusion.

1974–75

FURTIVOS (POACHERS)

DIRECTOR: JOSE LUIS BORAU

CREDITS: Screenplay: Manuel Gutierrez Aragon & Jose Luis Borau; Color Photography: Luis Cuadrado; Producer: Jose Luis Borau for Iman Films; Music: Vainica Doble.

CAST: Lola Gaos (Martina, the mother), Ovidi Montllor (Angel, her son), Alicia Sanchez (Milagros, his wife), Ismael Merlo (the priest), Jose Luis Borau (the provincial governor), Felipe Solano ("El Cuqui," Milagro's former lover and a petty thief).

BACKGROUND: Made just before the death of General Franco, *Furtivos* is a landmark film, since it directly challenged Franco's censorship policies with its scenes of stark violence, explicit nudity, its depiction of amoral characters and its display of the degeneration of the existing political regime, as well as the decline of the Catholic church and its own hypocrisies. "Spain is a cruel mother who devours her children," said Borau, and *Furtivos* is a cruel film.

Borau's battles with the Spanish censors paved the way for many other Spanish film directors to deal directly with controversial themes without fear of censorship, winning artistic freedom for himself and his colleagues. Banned in Spain when it was first released, *Furtivos* was finally shown at the Cannes and Berlin Film Festivals in 1976 as well as in other countries abroad without any cuts.

Although not a debut film nor one with international resonances, *Furtivos* is Borau's best and most Spanish film and his highest grossing success at the box-office.

PLOT: *Poachers* is the story of Angel and his mother Martina, who live in the forests around Segovia and earn their living by hunting wild game and selling the meat and skins for profit. Because trapping has been outlawed, Angel must resort to "furtive" deception of the local civil guards in order to survive while living off the forest.

Martina's foster-son, her favorite, is the local governor of the province (played brilliantly by the director), who comes to hunt deer with his entourage and visit his foster-mother.

One day, Angel (played by Ovidi Montllor) goes to the provincial capital to buy traps, rope and nooses and meets an under-age runaway girl, Milagros (played by Alicia Sanchez), who is the mistress of the well-known delinquent, El Cuqui. Milagros has escaped from the local girl's reformatory and immediately takes up with Angel (whom she picks up on the street), thinking him a fool. Angel returns to the forest with her after spending a clandestine evening in an out-of-the-way hotel, much to the displeasure of his mother (played by Lola Gaos). Milagros plans to leave Angel and hide out from the authorities until El Cuqui comes to reclaim her. The governor, however, intervenes and Angel decides to marry the wayward girl.

Happiness is brief, since El Cuqui returns sooner than expected and Milagros, although now genuinely fond of Angel, still plans to run off. Meanwhile, the local

Ovidi Montllor and Alicia Sanchez in *Furtivos.*

police discover El Cuqui's presence in the forest and Angel is hired to track him down. He pursues him and finds him, but lets him go because Milagros has promised to stay with him if her lover is spared from jail. El Cuqui escapes and Martina, Angel's mother, tells him that Milagros has fled as well, taking some of the family's possessions with her.

At first, Angel is distraught, but under the influence of the governor he becomes a Forest Guard and prospers. However, he is still obsessed by Milagros' disappearance. Searching their room, he finds some nostalgic possessions of Milagros' in a box she would never leave behind. He finally realizes that Martina, out of jealousy, has killed his wife. Martina takes communion at her last confession at Angel's insistence and on the way home from the Sunday church service, Angel shoots her in a field of snow.

COMMENTARY: *Furtivos,* one of the most brutal films ever made in Spain, portrays an oedipal relationship and its dire consequences.

Lola Gaos gives the performance of her life as the mother who cannot accept losing her son to another woman. As was stated earlier, the film was made in 1975, just before Franco's death, and Borau was forced to censor certain scenes of nudity, although there are still passages of unexpected eroticism and nudity that the censors allowed to remain, as well as some brutal hunting scenes.

Furtivos has a double meaning in Spanish: persons hunting game illegally (poaching) and persons who harbor secret thoughts. As a film, *Furtivos* is severely critical of Spanish brutality, both physical and mental. After much hostility, Borau finally won his battle with the Film Ministry to show *Furtivos* abroad without cuts. It has been widely distributed throughout North America under the auspices of the American Film Institute.

Shot principally in Segovia, it cost Borau some two hundred thousand dollars to make; it was filmed in color and the exteriors of the forest were very difficult to film because of constantly changing weather conditions. *Furtivos* became the top grossing film in Spain in 1976 after censorship objections were overcome, netting some three million dollars. Borau certainly deserves his success; he had the courage to reveal, overtly, the dark side of the Spanish character. Although the film begins with the statement, "Spain is a peaceful forest," Borau demonstrates the exact opposite and clearly dramatizes the rebelliousness and oppression of the Spanish people under the Franco regime.

Furtivos is a stark drama with powerful sexual undertones in which the primitive passions and emotions are the rule. Borau clearly built on his past directorial experiences (*Furtivos* was his fourth feature film) to mold this terse and suspenseful drama into a mordant critique of Franco's political and religious repression which continued to impoverish the spiritual and psychological life of the Spanish people.

Furtivos is not an oblique assault on present-day Spain but a well-told tale, excellently plotted, containing much development of character, and set against thrilling rustic backgrounds. It directly seeks governmental reforms and paves the way to new freedoms for Spanish filmmakers. Based on actual events, it is considered one of the cruelest stories in Spanish cinema. The realization of the incestuous relationship between Angel and his mother, especially when she is literally dragged and torn out of their bed to make room for Milagros, is one of the most startling scenes in Spanish cinema.

Also memorable is Martina's taking her aggressions out on animals, beating a trapped *loba* or she-wolf to death with an axe before our very eyes.

Most disturbing is the conclusion, the matricide scene where Angel shoots Martina without remorse, just as he had killed a beautiful wild stag, the governor's coveted but elusive prize, during one of his hunting excursions. *Furtivos* is one of the most memorable, most disturbing films of the decade of the seventies. Like *Spirit of the Beehive* and Ricardo Franco's *Pascual Duarte* of 1975, taken from Camilo Jose Cela's great but brutal novel, it will continue to haunt its viewers for years to come.

1974

LA PRIMA ANGELICA (COUSIN ANGELICA)

DIRECTOR: CARLOS SAURA

CREDITS: Screenplay: Rafael Azcona & Carlos Saura; Color Photography: Luis Cuadrado; Producer: Elias Querejeta; Music: Luis de Pablo.

CAST: Jose Luis Lopez Vasquez (Luis), Fernando Delgado (Anselmo), Lina Canalejas (Angelica), Lola Cardona (Aunt Pilar as a youth), Maria Clara Fernandez (Angelica as a child), Pedro Sempson (Luis' father), Encarna Paso (Luis' mother), Julieta Serrano (the nun), Josefina Diaz (Aunt Pilar).

BACKGROUND: The director once said about this film: "For years, I have been studying how memory, imagination and close reality form a complex and fascinating whole." Very much taken with Ingmar Bergman's Swedish masterpiece, *Wild Strawberries*, and still working under the constraints of Francoist censorship, Saura finally brought together all of his youthful memories into a surging, artful work which reveals as much about himself as about his preoccupations with his memories of the Spanish Civil War.

Winner of the Special Jury Award at the Cannes Film Festival, *Cousin Angelica* is Saura's most literary film, very Proustian in its textures and in its use of sight, sound, smell and touch to recall memories of the past. In fact, "petites madeleines" are dipped into Linden tea during the film as Luis, the protagonist, like Marcel Proust in *Swann's Way,* delves into his past.

PLOT: Photographed in color in Segovia and Barcelona, *Cousin Angelica* stars Jose Luis Lopez Vasquez in a dual role—as the younger and the older Luis, participating in the recall of his youth and also visiting his grown-up cousin Angelica.

Initially, Luis comes from Barcelona to Segovia to bury his mother's ashes in the family plot. (His mother died during the Civil War.) Arriving at Angelica's home, he discovers she is married and has a daughter, also named Angelica. In fact, the same young actress plays both the daughter and the "young" Angelica in Luis' recall of the past.

It seems that Luis, presently a bachelor, is still in love with his cousin; she, in turn, is having marital difficulties. Her husband, Anselmo, is a rather insensitive, gruff, materialistic Spaniard, in contrast to the sensitive, understanding and spiritually effete Luis.

As Luis gazes upon the rooms, the furniture and his relatives, he relives his past in Madrid, his adventures and love for Angelica in the summer of 1936. Saura delights in the use of flashbacks, Proustian triggers which recall Luis' "lost" love, how he and Angelica tried to run off together, only to be stopped by Falangist soldiers (which is the film's concluding scene.) Luis and Angelica cannot capture the past and Luis returns to Barcelona, somewhat richer for his memory recalls, but fated to be a solitary bachelor the rest of his life. As he leaves, he is still unable to reconcile the past with the present.

COMMENTARY: In *La prima Angelica* there is a chilling scene showing a bombardment of a religious school in which a little boy is killed by chards of flying glass, which is based upon a real event in Saura's own lifetime. In fact, the main titles of the

Jose Luis Lopez Vasquez and Lina Canalejas in *La prima Angelica.*

film's opening are played against this traumatic event, which is seen again later in the film. Saura's images of the war and his youth are "personal" ones and "dreamed" ones.

When he wrote the screenplay with Rafael Azcona, Saura deliberately used Proustian references to create a literary, artistic world of memories and images, a unique blend of nostalgia and realism unlike anything in his previous films.

A retreat to Italian neo-realism would have hampered Carlos Saura's new filmic style. In *Prima Angelica* he omits all the naturalistic elements used in his earlier films, such as *La caza* or *Los golfos*, transcends their limitations and evolves into an introspective, literary filmmaker of beautiful and sensitive demeanor, perhaps inspired by the works of his Swedish contemporary, Ingmar Bergman. And as in Bergman's films, Saura-Luis tries to recapture his past and revive his feelings of love with Angelica in present-day Madrid.

In one beautiful scene, Angelica and Luis meet in the attic of their old house. Leafing through old elementary school books and ink-stained penmanship notebooks, they discover poems written to Angelica by Luis, but realize that their past is completely gone. Luis returns to Barcelona enriched by his journey and explorations into memory but decidedly a frustrated romantic.

Saura purposely avoids the steamy emotionalism of the Hollywood nostalgia films like the hugely commercially successful *Summer of '42* in favor of a cool but artistically sensitive exploration of the Spanish character. *Prima Angelica* is his most controlled, unified, fluid and best conceived film work of the Seventies, in which autobiography is merged with filmic art.

Saura is to continue this successful merger and exploration of his past into the Eighties, emerging as one of Spain's most internationally recognized and best directors.

Prima Angelica is also a landmark film for Saura because it is, like *Furtivos*, one of the first to expose clearly the fascist elements of Francoism and to lead the way to freedom from political censorship. On its initial release, the film was a huge success, but because of the bombing of a theater in Barcelona in which it was being shown, it was pulled by the Franco regime because of its "subversive" political attitudes. It returned to the screen intact, without cuts, after the death of Franco. Saura claimed he was interested more in the psychoanalytic and literary dimensions of Luis' attitudes than in his political ones. *Prima Angelica*, one of the best films of the Seventies, also indicates the *ruptura* with Francoist censorship and the *apertura* of the new freedoms to come.

1976

RETRATO DE FAMILIA (FAMILY PORTRAIT)

DIRECTOR: ANTONIO GIMENEZ RICO

CREDITS: Screenplay: Jose Samano and Antonio Gimenez Rico, based upon the novel, *Mi idolatrado hijo Sisi* by Miguel Delibes; Color Photography: Jose Luis Alcaine; Producer: Jesus G. Gargoles for Sabre Films & C.B. Films.

CAST: Antonio Ferrandis (Cecilio Rubes), Amparo Soler Leal (Adela Rubes), Monica Randall (Paulina), Miguel Bose (Sisi Rubes), Gabriel Llopart (Luis Sendin) and Encarna Paso (Gloria Sendin).

BACKGROUND: The director considers *Family Portrait*, filmed in 1976, his best-known work either in or outside of Spain. A realist and a practitioner of realist cinema, Gimenez Rico considers himself "the Dickens of Spain" and consequently resuscitated Miguel Delibes' successful panoramic novel about the Rubes family and their plight during the Spanish Civil War for the subject of his fifth film.

Shooting took place in Burgos, the director's birthplace, although the real locale of the novel is Caceres, a village of Castilla la Vieja.

PLOT: *Family Portrait* is the story of the Rubes clan, headed by the aristocratic father Cecilio, a roué in love with another woman, Paulina, although he lives with his wife and his teenage son, Sisi (played by Miguel Bose, making his acting debut). His wife hates the thought and practice of normal sexuality in their marriage. Their son notes his parents' sexual frustrations but must experience his own initiation into the mysteries of love and sex. We watch Sisi grow, mature, and compete with his father for the attentions and sexual favors of the local actresses in Burgos.

One day, quite by chance, Sisi meets Paulina, his father's more or less discarded lover, and they begin a tumultuous affair. Sisi is then inducted into the army and goes off to war. News of his death arrives quickly. Apparently Sisi was killed by a land mine while driving an army truck. His father wants his wife to bear him another son, but she refuses. The old man, broken-hearted by Sisi's death, returns to his former mistress, Paulina, who tells him she is pregnant by his own son. With no legal heir, the elder Cecilio Rubes, desperate, jumps off his mistress's balcony and

Antonio Ferrandis, Miguel Bose, and Amparo Soler Leal in *Retrato de familia*.

commits suicide. Paulina had always wanted the elder Rubes' child but is now content with having one sired by his son.

COMMENTARY: Rich in historical detail, settings and costumes, *Family Portrait* is a marvelous film, capturing the spirit of Castille's provincial life during the 1930s. Miguel Bose, son of actress Lucia Bose and bullfighter Luis Dominguin, is superb as Sisi, the spoiled and handsome *senorito* who literally seduces every woman he meets. We watch him as a child go out on his first date. At the death of his grandmother, he arrives late for the funeral and is summarily slapped by his father for lack of respect. Sisi slaps his father in return, demonstrating his egocentric character and total lack of respect for family and authority, symbolic of the lack of authority during this period of Civil War.

The director is also adept at developing the entire group of characters who live in the apartment house, especially Sisi's next-door neighbors. Sisi is infatuated with the "piano-playing" daughter whom he genuinely respects and loves. When he is killed, she accepts his death as part of a "Great Cause," elevating his demise politically. Sisi's father cannot accept this explanation and rails against the Nationalist armies under Franco.

Family Portrait is one of the first films to show resentment against the winning side. Also, there are several sensual sexual scenes and scenes of total nudity which could never have appeared in Spanish films until after Franco's death, scenes that are quite torrid, erotic and sensational even for Spanish audiences of the late 1970s.

Family Portrait continues to be Gimenez Rico's best film, for several reasons. Its story is sensitively mounted, its production values are of a high caliber, the love story and the outbursts of political violence are all extremely well handled, and the performances by all the actors are all superb. (The director never expected Miguel Bose to turn in such a good performance. This rock performer had to completely change his image and cut his long hair, and his voice was dubbed because there is too much of an Italian inflection in his Spanish pronunciation.)

Also, the film is considered a transitional one because it attempts to straddle the pre- and post-Franco eras. Even its advertising campaign stressed its attitudes opposing the Spanish family, the Civil War, bourgeois attitudes and sexual hypocrisy. Although sometimes straightforward in its criticism of the preceding period, this film and others of the same era are transitional in that they have broken with past Francoist attitudes of disenchantment and censorship and are cautiously testing the new freedoms after the dictator's death in November, 1975.

1977

LAS LARGAS VACACCIONES DEL 36 (THE LONG VACATIONS OF '36)

DIRECTOR: JAIME CAMINO

CREDITS: Screenplay: Manuel Gutierrez Aragon & Jaime Camino; Color Photography: Fernando Arribas; Producer: Jose Frade; Music: Xavier Montsalvatge.

CAST: Analia Gade (Virginia), Ismael Merlo (the grandfather), Angela Molina (Encarna), Vicente Parra (Paco), Francisco Rabal (the teacher), Jose Sacristan (Jorge), Charo Soriano (Rosita), Conchita Velasco (Mercedes), Jose Vivo (Alberto).

BACKGROUND: The script for this film was written in the summer of 1975, just about the time General Franco was ill and script censorship had been abolished. Based upon Jaime Camino's family memories (since he was born in 1936) the film can be considered somewhat autobiographical. It is original and daring for its time because it shows the victors of the Civil War as evil and the losers (Communists or Reds) as good. Even its producer, Jose Frade, had a premonition of Franco's death and therefore risked his capital to produce what turned out to be a mildly controversial film. Although some censors demanded cuts of passages dealing with Catalonian nationalism and the use of the provincial flag to foment the separatist movement, the film was finally approved for release nearly a year after Franco's death.

PLOT: *Vacations* is the story of several families in a Catalonian town caught in the throes of Civil War, some on the side of the Nationalists, others on the Republicans. The film begins in 1936 and ends in 1939, and delineates a series of relationships between men and women over this three-year period.

The best "story" is that of Quique and Alicia. Quique dies in the war and Alicia mourns. The family, who supported the Reds, must leave their homes as General Franco marches into Catalonia. There is an interesting sub-plot about a father who refuses to fight and a son who enlists to maintain the family's pride and courage.

Angela Molina (*extreme left*) and family group in *Las largas vacaciones del 36.*

Angela Molina, one of Spain's most popular actresses, plays a maid, Encarna, who must return to her local village because her family needs her. We witness the trials and tribulations of the Catalonians as the children grow up and mature amid the adversities of war.

Francisco Rabal is surprisingly good in the small role of the "Red" school teacher who is ill, starving and left to die. Although the film suggests many political motivations, it is essentially not political in nature. It is really about how people survive during wartime, how children who began the summer of 1936 with childish games ended playing at war by the summer of 1939, and it demonstrates how war was the most traumatic phenomenon in their young lives. Rather than depict the war itself, Camino and his script writers have chosen an indirect approach in which political and military situations increasingly impinge on the life of the bourgeois families.

COMMENTARY: The film's best scenes are those which show the atmosphere of the Catalan family and the continuance of its life style through all the disruption created by the war. The film is richly textured and features a grand cast of well-known popular actors. Yet despite its truthful insights into everyday life, it is sometimes impaired by a sentimental treatment of the child characters and gives a grossly parodic and complacent view of the Francoist figures.

Certainly, *Vacations* is not the definitive film about family life during the Spanish Civil War era. It seems that Camino and his co-scenarist Manuel Gutierrez Aragon intended to collaborate on a purely commercial work for general consumption by the Spanish public. But like most films that combine commercial appeal with intellectual premises, Camino's films tend to be moderately successful in Spain. Few of them, however, are ever shown abroad. Many of Camino's films have lost their dramatic impact because of some censorship restrictions. Yet *Vacations* is still one of the most memorable films of the transition period because it dares to show "red" flags, the Communist rebels, sometimes victorious, and Franco's brutal Moorish Cavalry putting down a final insurgency as the Nationalists take control.

Vacations is beautifully photographed and contains images of strength, beauty and subtlety. In a film as long as this, however, certain characters falter dramatically because they have little motivation and much of their dialogue seems static because of the grandiose nature of the film. Too many characters and too much plot can confuse and bore the viewer. What saves this film from these excesses is Camino's willingness to leave the details and vigorously pursue the panorama of the Civil War and its effect on Catalonia. He has succeeded in creating a small but somewhat epic film.

1977

CAMADA NEGRA (BLACK BROOD aka BLACK LITTER)

DIRECTOR: MANUEL GUTIERREZ ARAGON

CREDITS: Screenplay: Jose Luis Borau & Manuel G. Aragon; Color Photography: Magi Torruella; Producer: Jose Acoste for Iman Films; Music: Jose Nieto.

CAST: Jose Luis Alonso (Tatin), Maria Luisa Ponte (Blanca), Angela Molina (Rosa), Joaquin Hinojosa (Jose), Manuel Fadon (Ramiro), Emilio Fornet (Joaquin), Petra Martinez (Librera).

BACKGROUND: Filmed eighteen months after Franco's death (after the end of forty years of Fascist rule) this is one of the most daring, startling, outspoken and controversial films ever to be made in Spain. It is a frontal attack on the old-guard Fascists and so violent that it had difficulty achieving release in other European countries, although its director won the Best Directing Award at the Berlin Film Festival in 1977.

During the film's production, there were many attacks on booksellers and art galleries in Spain because of the "fictional" events taking place in the film: the destruction of bookstores, clandestine shootings, etc. (Life imitates art!) The film's release was held up for several months, although Jorge Semprun, then a Spanish exile living in France (and presently Spain's Cultural Minister), said that a democratic government would, without doubt, declare *Black Brood* of national interest and that it should be required viewing for all citizens.

PLOT: *Black Brood* is the story of the "outlaw" political bands, anti-Falangist, anti-regime, that arose after Franco's death. Extremely well-acted by a professional cast including Joaquin Hinojosa as Jose, the leader of a young man's choir engaged in terrorist activities, and Maria Luisa Ponte as his mother Blanca, the ideological force behind the group, the film focuses on Jose Luis Alonso (Tatin), her teenage son who seeks to enter the group.

Blanca indoctrinates her sons into the choir's concept of heroism: keep a secret, avenge insults to a comrade and be ready to sacrifice one's nearest and dearest for the cause of the group. The fifteen-year-old Tatin secretly resolves to fulfill all these conditions. He assaults a girl who has insulted one of his brothers. While trying to rape her, he is caught by a young waitress (played by Angela Molina), with whom he shares a tragic love affair.

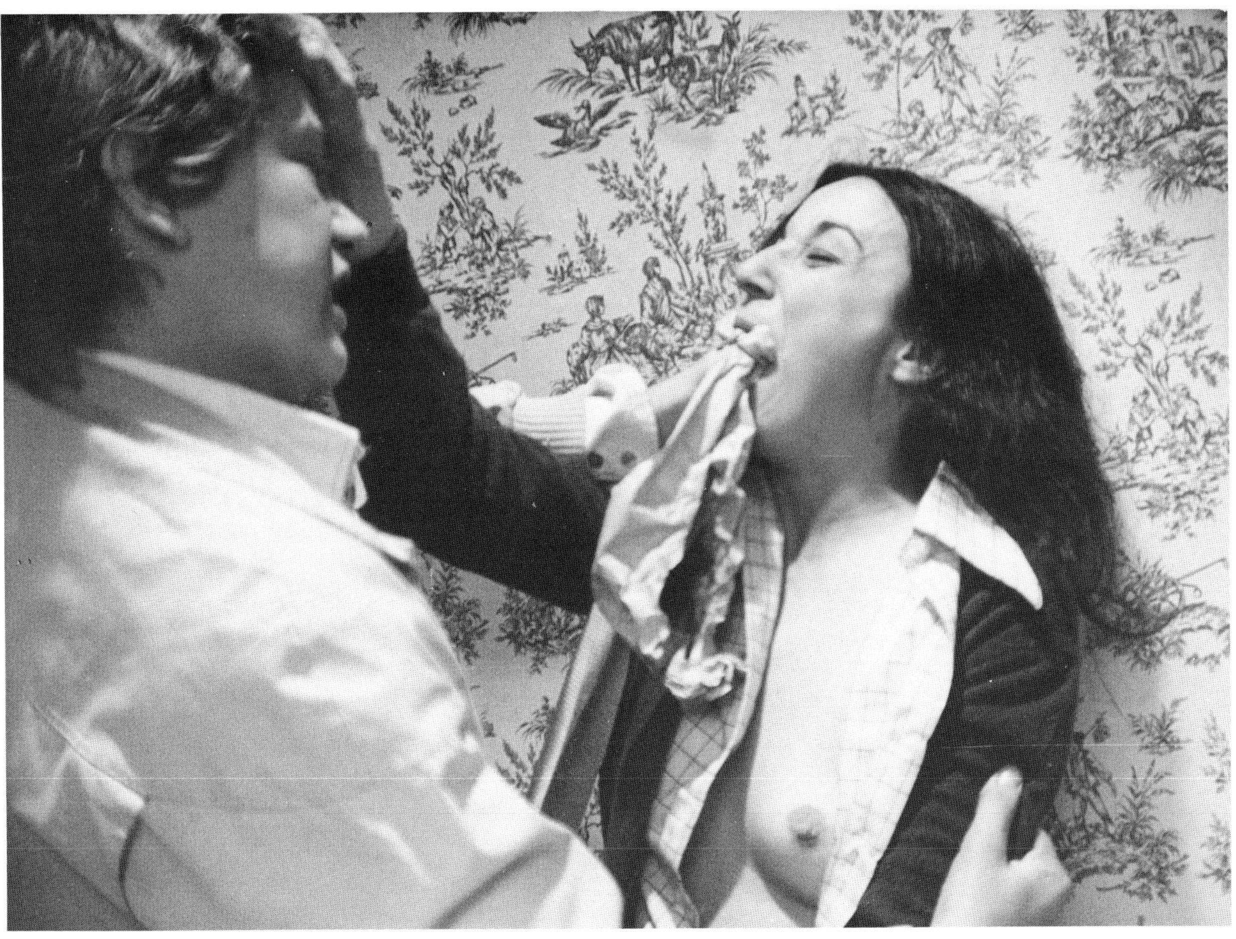

Angela Molina and Jose Luis Alonso in *Camada negra*.

Molina plays Rosa, a naive, warm-hearted girl, giving, tender, muddling along with her illegitimate child in a world she barely understands. Tatin becomes her protector, but in his desire to become a good Fascist-terrorist, he kills her, in one of the most shockingly brutal and cruel scenes ever filmed. He makes love to her and while she is in the throes of her passion, bashes her head in repeatedly with a stone, shouting, "For Spain! For Spain! For Spain!" He then hides the body in a hole, one of a large number dug for saplings which are being planted in a nearby forest. With this last act of extreme cruelty, Tatin has come of age and is officially inducted into the choral (terrorist) group.

The film ends as Rosa's baby boy searches aimlessly for his mother, only to become lost and probably die in the forest.

COMMENTARY: *Black Brood* is a direct attack on the Franco establishment, and much more than just a political thriller made in the style of Costa-Gavras. When I interviewed the director in Madrid in 1982, he told me that with this film he tried to demonstrate the fascism latent in so many situations in our lives.

At the film's conclusion, any hero can objectively be a right-wing Fascist. But, according to the director, the most tragic hero is one who fights against something he cannot change, such as history, because *that* is the most irrational fight of all. The director found audiences very resistant to his film because of its excessive violence and its strong narrative.

1977

A UN DIOS DESCONOCIDO (TO AN UNKNOWN GOD)

DIRECTOR: JAIME CHAVARRI

CREDITS: Screenplay: Elias Querejeta & Jaime Chavarri; Color Photography: Teo Escamilla; Producer: Elias Querejeta.

CAST: Hector Alterio (Jose), Javier Elorriaga (Miguel), Maria Rosa Salgado (Adela), Rosa Valenty (Clara), Angela Molina (Soledad), Margarita Mas (Soledad as an adult), Mercedes San Pietro (Mercedes), Jose Joaquin Boza (Pedro).

BACKGROUND: Testing the new freedoms of post-Franco cinema, Jaime Chavarri decided to deal with the problem of homosexuality, formerly a taboo theme. Under no censorship restrictions from the Spanish government whatsoever, *To an Unknown God* is based upon the life of poet Federico Garcia Lorca and his sexual preferences. When the poet's sister, Isabel, saw the film at the Cannes Film Festival in 1977, she made no criticism of Chavarri's handling of the homosexual theme.

PLOT: Jose is an actor-magician, an elegant homosexual who lives alone and has

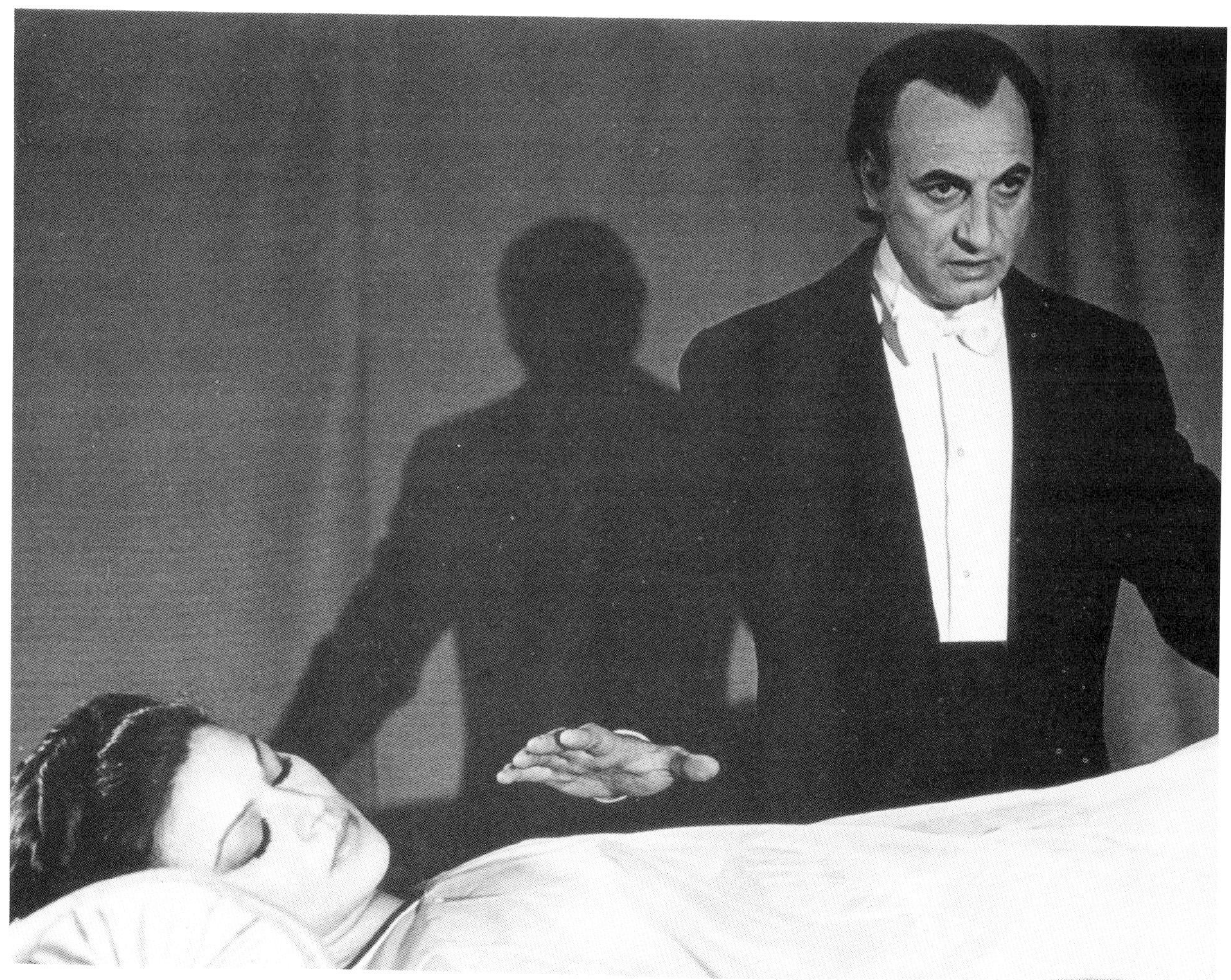

Mirta Miller and Hector Alterio in *A un Dios desconocido.*

an occasional affair with Miguel, a young politician who finds it more convenient in Madrid's high society to marry than assert his homosexuality. We follow Jose, the magician, through his daily experiences. He is a man romantically possessed and obsessed by his childhood in Granada during the outbreak of the Spanish Civil War in the spring of 1936.

Now in his fifties, Jose returns to Granada and relives his childhood there (in flashback), a time when he fell in love with Garcia Lorca and had a youthful affair with Lorca and/or one of Lorca's own lovers. Memories come flooding back to the mature Jose, of youthful sexual conquests, of Lorca's murder at the hands of Franco's agents, and of his own early homosexual affairs. Jose's entire life is colored by his obsession with Garcia Lorca, his "unknown God," to whom the film is dedicated.

During the course of the film, we travel twice to Granada with Jose: first, he revisits a woman who is also obsessed with Garcia Lorca's memory, and steals a photograph of the boy with whom he had his first sexual encounter; later, Jose returns to Madrid, to a party in search of his youth, and meets a pianist with whom he had sexual relations many years before but now does not remember.

When Jose returns to Madrid, he is man tormented by his past, and in search of peace. Listening to a taped recording of Garcia Lorca's famous *Ode to Walt Whitman*, he desires nothing more than to face the rest of his life in loneliness, although his recent lover, Miguel, has returned to his bed and wants to continue their affair. Jose realizes that he is really all alone in the world, alone with his God, Garcia Lorca, perhaps his fantasy lover.

COMMENTARY: Many European and Spanish critics were astonished by Chavarri's frank and unhysterical treatment of homosexuality. The film is a totally mature exploration of an extremely controversial theme, never before dealt with by a Spanish director and aimed at a Spanish audience. There is not a single jarring note.

Chavarri keeps the sex and poetry beautifully under control. The film is lovely to look at, highly cultivated and poised, and probably the director's best film to date. It is sensitive, allusive, graceful, intelligent, moving—in short, a masterpiece of Spanish cinema.

It was the Grand Prize winner at the Chicago Film Festival of 1978 and was part of the American Film Institute series of Spanish films which traveled throughout North America in 1979–1980. Hector Alterio also won the Best Actor award at the San Sebastian Film Festival in 1977 for his performance as Jose. *To an Unknown God* is controversial and symbolic cinema at its peak, representative of the Juan Carlos government's attempt to bring freedom and an audacious spirit to the Spanish cinema.

1978

LA VERDAD SOBRE EL CASO SAVOLTA (THE TRUTH ABOUT THE SAVOLTA CASE)

DIRECTOR: ANTONIO DROVE

CREDITS: Screenplay: Antonio Larreta & Antonio Drove, based upon the novel by Eduardo Mendoza; Color & CinemaScope Photography: Gilberto Azevedo; Producer: Andres Vicente Gomez for Domingo Pebret Film (Barcelona), Nef Diffusion (Paris) & Filmalpha (Rome); Music: Egisto Macchi.

CAST: Charles Denner (Leprince), Jose Luis Lopez Vasquez (Pajarito de Soto), Omero Antonutti (Savolta), Ovidi Montllor (Javier Miranda), Stefania Sandrelli (Teresa, Savolta's daughter), Ettore Mani, Alfredo Pea & Virginie Billetdoux.

BACKGROUND: In another of the transitional films testing the new freedoms from government censorship, Drove, who considers himself a director of strong political convictions, demonstrates his preference for working in "revisionist cinema," political films that change one's thinking. *Savolta* is an epic film, a political statement against tyranny, not just entertainment.

This French-Italian-Spanish co-production is the first of Drove's films to go uncensored in Spain and the first for which he feels totally responsible. He had to face some adversities while filming it, especially a four-month strike of technicians when the producers tried to remove him as director for unknown reasons. (In fact, on some of the poster art Jose Maria Forque is cited as the film's director.)

Drove suffered other harassments in his professional life because of his essential honesty and his desire to preserve a truthful story on the screen. His disputes with his producers over the film's ideological center caused him to be fired at one point. In fact, Argentine director Diego Santillan worked on several scenes while Drove argued to retain his political viewpoints. *Savolta* is the result of his uncompromising attitude and artistic courage.

PLOT: *La verdad sobre el caso Savolta* is based upon real events, emphasizing the true story behind munitions contracts negotiated in Barcelona between 1917 and 1923. Savolta is a Catalan munitions manufacturer who is trying to obtain war contracts with both French and German governments before World War I. The factory workers are treated badly by the Savolta family and labor strikes ensue. The labor unions urge reforms but have no leverage in obtaining them until a journalist named Pajarito obtains secret information from Savolta's accountant that a French representative of the firm, Leprince, has been selling arms secretly to the Germans as well as smuggling war materials and falsifying bills.

Leprince is the real Machiavelli of the

Antonio Drove (*center*) directing Charles Denner (*left*) and Jose Luis Lopez Vasquez (*right*) in *La verdad sobre el caso Savolta*.

plot. It is he who orders the deaths of the strike leaders and later kills Savolta himself, realizing that the strikers will be blamed for the murders. Leprince extracts all the pertinent information from the journalist about incriminating documents that prove that Savolta had sold arms to the Germans. When the journalist's wife discovers that her husband is blamed and called a traitor, she commits suicide and her lover, played unctuously by Ovidi Montllor, becomes Leprince's number one henchman. Savolta himself loses control, apparently because of the demands of the anarchist unions, although actually as a result of Leprince's plotting to wrest total control of the company.

The film concludes with a bloodbath caused by the murder of union leaders by paid thugs, sometime between the end of World War I and the imminent dictatorship of Primo de Rivera in Spain in 1931. Leprince and his henchman, Miranda, remain on the periphery of the action, although they are directly responsible for the murders of the union leaders.

In one wonderful scene, Miranda wants to kill Leprince because of the havoc he has wreaked in his own personal life while both are touring the Savolta munitions factory, but Leprince talks Miranda out of shooting him—to their mutual advantage.

Another wonderful scene takes place during a masked ball at Savolta's home. Leprince, dressed as Pierrot, is engaged to Savolta's daughter. Savolta is costumed as Julius Caesar, suitably robed for his demise, and Miranda wears the appropriate costume of a fifteenth-century inquisitioner under Torquemada's aegis.

COMMENTARY: *La verdad sobre el caso Savolta* (*The Truth About the Savolta Case*) is a fine political thriller, rich in color, action, character development and period detail, conceived much in the manner of Costa-Gavras' films, *Z* or *State of Siege* or *Missing*. Drove stayed as close to historical events as possible and did not kill the villains off because historically such a denouement was not accurate, even though it might have been dramatically desirable. Drove's intent was to depict the dangerous disguise of fascism—to show that fascists are human beings who can also be villains, not necessarily big political criminals but perhaps the perpetrators of big political crimes. Drove's aim is to have audiences recognize fascism and its instigators, and to persuade the public to guard against fascism in the future.

Unlike the *film noir*, where crime is considered big business, Drove intends *Savolta* to show how big business can become a crime. His film ends with the defeat of the Worker's Movement and the rise of fascism. The film corroborates his historical conclusion but opposes the very ideology it upholds. *Savolta* ends with a quotation from Bertolt Brecht: "Only violence can help where violence is the rule." One must fight fire with fire. Drove reminds Spaniards and his viewers that they must never be suborned by fascism.

The resultant film is an intelligent and effective work which advances Drove's anti-fascist views and keeps his integrity intact. It testifies to his talent as one of Spain's leading, most serious, politically-engaged directors, willing to test the new freedoms after the abolition of censorship.

1979

EL CRIMEN DE CUENCA (THE CUENCA CRIME)

DIRECTOR: PILAR MIRO

CREDITS: Screenplay: Salvador Maldonado & Pilar Miro, based upon an idea by Juan Antonio Porto; Color Photography: Hans Burmann; Producer: Alfredo Matas for Incine & Jet Films; Music: Anton Garcia Abril.

CAST: Jose Manuel Cervino (Leon Sanchez Gascon), Daniel Dicenta (Gregorio

Valerio Contreras), Amparo Soler Leal (Varona), Hector Alterio (Isasa, the Magistrate), Fernando Rey (Contreras, the Political Boss), Jose Vivo (Don Rulfo).

BACKGROUND: One of the few women directors working in Spain today, Pilar Miro is certainly the most outstanding and controversial, especially after filming *El crimen de Cuenca.*

Although this film was made in 1979, it was released to packed theaters in Madrid in 1981 and was sent to compete at the Berlin Film Festival that year. The film was confiscated by a military court, which also attempted to try Miro and her producer, Alfredo Matas, because *Cuenca* revealed illegal methods of interrogation by police under the Franco regime, now strongly prohibited by the current Constitution.

It is interesting to note that when the military embargo placed upon the film was lifted on March 30, 1981, and the case against Miro and Matas was withdrawn, *Cuenca* became the box-office champion of the Spanish film industry, seen by nearly two million people and taking in nearly $4 million in receipts.

PLOT: In 1913, Gregorio Valerio Contreras and Leon Sanchez Gascon, friends from the small village of Osa de la Vega in Cuenca, are arrested for the robbery and murder of a shepherd friend, Jose Maria Grimaldos Lopez. The entire village accuses the pair of the crime, including the shepherd's mother, Dolores Varon Pavo, who gathers evidence against them. Pleading their innocence, they are brutally tortured by the Civil Guard, finally confess, and are brought to trial by the Provincial Courts of Cuenca, where the

Franciso Casares and Daniel Dicenta in *El crimen de Cuenca.*

death sentence is commuted to eighteen years in jail.

The tortures, which follow trumped-up charges, are ordered by Contreras, a local right-wing Congressman and political boss, and Isasa, an ambitious judge seeking to elevate his status in the province.

After eight years, Jose Maria Grimaldos Lopez, the supposed victim of the robbery and murder, shows up in another small town, Mira de la Sierra in the province of Cuenca. His reappearance brings to light the monstrous judicial error committed by the Political Boss and the Magistrate, since the two men were "forced" under torture to confess to a crime they never committed.

As a fitting conclusion, three of the people directly implicated in this miscarriage of justice commit suicide when the case is brought before the courts once again and the shepherds are exonerated.

COMMENTARY: *El crimen de Cuenca* deals very realistically with an actual historical event. It is a wonderfully evocative, detailed film shot in the actual locales where the "supposed" crime took place.

The film contains about fifteen to twenty minutes' worth of torture scenes that portray graphically the police methods of the *Guardia Civil* during the early twentieth century. The men served only six years in jail of a fifteen-year term, being given time off for good behavior, and the film concentrates on their great friendship, showing them embracing each other in the last minutes of the conclusion, after living through torture, self-hate, self-torment and hatred of each other. They are finally vindicated by the judge and the political boss who originally fomented the trial and wanted to see "justice" done at the expense of real truth.

The director, Pilar Miro, has taken a documented story and portrayed graphically and realistically the political, emotional and social behavior of the protagonists of the period. The film stands as a plea to end police brutality, political subversion and provincial ignorance in Cuenca and throughout Spain.

Cuenca is a strong film made by a forceful feminist director. Her aggressive stance was supported by the film industry when, in 1984, she was appointed Director General of the Film & Theatre Division of the Ministry of Culture and helped to promulgate the *Miro Law*, which encouraged the Spanish government to invest in grants up to 50% of a film's budget for worthy projects.

Since 1978, Miro has also fought for total freedom from government censorship, and was crucial in the formation of the *Junta de Clasificacion*, an impartial group elected by the film industry on an "advisory" basis to classify films on a "rating" system, similar to the ones in Great Britain and the United States. With this new system of classification and assurance of total freedom for filmmakers, (battles won by *Cuenca* and Miro's *politique des cineastes*), she has set the tone for filmmakers of the next decade in Spain, the fabulous Eighties.

IV. THE EIGHTIES

During this decade, more feature films were produced than in any other, especially in the first six years. But because of the rise in production of videocassette recorders (VCR's) and the huge sale of videocassettes, audience attendance in Spanish cinemas dropped sharply towards the end of the decade. As this book goes to press, however, there have been some signs that Spanish films are recapturing their formerly gigantic box-office ratings.

Government subsidies to the motion picture industry have also been on the wane, reflecting the roller-coaster changes in political policies so typical of Spain, and causing detrimental effects on Spanish film production. Various Ministers of Culture and Presidents of the *Filmoteca Nacional* have been appointed and have served brief terms, to be replaced by other "political" appointees who know very little about Spanish cinema. Some film directors profited from these changes but others suffered at the hands of often inexperienced "politicos" who sat in judgment on worthy film projects but did not provide funds to keep up the momentum of the film industry.

At least two major developments took place in the industry itself: token attention was paid to worldwide distribution (e.g., Spanish Film Festivals in New York City and elsewhere) and many new Spanish films were made in English and other foreign languages, utilizing foreign locales and talent from other countries as drawing cards to counteract waning audience attendance. The co-production became the norm in the late eighties, as did monies invested by RTVE (Spanish Radio & Television) in feature film production.

As this book goes to press, more than one thousand new feature films had been produced in the eighties, with two hundred more projected before the close of the decade. The Ministry of Education, under the leadership of author Jorge Semprun, continues to perpetuate the industry motto: Spanish Films for the World! *Vale!*

1980

OPERA PRIMA (FIRST WORK)

DIRECTOR: FERNANDO TRUEBA

CREDITS: Screenplay: Fernando Trueba & Oscar Ladoire; Color and CinemaScope Photography: A. Luis Fernandez; Producer: Fernando Colomo; Music: Fernando Ember.

CAST: Oscar Ladoire (Matias), Paula Molina (Violeta), Antonio Resines (Leon), Gonzales Regural (Nicky), Kitty Manver (Ana), Marisa Paredes (Zoila), David

Thompson (Warren Belch), Alejandro Serna (Alejandro).

BACKGROUND: Beginning with its title, a bilingual pun referring to the hero's work on his first novel, and to his accidental meeting with his cousin (*prima*) at the Madrid Metro station Opera, *Opera prima* is considered the first major work of Fernando Trueba, a new filmmaker then under thirty. It was both produced and directed by him and acted by a group of unknown Spaniards who succeeded in making a lively comedy which is fully attuned to today's Spanish society (at least the under thirty generation). It is a sprightly film which represents a new comic spirit in commercial Spanish cinema.

PLOT: *Opera prima* has a simple story-line. Boy (Matias) meets girl (Violeta, his cousin) one morning in Madrid at the Plaza de Opera subway station. They are two opposites who improbably attract and fall in love with each other. Apparently Matias had lived with Violeta and her family several years before, but now Violeta is nineteen, has her own apartment and is studying the violin. Matias at twenty-five is a divorced journalist who lives alone and would like to recapture with Violeta the happiness of their youth.

But so many things separate them. Violeta is a vegetarian and Matias loves meat. Matias hates foreign travel and Violeta adores it. Nevertheless they fall in love again and Violeta seduces Matias. He moves into her apartment but she decides to leave for Peru and the wonders of Machu-Picchu in spite of her new-found happiness with Matias. He is insanely and irrationally jealous of Violeta's other male friends. When Violeta informs him of her impending trip, Matias insincerely tells her that it is a wonderful idea. But as she leaves for the airport, Matias realizes he loves her too much to lose her. At the Aero Peru gate, Violeta decides to return to Matias. When she turns around at the Opera Square, they start running towards each other and embrace.

COMMENTARY: An extremely romantic comedy about intense, moody young people who lead complicated lives and tend to complicate them further with a variety of sexual liaisons, *Opera prima* deserves its success because its actors are charming and easy to look at and never seem to take the plot or themselves too seriously. (Incidentally, Oscar Ladoire won the Best Actor award at the Venice Film Festival for his role.)

The film captures the spirit of daily life in Madrid from the "hippie" vantage point. Ladoire is perfect as the skinny, foul-mouthed, cynical *madrileno* looking for love and finding it with the somewhat corpulent and sexy Paula Molina, who made her screen debut in this film. *Opera prima* is full of youth, charm, scintillating language, delightful dialogue. It is one of the best written and directed films of 1980 and shows off Madrid and its young lovers to their mutual advantage.

The character of Matias, the Madrillian version of all the Seventies gentle, angry young men in Western European films, is most easily compared to Francois Truffaut's creation, Antoine Doinel. But Matias has wit, a sense of humor and a beguiling self-confidence that his French counterpart seems to lack.

Trueba also inserts Matias as an interviewer into a world of pseudo-literati and porno filmmakers, all to fine comic effect. He seems to share with Woody Allen an affinity for bubble-headed bumblers. This is especially evident during Matias' outrageous interview with an American author, Warren Belch, who has just successfully published his first novel, *A Trip to the End of My Anus*, and is writing its successor, *Dried Shit*. (Sometimes, Trueba's humor and lampoons are a bit too broad and off-color.)

Yet *Opera prima* can be so hysterically funny that one sometimes finds it hard to understand how this very amateur and yet

Paula Molina and Oscar Ladoire in *Opera prima*.

sophisticated film was ever produced in Spain. Gone are the morbid metaphors of Carlos Saura and his recapturing of the past, Francoism and the Civil War. *Opera prima* is the very first light-hearted film to come from Spain and demonstrates a kind of renaissance in Spanish filmmaking.

Trueba has paved the way for Colomo and Almodovar. His is the first Spanish comedy film in the manner of Truffaut or Woody Allen, and has a true charm in its reflection of the trendy new post-Franco era of cultural and sexual freedom. Trueba's dialogue is snappy, ribbing the stodgy old values of the Franco regime; his cynicism is freshly imbued with an eighties' morality. For example, women like Violeta are portrayed as emancipated, sophisticated, outwardly sexual. No *tia Tula* here. Sexuality and its variations and combinations are all portrayed openly, easily on the screen, and for the first time, in amazingly good taste. The film is a light, upbeat comedy, aimed at a very articulate youth market.

Opera prima is a marvelously controlled film, largely made up of two-shots. It is also a wonderful example of classical filmmaking, a tribute to Trueba's intelligence in not treating flamboyantly such potentially flamboyant material. Notice how he handles Matias' jealousy scene, playfully beating up his rival Nicky off-camera, and Zoila's *ménage à trois* invitation is carefully handled, with Matias' friend Leon reporting what happened to him off-camera, where Zoila expertly ravaged him, practically against his will.

Trueba avoided many temptations to "jazz up" his screenplay with excessive zaniness on the part of his actors or to include a soundtrack with too many "hip" or "mod" or "rock" songs and sounds. He succeeds in convincing us of the romance between Matias and Violeta, the cranky intellectual and the earthy sensualist, because he employs directorial restraint. Although the film originally was a pun on the words opera (work) and prima (first), Trueba decided to have a musical *prima* (cousin), who lives near the "Opera" metro station, meet her cousin and begin their romance.

Trueba is a new, young director who has brought humor into the somewhat airless world of the Spanish cinema. He has caused laughter to ring out once again in the capital's best cinemas along the Gran Via (the Broadway of Madrid). *Opera prima* has also been very successful in the U.S. and abroad.

1980

EL NIDO (THE NEST)

DIRECTOR: JAIME DE ARMINAN

CREDITS: Screenplay: Jaime de Arminan; Color Photography: Teo Escamilla; Producer: A Punto E.L.S.A. Films; Music: Haydn's *Creation*, anonymous music from the seventeenth century, and selections of Maxence Cantelobe.

CAST: Hector Alterio (Alejandro), Ana Torrent (Gregoria, or "Goyita"), Luis Politti (Eladio, the priest), Agustin Gonzales (the Sergeant), Patricia Adriani (the schoolteacher), Maria Luisa Ponte (the housekeeper), Mercedes Alonso (the antique dealer), Ovidi Montllor (the father).

BACKGROUND: Only slightly reminiscent of the films made before Franco's death, when writers and directors alike, in order to circumvent censorship, used allegory, understatement, allusions and ellipses, and transformed their screenplays into a national cinema style of "possibilities" typical of Spain during this repressive era, *El nido* attempts to break with this tradition. De Arminan emerges as a courageous director, executing with originality and lyricism the somewhat "ambiguous" themes of this film with supreme good taste.

Following the success of *Mi querida senorita* (*My Dearest Senorita*), *El nido* is a breakthrough film, a love story between a teenage girl and a widowed aristocrat in his sixties. As in his earlier films, De Arminan preserves his reputation as a careful, lyrical teller of unusual stories of extraordinary—and sometimes, ordinary—behavior filmed with sensitivity, charm and psychological acuity. It was the Foreign Language Nominee from Spain for the Academy Award in 1981.

PLOT: Set in the environs of Salamanca, *El nido* is the story of an aging *hidalgo* (gentleman), Alejandro, who lives in an ultra-modern but rustic country house, and his relationship with a girl on the verge of puberty named Goyita. Alejandro lives a purposeless life filled by computer chess, horseback riding, and an elaborate stereo system to which he conducts to the sounds of Haydn's "Creation." His wife had apparently died several years earlier (there were no progeny) and Alejandro is easily disposed to meeting the thirteen-year-old village school girl Goyita. Their meeting is well-planned by her. Since both have a fondness for identifying birds and hunting nests, on one particular sunny day she hits him on the head with a rook's egg and leaves him notes and clues so that he can identify her as the young student playing Lady Macbeth in the local village play.

Because this serious, mature and reflective teenager is just as alone as Alejandro when they meet, she insinuates herself into his life and a strange, overpowering relationship develops between them, at first Platonic but later with covert sexual overtones. The older man acts much like a child and later forbids Goyita to see him. Goyita, the daughter of a Civil Guardsman, makes more elaborate demands upon Alejandro. He balks at first, then complies, burning his wife's clothes at her

Ana Torrent and Hector Alterio in *El nido*.

insistence. Finally, they swear an oath of allegiance (and love) in blood. She asks Alejandro to avenge her hate for the local Civil Guard sergeant (her father's superior officer) who set free her pet hawk.

Aware of the "love" he feels for Goyita, Alejandro nevertheless cannot stop her family from sending her off to relatives in Salamanca, to discourage their relationship. Following Goyita there, Alejandro realizes he must fulfill the pact, challenge and kill the sergeant out of love for Goyita. From high above, on horseback in the mountains, Alejandro fires at the sergeant, who is riding with Goyita's father, but Alejandro is shot and killed by the Civil Guards. (Apparently his rifle contained only blanks, indicating his wish to die for his unfulfilled and impossible relationship with Goyita.) He is buried on a hillside on his own estate. Several years later, Goyita returns to the grave site, and promises never to give herself sexually to anyone else, a reaffirmation of the love pact they had sworn for eternity.

COMMENTARY: *The Nest* has some especially well-played scenes between Hector Alterio and Ana Torrent—they lead an orchestra together in the open forest, hunt for birds and nests, and just play and ride horseback together. Torrent enacts the role of child-woman with extraordinary charm and grace. Alterio realizes, although he was once married, that he had never really lived passionately until he met Goyita (Torrent) and that hers is the only "game in town" he wants to play. He is doomed to die.

The Nest is an extraordinarily sensitive and beautiful film. The nest itself is symbolic of a comfortable place, a sanctuary which one finds only in death. Torrent may be thought of as a Spanish "Lolita," a nymphette who leads and even tantalizes Alejandro to his death. It is also possible to read Alejandro's role differently: he is Don Quixote on a white steed, living a chivalric Middle Age romance with his lady, performing a "boon" for her that ultimately leads to his demise. Notice Alterio's patriarchal greying beard and his willingness to give himself over to their fantasy world of love and solitude.

If this film had been made before Franco's death, Alejandro's suicide scene would have not been permitted and *El nido* would have been turned into a genteel love story between an older man and a young girl, devoid of any sexuality or eroticism. Defamatory references to the Catholic church would also never have been permitted. The film has several extraordinary performances, especially Torrent's Goyita, who expresses everything in her face, while literally doing nothing. Her performance and Alterio's are believable and larger than life. Although Goyita may act out both incestuous and patricidal desires, the director has succeeded in sounding the death knell of the strength and indestructibility of the family unit. Gone forever is the Francoist esthetic of the glorified ideals of patriotism, Catholicism and the family. With *El nido*, Spanish cinema departs from the "official styles" of glorification into the new realm of a personal, individualized, controversial and dynamic cinema.

1981

BODAS DE SANGRE (BLOOD WEDDING)

DIRECTOR: CARLOS SAURA

CREDITS: Screenplay: Alfredo Manas, based upon the play *Blood Wedding* by Federico Garcia Lorca; Color Photography: Teo Escamilla; Producer: Emiliano Piedras; Music: Emilio de Diego.

CAST: Antonio Gades (Leonardo), Cristina Hoyos (the bride), Juan Antonio (the bridegroom), Pilar Cardenas (the mother), Carmen Villena (the wife).

BACKGROUND: After a career spanning over thirty years directing Spanish films, Carlos Saura emerges in the 1980s as a truly artistic director for the first time, acting as the interpreter of this classic Spanish play. While adhering to the drama, however, he chooses to tell the entire story through the dance.

Bodas de sangre begins backstage at a rehearsal hall. The actor-dancers are putting on makeup and costumes, practicing steps. Saura as director is a participant, asking questions, interviewing the dancers in semi-documentary fashion, using his camera to capture their pre-performance conversations, thoughts, actions, jitters.

The star of the film is Antonio Gades, with his entire troupe of Flamenco dancers. In a long, rambling monologue, Gades, as he applies his makeup, reveals how he got his start in flamenco ballet. (In the pressbook, Gades is listed as the "first" dancer and choreographer of the "ballet," *Blood Wedding,* as directed by Saura.) As the dancers prepare for the performance, we can see why Saura made a conscious choice to film Lorca's play as dance rather than as a literary or theatrical work.

PLOT: The action of the film takes place in six scenes.

In the first, the Mother is helping the Bridegroom into his wedding suit. She discovers he is carrying a knife and takes it away from him as her son tells her it may be used for cutting a bunch of grapes or an imaginary flower, which the Bridegroom gives her as she hears a horse's gallop, which is considered a bad omen. The Mother keeps the knife.

In the second scene, it is the morning of the wedding. Leonardo's wife, already dressed for the ceremony, is waiting, somewhat agitated and upset by the late arrival of her husband. Leonardo always arrives late and stays away from home for days on end or sometimes does not come home at all. On this occasion, when he enters the house, his wife is rocking their baby, singing a lullaby. (The song is delivered by Marisol, the real wife of Antonio Gades.) His wife ceases her singing when she hears the horse's gallop previously heard by the Bridegroom's mother. Leonardo and his wife dance a ballet of jealousy and reproach. Later he rocks the baby's cradle but his wife takes the baby away from him and Leonardo leaves.

In the third scene, Leonardo is alone, serious, deep in thought about someone else. That "someone" is far away, but his imagination brings her within view; it is the Bride, dressed in underclothes as women prepare her for the wedding ceremony. In his imagination, a love dance begins between Leonardo and the Bride. They are united in their passion, their ecstasy, dancing a lyric dance of pure sensuality. When one of the bride's attendants comes to dress her in the wedding dress, the image of Leonardo fades.

The fourth scene begins as Leonardo enters the Bride's house after the ceremony and sees the entire wedding cortege. Everyone celebrates the wedding in classical village fashion. As the Bride and Bridegroom dance to "Long live the happy couple!" Leonardo is found alone, brooding. When Leonardo's wife leaves him to dance with another man, Leonardo seizes the opportunity to dance with the Bride, precipitating a jealous rage on the part of his wife. The Bride and Bridegroom dance once again after this "interlude" of jealous rage. Leonardo's wife, once again, watches Leonardo seek out the Bride and sees them decide to elope on horseback. The Bridegroom's mother now looks for the knife, gives it back to her son and urges him to redress their honor by killing Leonardo.

In the fifth scene, Leonardo and the Bride are riding on "imaginary" horseback, literally flying, locked in their passion. The Bridegroom appears with four more riders, following them closely.

In the sixth and last scene, Leonardo and the Bride appear, she still in her wedding dress. The Bridegroom's horse

Poster art for *Bodas de sangre*.

approaches and both men dismount. As the Bride tries to place herself between them, they push her aside, open their knives in true Gypsy fashion and begin an intense, agonizing fight in the final ballet sequence of the film, a literal dance to the death. Leonardo thrusts his knife into the Bridegroom's belly as the latter thrusts his knife into Leonardo's heart. Before they both fall, the Bride embraces them and both die at her feet.

COMMENTARY: Gades' choreography for *Blood Wedding* shows tremendous literary respect for Lorca, and Saura felt that through the dance, he could best reach the heart of Lorca's drama of jealousy and vengeance. This 72-minute film adeptly captures the drama—in the faces, the feet stamping in throbbing closeups, the virtuosity of Gades and his troupe—of Lorca's tale of love, seduction and murder. The camera both records and participates in the telling of Lorca's tale of deceit.

One of the most thrilling uses of the rhythmic camera occurs in the climactic switch-blade fight, beautifully photographed in 360-degree turns. The camera "dances" itself. Sometimes Saura will begin a sequence with a closeup of one foot tapping and then cut away brilliantly, unexpectedly, breathlessly into a panning shot of the entire ensemble dancing a spirited fandango. It is a film of bewitching beauty, a spell-binding aesthetic experience.

In nearly thirty years of filmmaking, Carlos Saura's career has matured extensively. This film, *Bodas de Sangre,* blends his early naturalistic style with his later literary qualities into an imaginative and aesthetically beautiful film that transcends Saura's own sense of style, into something lyrical beyond it. *Blood Wedding* transports us into a dimension of illusion, beyond personal significance into a poetic and spiritual union with Spain, flamenco, life and death.

The film is a literal explosion of energy, a pure celebration of Spain, its people, its great emotions. It is a passionate experience celebrating *machismo,* lyricism, flamenco, great art. Saura is to reprise this aesthetic celebration in *Carmen* (1983) and again in *El amor brujo* (1985), both dynamic tours de force in a trilogy where fiction, reality and flamenco merge to create true cinema magic.

1982

LA COLMENA (THE BEEHIVE)

DIRECTOR: MARIO CAMUS

CREDITS: Screenplay: Jose Luis Dibildos, based upon the famous Camilo Jose Cela novel; Color Photography: Hans Burmann; Producer: Jose Luis Dibildos for Agata Films; Music: Anton Garcia Abril.

CAST: (in alphabetical order): Victoria Abril (Julita), Francisco Algora (Ramon Maello), Rafael Alonso (Julian Suarez), Ana Belen (Victorita), Jose Bodalo (Don Roque), Mary Carillo (Dona Asuncion), Camilo Jose Cela (Matias Marti), Fiorello Faltoyano (Filo), Agustin Gonzales (Mario de la Vega), Emilio Gutierrez Caba (Ventura Aguado), Charo Lopez (Nati Robles), Jose Luis Lopez Vasquez (Leonardo Melendez), Encarna Paso (Victorita's mother), Maria Luisa Ponte (Dona Rosa), Elvira Quintilla (Dona Visi), Francisco Rabal (Ricardo Sorbedo), Antonio Resines (Pepe "El Astilla"), Jose Sacristan (Martin Marcos), Concha Velasco (Purita).

BACKGROUND: Winner of the Golden Bear Award for Best Movie of the Year in 1983, *La colmena* is one of the most lavishly produced adaptations of Camilo Jose Cela's epic novel about the lives of more than sixty

Francisco Rabal, Mario Pardo, Francisco Algora, Luis Barbero, and Jose Sacristan in *La colmena*.

characters in post-Civil War Madrid *circa* 1943. It features a cast of all-star actors from the modern Spanish stage and screen.

PLOT: Martin Marcos, a poor poet, spends much of his time at "La Delicia," an enormous cafe owned by Dona Rosa. The film repeats many of the plots of M-G-M's *Grand Hotel*, Vicki Baum's filmed novel set in Berlin in 1932. Instead of the hotel, we are in a huge cafe in Madrid, either in 1942 or 1943, witnessing how the people live in an atmosphere of economic duress and political fear. Everyone is hungry, tired, short tempered, destitute, but all have an indomitable will to survive.

The cavernous cafe is always crowded with people who want not only shelter from the cold winter, but to take refuge in their conversations, in each other's company and in their dreams.

During the course of the film, over sixty characters are observed inside and outside the cafe, in the streets and in the houses of Madrid. An avalanche of people, sometimes happy and at other times not so happy. From these thumbnail sketches of various characters, we glimpse each person's plight and peril.

For example, Jose Luis Lopez Vasquez plays an ex-Communist scratching out an existence in Francoist Spain; Ana Belen is a prostitute working so that she and her tubercular lover will be able to survive the winter; Concha Velasquez reprises her "prostitute" role, ironically called "Purita" ("Purity"); Victoria Abril, who plays Julita, is desperately in love with the poet, Martin Marcos (Jose Sacristan), who is unable to respond to her needs. Francisco Rabal plays another poet, Ricardo Sorbedo, who comments upon the actions of most of these characters set against the urban post-war background of Madrid.

There is an occasionally humorous scene. One of the most memorable and funniest takes place when the poets (Sacristan and Rabal) discover that the tables in the cafe are marble slabs stolen from the local cemetery.

Although we may enter into the lives of this bustling cast of characters, this crowd, this "beehive," and experience their innermost thoughts and feelings, there is never a solution to their depressing problems on screen. The author felt that we must accept these people and their situations, even if they disgust us, since they are not worth our sadness. Sadness is an atavism, too, Cela believes.

Agustin Gonzales and Ana Belen in *La colmena.*

COMMENTARY: All the characters in *La colmena* come and go as in Vicki Baum's *Grand Hotel,* and nothing significant ever happens. However, Spaniards, like Americans, love to see film versions of their own classic literature and Mario Camus is one of the best practitioners of this kind of artful transposition. He is a skillful and efficient narrator of almost intractable material.

La colmena suffers from an unwieldy number of characters and incidents but Camus deftly interweaves together a series of short, incisive tales, creating a dramatic mini-cosmos from this flotsam of Spanish society. The film was the box-office champion of 1982 because Spaniards flocked to the cinemas to discover in this florid recreation of the post-Civil War years, a Spain unknown to a generation born in the Sixties. *La colmena* has the feeling of an authentic recreation of the period and is deservedly Mario Camus' earliest success in a string of successful films based upon modern Spanish novels.

1983

CARMEN

DIRECTOR: CARLOS SAURA

CREDITS: Screenplay: Carlos Saura & Antonio Gades, based upon the Prosper Mérimée novella, "Carmen," and the Bizet opera; Color and CinemaScope Photography: Teo Escamilla; Producer: Emiliano Piedra for C.B. Films; Music: Paco de Lucia, and fragments from the opera "Carmen" sung by Regina Resnik and Mario del Monaco.

CAST: Antonio Gades (Antonio, the choreographer), Laura del Sol (Carmen, the dancer), Paco de Lucia (the guitarist), Cristina Hoyos (Cristina, the teacher), Sebastian Romero, Jose Yepes, Pepa Flores (dancers).

BACKGROUND: *Carmen,* the film, is now a flamenco dance drama, the result of the second collaboration between Saura and Gades. It is the eternal story of love and jealousy, inexorably mixed, leading to tragedy. This film version merges the flamenco form of Spanish music and dance with the Bizet opera, an eternal, almost mythical story of an all-consuming passion, jealousy, leading the characters to their destruction. It was a contender for the Foreign Film Oscar in the United States that year.

PLOT: In 1983 in a rehearsal studio on the outskirts of Madrid, Antonio is looking for the perfect Carmen for his new dance version combining the Mérimée-Bizet versions of their idea of Carmen—the *tabacalera,* the seductress, the treacherous siren, sexually leading men to their doom.

He meets the young Carmen in a school for flamenco. Carmen dazzles Antonio, sleeps with him, but neglects to tell him about her husband who is serving time in a Madrid jail for selling (or using) illegal drugs. Under Cristina's and Antonio's tutelage, Carmen ascends to her role of the mythical "Carmen" but assimilates all the malevolent traits of the Mérimée character. Antonio offers to buy her husband off so that Carmen will move in with him. Carmen, however, wants to be free to sleep with any man she likes, even though she says she "loves" Antonio.

On the evening before Antonio's birthday celebration and the bullfight of the following day, Carmen is caught by Antonio *in flagrante* with one of Antonio's male dancers. Antonio throws them out, but the flamenco performance continues the next day with the arrival of the bullfighter. Carmen makes amorous overtures to the latter, but Antonio intervenes and kills Carmen with a knife in the wings of the rehearsal hall.

COMMENTARY: Utilizing Gades' flamenco troupe once again to fine advantage, the film contains some spectacular

Laura del Sol and Cristina Hoyos in *Carmen.*

dancing, performed without real sets or props. Unlike *Bodas de sangre,* which already had a script and choreography, *Carmen* had to be created anew, reinvented with a script by Saura and choreography by Gades, whose intention was to dance the ballet of *Carmen* in theaters after a successful commercial run of the film at international cinemas.

If Saura had kept to his notion of a dance film made in the high style of a Franco Zeffirelli-mounted opera, *Carmen* might have been a more transcendent work of art. Although it was more successful than *Bodas de sangre* at the box office, I feel that Saura erred in transfering the romantic plot of the fictional intrigue acted out by Gades and Laura del Sol to a contemporary setting—Madrid society in 1983. When Gades murders his ballet dancer, Carmen, because of her infidelity (as Don Jose kills the Carmen of Mérimée's novella), the scene echoes its nineteenth-century counterpart but has no reality in contemporary Madrillian society. Carmen is a modern "liberated woman," and Gades should have just walked away at the conclusion. Post-Francoist cinema has gone way beyond the old clichés of *machismo* and female sexual naiveté.

If this is a structural fault, this version of *Carmen* is still a truly mesmerizing experience, especially because of the dance sequences, the true highlights of the film. This film had such great international success because it demonstrates Saura's artistic growth and ability to interpret a truly Spanish theme through the medium of Gades' ballet. And Gades is undeniably a true star, resilient, creative, immortal. Saura and Gades have somewhat successfully used the device of life mirroring art, offstage and on, at times blurring the dividing line between rehearsal hall (reality) and the drama (fiction). But it is Gades' brilliant choreographic pyrotechnics, executed with breathtaking expertise, that make this version of the *Carmen* genre truly memorable.

1983

EL SUR (THE SOUTH)

DIRECTOR: VICTOR ERICE

CREDITS: Screenplay: Victor Erice; Color Photography: Jose Luis Alcaine; Producer: Elias Querejeta for Chloe Productions (A Spanish-French Co-production); Music: Granados, Ravel, Schubert.

CAST: Omero Antonutti (Agustin, the father), Sonsoles Aranguren (Estrella, his daughter, age eight), Iciar Bollain (Estrella, age fifteen), Lola Cardona (Julia), Rafaela Aparicio (Milagros), Maria Caro (Casilda), Francisco Merino, Aurore Clement and Germaine Montero.

BACKGROUND: Erice's second film in ten years after *Spirit of the Beehive, El sur* opened to successful reviews in Madrid and in New York at the 1983 Spanish Film Festival. But as a result of some cuts made by the producer, Elias Querejeta, Erice supposedly never finished the film, or the "second" part of the film was abandoned by him because of the producer's "interference." Whatever the situation, Querejeta edited the footage and released it under the director's name.

PLOT: Agustin, a doctor and water diviner, lives with his wife Julia, a teacher (who is not allowed to teach after the Civil War), and their young daughter Estrella, in "La Gaviota" ("The Seagull,") a house with a weather vane, on the outskirts of a town in the northern part of Spain in the late fifties. The story shows Estrella growing up and the fascination exerted upon her by her Republican father.

One day, almost by chance, Estrella discovers some letters which make her suspect that there is (or has been) another woman in her father's life, perhaps an actress. From that moment on, her life changes at "La Gaviota." She begins to imagine things about her father and the south, where he had lived.

We discover that her father left the south because of ideological differences over the Civil War. The film concentrates on developing the relationship between father and daughter, revealing the father's past love affair with an actress, his disillusion living in the north, his suicide. But even in her final conversations with her father, the now adolescent Estrella is unable to discover the identity of the woman who, Agustin knew, definitely remained in the south. Left with her mother, Estrella decides to go south, to visit her grandparents and aunts and perhaps to penetrate the mysteries of her father's strange behavior.

COMMENTARY: Filmed in the distinctive elliptical style Erice introduced in *Spirit of the Beehive* in 1973, and once again dealing with the pains of childhood, memory and the Spanish Civil War as seen through the eyes of a child, and later an adolescent, *El sur* is a masterful drama and confirms Erice as a rare and major talent of Spanish cinema.

It is a richly textured film, with beautiful, lyrical photography reminiscent of impressionist paintings, and extends the lyricism of *Spirit of the Beehive* into the

Omero Antonutti and Sonsoles Aranguren in *El sur*.

1980s. One scene that demonstrates this quality is Estrella's Communion celebration, where her face is highlighted and the background remains in palpable darkness as father and daughter begin to dance, round and round, the camera swirling in 360-degree turns to music identified as "their" song, which the father later forgets near the end of his life. Erice's world is poetic, mythical, elusive and mysterious, like the relationship of the father and child-daughter woman in the film.

Antonutti's role is masterfully played, especially in the scenes where there is virtually no dialogue and we are forced to watch and read the father's gaze, which is the heart of the film. In fact, there is a wonderful scene when Estrella follows her father to a movie theater and spies on him after he had seen *Flower in the Shadow* starring Irene Rios, as he sits in a local cafe, lost in dreams after the film, in reveries of the past. He seems emotionally despondent, miserable, plagued by his Leftist past, uncomfortable in this desolate village of the north.

Just as Erice made a homage to movies in *Spirit of the Beehive,* he does so again in this film. But *El sur* is a difficult film to decipher. We never reach the south, Estrella's birthplace, the land of sun and hope, where all mysteries are resolved, the elusive, unattainable future. It is there that Estrella would have reconstructed her father's past life, solved the mystery of his "love affair" and perhaps received the enlightenment and fulfillment necessary to carry on with her own life or her father's mission. (Just before committing suicide, Agustin put his magical pendant for water divining under Estrella's pillow, lovingly entrusting to her the sacred object that unites them both and mandating her to go south, to return to their homeland, perhaps figuratively uniting northern and southern Spain.)

In many interviews after *El sur* was released, Erice discussed his frustration and the remaining second part that should have been filmed in the south. It seems that the father had an affair with a minor actress, Irene Rios, and they had an illegitimate son whom Estrella now meets and becomes romantically involved with on her trip south. In fact, her half-brother/lover called "Octavio" wants to be a writer and is given the diviner pendulum by Estrella, thus carrying on the tradition for his father Agustin. However, Estrella's aunt, fearful of an incestuous relationship and reluctant to tell the boy about his father who had been living all of these years in the north, tries to discourage the relationship. Besides giving *El sur* the satisfying ending it deserved, this section, had it been filmed, would have raised Erice's stature beyond the "rare" directorial talent that he already is, to the level of ethereal myth-maker and illusionist. Still, *El sur* is brilliant cinema and like its predecessor, *Spirit of the Beehive,* one of the very best films to come from Iberia.

1984

TASIO

DIRECTOR: MONTXO ARMENDARIZ

CREDITS: Screenplay: Montxo Armendariz; Color Photography: Jose Luis Alcaine; Producer: Elias Querejeta; Music: Angel Illarramendi.

CAST: Patxi Bisquert (Tasio as an adult), Isidro Jose Solano (Tasio as an adolescent), Garikoitz Mendigutxia (Tasio as a child), Amaia Lasa (Paulina, Tasio's wife), Enrique Goicoechea (Tasio's father), Elena Uriz Etxaleku (Tasio's mother), Ignacio Martinez (Tasio's brother), Jose Maria Asin (Tasio's friend), and a cast of fifty-six Basque actors.

BACKGROUND: In the early eighties, Basque cinema began to attract large audiences in Spain and elsewhere. In fact, *Tasio* was the unqualified hit of the Second Spanish Film Festival in New York in 1986. The Basque government also instituted a new and enlightened film policy, subsidizing up to one-quarter of a film's budget, providing all filming was done in the Basque provinces and that mostly Basque actors and technicians were utilized, although the films did not have to be made in the Basque language.

Taking its cue from the Basques, the Spanish government, in 1984, under the Ministry of Culture, decided to provide up to 50% of funding for worthwhile projects, with similar stipulations. The Catalan government followed suit, making seed money available for films shot in Catalonia (Barcelona) and in the Catalan language, as well as offering loans up to ¾ of a million dollars for viable film projects.

During the early eighties, the encouragement of "regional" films, especially in the *vascuence* (Basque) and *catalan* (Catalonia) languages, was rife and a Spanish cinema took a more urgent, political, committed tone, free of censorship and steeped in folkloric traditions of the outlying provinces, encouraging "separatist" cinema. *Tasio* is one of the best examples of this new movement in Spanish films.

Amaia Lasa and Patxi Bisquert in *Tasio*.

PLOT: *Tasio* is the story of a man born in a Basque hamlet at the foot of the hills of Urbasa. We see him at age eight, forced to work up in the hills because of his family's poverty.

At fourteen, following the tradition of the valley, he becomes an apprentice coal-miner. At this time, he meets Paulina, the young girl who some years later will become his wife.

Married at age twenty, he and Paulina have their only child, Elisa. With this added responsibility, Tasio not only continues his job as coal-miner but begins to poach illegally in the forest, making an enemy of the game warden.

One day, after killing a huge boar, Tasio is told that Paulina is gravely ill. She dies, and this is the most difficult moment in Tasio's life. His parents try to convince him to abandon the hills as a coal-miner/poacher and take a steady job in the nearby city. But Tasio refuses.

Tasio's daughter, already grown up into a beautiful young woman, hurriedly marries a local villager—she is already pregnant—and will move with him to the big city. Tasio is invited to live with them, but he refuses; he prefers to remain in his solitude with his memories of Paulina, tending to the coal pyres and occasionally poaching, to the chagrin of the game warden.

COMMENTARY: A unique and sensitive drama, *Tasio* is an especially good film because of the natural performances elicited from a series of new actors who speak in *vascuence* (Basque) and at times in Castilian. They are fresh, new faces on the Spanish screen. Tasio is the center of the film. It is essentially his story, from birth and childhood to adolescence to old man, all witnessed in two hours. At the end of the film, we watch him giving away his daughter in marriage, and know that he's destined to remain alone till his death.

Tasio, the man, incarnates the rebellious

nature of the Basques and will work for no man but himself. He has an indomitable sense of freedom. This single characteristic is the essence of the film. Tasio is a rude peasant who has fulfilled his life the best way he could. Though his life is a lonely one now, stoking coke for sale is the only job he really knows and at which he is supremely happy. The director emphasizes that loneliness is preferable to giving up one's personal freedom, and Tasio's life is testimony to this philosophy. He lives what he is, a totally free man.

Tasio, is a tribute to Basque liberty. Armendariz' filming of this fictional biography also gives credibility to the concept that the individual is no longer prisoner of his environment but also profits from it, identifies with it, triumphs over it—certainly a new concept in post-Franco cinema.

1984

LA MUERTE DE MIKEL (THE DEATH OF MIKEL)

DIRECTOR: IMANOL URIBE

CREDITS: Screenplay: Jose Angel Rebolledo & Imanol Uribe; Color Photography: Javier Aguirresarobe; Producer: Jose Cuxant for Aiete/Jose Esteban Alenda/ Cobra Films: Music: Alberto Iglesias.

CAST: Imanol Arias (Mikel), Monserrat Salvador (Dona Maria Luisa, his mother), Fama (Fama, a transsexual), Amaia Lasa (Begona, his wife), Ramon Barea (Yon Uriarte), Martin Adjemian (Martin), Juan Mari Segues (Don Jaime), Xabier Elorriaga (Inaki, his brother), Daniel Dicenta (Inspector).

BACKGROUND: Often shown at gay film festivals in the United States, *La muerte de Mikel* is another post-Franco Basque film that deals with a formerly forbidden theme—homosexuality. Unlike the films of Eloy de Iglesia, a contemporary of Uribe's who seems to extol the virtues of the "gay" Spanish population (*El Diputado* and *Colegas* among others), Uribe is more interested in the social and political aspects of homosexuality in Spain.

PLOT: *La muerte de Mikel* tells, in a series of flashbacks, the story of Mikel, a Basque pharmacist, unhappily married, at war with his wife, his country, his repressed homosexuality.

We first meet Mikel after his wife returns to him from a European vacation-cum-trial separation. As Mikel and his wife make love after her return, we witness a horrible sexual scene in which Mikel, feigning drunkenness, sinks his teeth into his wife's genitals, creating great pain and mental agony for Begona. Mikel's best friend, a local doctor, recommends him to a psychiatrist because of this outrageous event, but therapy does not seem to help him.

As the film progresses, Mikel meets a transvestite (played by Fama), beds him and falls in love thereafter, coming slowly "out of the closet" from his "latent" homosexuality.

Mikel's "politics" become the larger issue as the film moves towards its conclusion. Formerly a member of ETA, the Basque Revolutionary Party, Mikel is arrested, tortured, sequestered. He dies off screen, and we assume that he committed suicide because of the psycho-sexual-political vortex in which he became involved. Or perhaps, he was poisoned by his own mother, since she could not share Mikel's gay pride or his political and/or social behavior.

COMMENTARY: The entire film was made in a small town outside of Bilbao in Northern Spain. Some scenes were also

Imanol Arias and Fama in *La muerte de Mikel.*

shot in Bilbao, especially the gay-club scenes with Fama. Imanol Arias plays the Mikel character with care, depth and multifaceted shadings. Fama is equally moving as the object of Mikel's affections.

The director, Uribe, emphasizes the provincialism of the town, the gossiping of its inhabitants and the consequent deleterious effects upon Mikel, his brother (Xabier Elorriaga) and their mother (Monserrat Salvador).

Mikel's mother is caught in conflict between her son's professed homosexual behavior and her own pride as head of an aristocratic clan. Her conflict creates a lapse in the continuity of the film's final moments. It is difficult to perceive whether or not Mikel was let out of prison and came home before his "death" occurred, since the death scene is never seen on camera. His demise continues as a puzzlement, especially since the Basque Separatists claim him as one of their fallen, dispelling entirely the notion of Mikel's homosexuality as the prime cause of his death.

The film's rather ambiguous ending does not serve well as a political message or a proper dramatic conclusion. Audiences will clearly sympathize with Uribe's depiction of gay men asserting their sexual preference. But the director hops off the track and the film dissipates its own impact, because of the ambiguous conclusion and through the use of flashbacks that tend to confuse rather than illuminate.

Uribe is a strong, forthright director and this film reveals that behind the physical beauty of Northern Spain lie the inner political and sexual conflicts of many Spanish males. Yet curiously, *La muerte de Mikel* leaves one saddened because the denouement provides only a personal conclusion for Mikel; it cures the gossip directed towards his aristocratic family, but neither solves the sexual repressiveness nor offers political solutions for the problems of the Basque country of the mid-eighties.

Uribe's film is more of a direct assault on bourgeois life, Spanish police methods and Basque politicos than we have seen before from this part of Spain. This is Uribe's watershed film and it made him the top Basque filmmaker in Iberia because he dared to criticize contemporary Basque society. *La muerte de Mikel* did very well at the box office and precipitated interest in regional Spanish cinema. Uribe's fame as the best-known Basque filmmaker is rightfully deserved and *Muerte* is his strongest film to date.

1984

LOS SANTOS INOCENTES (THE HOLY INNOCENTS)

DIRECTOR: MARIO CAMUS

CREDITS: Screenplay: Antonio Larreta, Manuel Matji & Mario Camus; Color Photography: Hans Burmann; Producer: Julian Mateos with the collaboration of RTVE (Spanish Television); Music: Anton Garcia Abril.

CAST: Alfredo Landa (Paco, el bajo), Terele Pavez (Regula, his wife), Francisco Rabal (Azarias, his brother-in-law), Belen Ballesteros (Nieves, his daughter), Juan Sanchez (Quirce, his son), Susana Sanchez (his retarded daughter), Agata Lys (Dona Purita), Agustin Gonzales (Don Pedro el Perito, the aristocratic landowner), Juan Diego (Senorito Ivan, the hunter), Mary Carrillo (Senora Marquesa), Maribel Martin (Miriam, her daughter), Jose Guardiola (Senorita de la Jara, her grandson), Manuel Zarzo (the doctor).

BACKGROUND: *Los santos inocentes* replaced *El crimen de Cuenca* as the top box-office champion of 1984 and also earned the top acting awards for both Alfredo Landa and Francisco Rabal, who shared the prize at the Cannes Film Festival that year.

Based upon the Miguel Delibes novel of the same name, and considered a five-handkerchief festival film by most critics, it was shown at both the Toronto and New York Film Festivals and continued to garner praise. It is one of the few great Spanish films available on video in the United States and has been shown internationally with great success.

This boldly critical film uses hunting as a metaphor for class oppression, attacking the villainous gentry for their cunning and guile and for keeping the pure-hearted peasants as medieval slaves, always "in their place."

PLOT: The setting is rural Extremadura in the sixties. We are introduced to a family of peasants who, like many others, live under the class that owns the land and always orders them about.

Paco, father of three children Nieves, Quirce and Rosarito (the retarded daughter) and husband to Regula, is the family's chief servant and retriever of game during the hunting season. Regula's brother, Azarias, a grizzled, retarded old primitive with unfortunate toilet habits (he defecates anywhere at any time and covers his hands with his own urine to keep them from chapping), also has a Franciscan rapport with birds (he raises and trains goshawks) and lives with the family in a farmhouse which is devoid of toilet facilities and electricity.

The family never complains to the aristocrats and is always available to serve them. They meekly obey, accepting stoically what must be endured to survive in

Extremadura. Paco and Regula hope their children will become educated and not be condemned to the hard life they experience on a day-to-day basis.

The story of the peasant family is interwoven with revelations about the aristocrats in a series of flashbacks told by each character.

In the first part, we meet Quirce, now a soldier in Franco's army, who remembers how he drove a tractor, and never questioned the authority of Senorito Ivan who used him to retrieve game after his father, Paco, had fallen from a tree, breaking his leg. Paco taught Quirce to read and write, so that one day he would be free from bondage to the aristocrats.

Nieves, now working in a factory in a nearby city, remembers, in the second flashback, how she was forced to work as a maid for the adulterous Dona Purita, wife of Don Pedro and mistress of Senorito Ivan. She, too, remembers the cruelty of Senorito Ivan, who mercilessly ordered her father to retrieve game with an already broken leg, causing him to limp for the rest of his life.

The third flashback is assigned to Paco, who remembers how his family was finally moved to a house with electricity and bathroom facilities, how cruelly Senorito Ivan treated him, forcing him to retrieve game with his broken leg after Ivan was warned by the doctor that Paco could be crippled for life, and how the Marchioness came, giving gold coins to her servants as tokens of gratitude for spending their lives practically as indentured servants on her lands.

Juan Sanchez and Francisco Rabal in *Los santos inocentes.*

The final flashback is seen from Azarias' point of view. Aware of the cruelty of Senorito Ivan towards Paco, and enraged over Ivan's killing of his pet goshawk out of petulance because he had killed no game on that day, Azarias tosses a rope around Ivan's neck and suspends him from an old oak tree, strangling him. Azarias is condemned to spend the rest of his life in a mental institution in a large city. He is visited by Quirce, whose memories began the film. Quirce had just visited his parents, who had aged badly. Paco was limping and Regula, almost blind, was trying to mend a slip cover; both were bent and spent from a life of hard work and had little left to comfort them except for pride in the accomplishments of their children, who escaped their own self-sacrifice and the misery of generations of servitude.

COMMENTARY: *Los santos inocentes* is a rare film of exceptional beauty, both geographical and spiritual. Its success confirmed Mario Camus' reputation as one of Spain's top filmmakers.

Camus took his crew to Extremadura to film this poignant indictment of the Spanish aristocracy under Franco's rule. The film could never had been made until after Franco's death, since it squarely places the burden of guilt (or blame) upon the aristocracy for the poverty, misery and exploitation of the lower classes.

Camus followed Delibes' novel carefully, deliberately, utilizing the recollections of the author's characters to serve his own flashback techniques, which reveal the entire grim truth of the feudal landlords who even impeded the freedom of the peasant's individual spirits.

The actors are remarkable, especially Francisco Rabal, who plays the retarded Azarias as simultaneously pathetic and repulsive. All of the characters are "ugly," the suffering peasants as well as the exploitive aristocrats. Juan Diego, who plays Ivan, offers a wonderful portrayal of the Spanish authoritarian mind, completely soulless and amoral. But the retarded Azarias elevates the film by his single act of murder and retribution for all the injustices committed by the aristocrats, especially the shooting of his pet goshawk. It is this violent act that frees the peasants from a life decreed them for generations and supported by the Franco regime. The film, chock full of colorful panoramas, is naturalistic in intent, glossy in execution, but it captures, so aptly, the ugliness under the burning Spanish sun.

1984

QUE HE HECHO PARA MERECER ESTO? (WHAT HAVE I DONE TO DESERVE THIS?)

DIRECTOR: PEDRO ALMODOVAR

CREDITS: Screenplay: Pedro Almodovar; Color Photography: Angel L. Fernandez; Producer: Herve Hachuel for Tesauro/Kaktus Films; Music: Bernardo Bonezzi.

CAST: Carmen Maura (Gloria), Luis Hostalot (Polo, her son), Angel de Andres-Lopez (Antonio, her husband), Veronica Forque (Cristal, prostitute and Gloria's neighbor), Gonzalo Suarez (Lucas), Chus Lampreave (Gloria's grandmother), Kiti Manver (Juani, another neighbor), Juan Martinez (Toni), Emilio G. Caba (Pedro, Antonio's friend), Katia Loritz (Ingrid Muller, Antonio's ex-mistress), Amparo Soler Leal (Patricia, Pedro's wife), Jaime Chavarri (a client), Tinin Almodovar (a cashier).

BACKGROUND: This is Pedro Almodovar's fourth feature film. It was preceded by many other film "efforts" since 1974, minor, short works in super 8mm., with titles such as *Two Whores, or Love Story That Ends in a Wedding* (his first film, in 1974) and *Folle, Folle, Folleme . . . Tim* (*Fuck, Fuck, Fuck me, . . . Tim*), his first "long" feature in super 8mm.

However his "real" feature film debut began in 1980–81 with *Pepi, Luci and Bom,* about a group of teenagers who talk about sex, love and drugs. It was a great hit at Madrid's Cine Alpahaville (named after Luc-Godard's famous cult film), which produced Almodovar's second feature, *Labyrinth of Passions* in 1982, dealing with sexual aberration, transvestism and multiple sexual couplings on screen, clearly testing the limits of Spanish censorship under the "new freedoms."

His third film, *Entre tinieblas* (*Sisters of the Night*), made in 1983, is a farcical send-up of the Catholic church. But his most controlled work is *What Have I Done to Deserve This?* Almodovar believes in a totally free Spanish cinema. For him, Franco and censorship never existed. His pre-AIDS, homosexual bias is evident in all of his films; his gay sensibility is campy, pervasive, all-encompassing.

Almodovar is the most successful, internationally-known Spanish film director since Carlos Saura. However, he admits that we should not take his films too seriously. They are entertainments, creations for the moment, although there are some serious underlying themes in many of his scenarios, especially in *What Have I Done to Deserve This?* (1984), *Matador* (1986), *Law of Desire* (1987) and *Women on the Edge of a Nervous Breakdown* (1988).

PLOT: Gloria works as a housemaid and never has a minute to herself during her eighteen-hour work days. She lives in a high-rise project, in a cramped apartment which she shares with her taxi-driver

Pedro Almodovar, director, and Gonzalo Suarez in *Que he hecho para merecer esto?*

husband, Antonio, their two sons, her mother-in-law and a lizard. She never has time to do her house work and is very unhappy with her life because her husband treats her like a servant and a sexual object, available only for his pleasure at any moment he desires. Also, one of her sons is homosexual, which deeply disturbs her. And her husband is faithful to the memory of his former mistress, a German woman with whom he had an affair during World War II.

One day, Ingrid Muller calls Gloria's husband, urging him to forge some of Hitler's "supposed" diaries. Antonio decides to go to meet Ingrid at the airport, since she is flying to Madrid that afternoon. He orders Gloria to iron his shirt. Gloria, used to taking amphetamines to get her through the day and suffering withdrawal symptoms because various pharmacists refuse to sell her drugs without a prescription, becomes so enraged with Antonio's request that she strikes him in the head with a Serrano ham which was hanging on the kitchen wall. (She then throws the bone into a pot of soup simmering on the stove, a homage to Alfred Hitchcock's TV play, "Lamb to the Slaughter.")

A police investigation ensues, but no evidence reveals the identity of the murderer. Meanwhile, Gloria's son Miguel, tired of living with a homosexual dentist (to whom he was "sold" by Gloria), decides to return home. Antonio's mother decides to leave the apartment with her lizard. Toni, Gloria's other son, who has been dealing drugs on the street at age fourteen, decides to leave Madrid with his grandmother for the healthier atmosphere of the country. Gloria is left virtually alone, except for her kooky neighbors—a young prostitute/actress who wants to make it "big" in Las Vegas and a manic, bitter, cleanliness freak whose daughter possesses telekinetic powers.

Realizing the emptiness in her life, Gloria goes out on to her balcony, overlooking the neighborhood, one of the ugliest legacies left by Franco's modernization program for the working-class during the economic boom of the sixties. As she breathes the polluted air from the nearby freeway which is clogged with traffic and considers suicide, her youngest son Miguel returns home, taking his father's place. Nothing much has really changed for Gloria since she still has the same day-to-day problem: survival. But now she is no longer alone and, somewhat ironically, she will have a "man" to take her husband's place.

COMMENTARY: Almodovar's film was popular in and outside of Spain because it was a send-up of Spanish *machismo* (male domination), dedicated to all housewifes who do *all* the work, provide sex and good cheer for their husbands, and get *nothing* in return but abuse for their efforts.

Carmen Maura is a supremely intelligent actress whose forte is "black comedy." And *What Have I Done to Deserve This?* is a Buñuel-esque tribute to Almodovar's perverse sense of humor and acute perception. It is a surprisingly funny, brave, tragic and bittersweet film, bawdy, witty, satiric, an extraordinary small masterpiece of its genre. The film is a "comedy," but its comic sense is so outrageous and provocative that it leaves viewers reeling and roaring with laughter.

For example, there is a cameo role played by film director Jaime Chavarri, in the role of an insatiable satyr, who needs an audience to watch his sexual mastery of a bored prostitute who titillates him with her "lies" about multiple orgasms in order to reinforce her client's *macho* sensibility and prowess.

Although the title of this film is somewhat ironic, Almodovar has succeeded in making a campy, yet pointedly serious drama of Spain's socially underprivileged in a neo-realistic style reminiscent of the early Spanish films of the fifties, but with the added dimension of his sense of satire and humor. One senses that the director feels the pleasure of his creative freedom and that Franco and the era of censorship are really dead. Almodovar is enjoying his personal freedom, mockingly jubilant, defiant. Considered the creator of *La movida* (the newest "new wave"), Almodovar is the one Spanish director with a gay sensibility, dominating Madrid's film scene and reaping the rewards of national as well as international success. His earliest films, short works in super 8mm., became cult favorites and were usually shown at midnight and thereafter. Almodovar has come a long way since those defiant "cult" days, but his films still project an attitude of defiance, which is at the center of Almodovar's personality. His movies made after 1984 are even more daring and disturbing.

1985

LA CORTE DE FARAON (THE COURT OF THE PHAROAH)

DIRECTOR: JOSE LUIS GARCIA SANCHEZ

CREDITS: Screenplay: Rafael Azcona & Jose Luis Garcia Sanchez; Color Photography: Jose Luis Alcaine; Producer: Luis Sanz for Lince Films; Music: Lleo, Perrin & Palacios, based upon the 1910 *zarzuela* (operetta).

CAST: Ana Belen (Lota/Mari Pili), Fernando Fernan Gomez (Roque), Antonio Banderas (Fray Jose), Josema Yuste (Putifar/Tarsicio), Agustin Gonzales (Father Calleja), Quique Camoiras (Corcuera/King), Mary Carmen Ramirez (Fernando/Queen), Juan Diego (Roberto), Guillermo Montesinos (Anto-

Antonio Banderas and Ana Belen in *La corte de Faraon.*

nio), Maria Luisa Ponte (Patricia), Millan Salcedo (Copero), Jose Luis Lopez Vasquez (Police Chief), Antonio Gamero (Ramirez), Guillermo Marin (Prior).

BACKGROUND: Based upon an actual event in 1940, when the censors under Franco's mandate banned this operetta from being shown because a priest raised objections to its licentious language and scantily clad actors and actresses, the screenwriters used the event itself as the focal point to present the operetta to the Spanish public in 1985. It was a huge box-office triumph.

PLOT: Toward the end of the 1940s, an amateur theater group decides to stage a musical, *The Court of the Pharaoh,* without trying to obtain the permits and licenses required by the Office of Censorship.

The work is widely known by the public because of its shocking political, erotic and religious audacities. During a long night at the local police station, the chief attempts to ferret out the reasons why this group has undertaken such an "insane" project.

As the interrogation proceeds, we witness a series of flashbacks, presenting the history of the show's production, its staging, the relations between its actors. When daybreak comes, most of the actors are held by the police, while the impresario, Don Roque, who has backed the play financially, is allowed to return home after several revelations have astonished the viewers of the film.

COMMENTARY: *La corte de Faraon* is a colorful, wonderfully witty, well-acted and highly stylized "film within a film."

Through a series of flashbacks, we learn how the impresario convinced his homosexual son to write the operetta, how the son is trying to overcome his sexual bent with the operetta's star, Mari Pili (Ana Belen), *her* sexual attraction to the monk, Fray Jose (Antonio Banderas), who serves as liaison between the Catholic church, the Guardia Civil (police) and the actors as he attempts to correct the ribald libretto of the *zarzuela*.

The entire plot of the operetta itself is revealed in flashbacks that are completely sung: virginal queen prefers young slave to old king and winds up with young slave with the approval of the entire court. The songs are intermittently cute, raucous, funny, sexual, loaded with double entendres, and are all beautifully performed.

At the conclusion of the film, the impresario (Gomez), his wife and son are released by the bumbling police inspector (Lopez Vasquez) after all eat an entire *paella de mariscos*. The last "act" of the play is performed in flashback, as we watch the entire cast once again hauled into jail. The story within a story comes full circle. Mari Pili is indeed sexually fulfilled by the desires of "Fray" Jose.

The film was a success in Spain and American audiences who saw it at the Second Spanish Film Festival in New York found that they too were entertained by the ribald humor of the Spanish *zarzuela*. M-G-M musicals of the forties and fifties were never as clever or as sensual as this one. The screen-writers obviously found the right combination: political commentary, a musical and a comedy of manners mixed with satire, making it the hit of the 1985 film season.

1986

TIEMPO DE SILENCIO (A TIME FOR SILENCE)

DIRECTOR: VICENTE ARANDA

CREDITS: Screenplay: Vicente Aranda & Antonio Rabinat, based upon the novel *Tiempo de silencio* by Luis Martin Santos; Color Photography: Juan Amoros; Producers: Oriol Regas & Francisco Lara for Lola/Morgana Films.

CAST: Imanol Arias (Pedro), Victoria Abril

(Dorita), Charo Lopez (Charo/mother), Francisco Rabal (Muecas), Juan Echanove (Matias), Francisco Algora (Amador), Joaquin Hinojosa (Cartucho), Diana Penalver (Dorita), Enriqueta Claver (Dona Luisa).

BACKGROUND: The director, Vicente Aranda, a Catalonian, has been making films in a wide variety of genres since 1964—science fiction, political thrillers, horror stories, psycho-sexual dramas, *films noir*. But his career began to soar with this transposition of Luis Martin Santos' classic novel, *A Time for Silence,* to the screen. The novelist himself was a doctor, and his tale deals with the struggle of a young Spanish medical student/doctor in the early fifties. Aranda has a keen interest in medicine and in fascinating stories. Since Martin Santos' novel combines these elements, Aranda was clearly the right director to mount this film.

PLOT: Madrid, *circa* 1945. Pedro is a scholarship student working at a research lab in the city, studying the growth of cancer in rats. He is unable to finish his research because he has run out of specimens. His lab assistant, Amador, tells him about Muecas ("grimaces") who breeds rats in his own house, a slum dwelling that he and his wife, Ricarda, and their two daughters share. Pedro decides to visit the shanty, fascinated by the thought of their immunity to cancerous rats.

Pedro himself lives in a modest boarding house run by a militant widow and her daughter Dora, who is also the mother of the widow's illegitimate "niece," the beautiful Dorita. The widow plans a wedding between Pedro and Dorita, so that his medical career may release them all from a life of squalor and penury.

Pedro visits Muecas, meets his eldest daughter, Florita, as well as her knife-wielding *macho* boyfriend, Cartucho. Pedro then spends the usual Saturday evening at a gathering of literati, but this time is influenced by his university friend Matias to spend the night at a house of prostitution. Returning to his boarding house, Pedro then makes love to Dorita.

At dawn, Pedro is visited by Muecas, who is in search of a doctor to cure his daughter, Florita, who is severely hemorrhaging from a botched abortion attempt after an incestuous relationship with her father. Florita dies and her boyfriend Cartucho suspects that Pedro is the father of the aborted fetus. Later that day, Pedro is sought by the local police. Dorita warns him and Pedro hides in the local brothel run by Dona Luisa. Meanwhile, Matias begs Amador to tell the police the truth of Pedro's innocence.

The police finally apprehend Pedro. Pedro, surprisingly, confesses rather than admit the truth because of the "absurdity" of this situation. However, Ricarda, Florita's mother, suspects her husband of incest. The body is exhumed, an autopsy performed and Ricarda reveals Muecas' guilt. Pedro is freed and returns to his research. But the director of the research institute fires Pedro, believing him guilty, and forces Pedro to do his cancer research privately.

Pedro and Dorita become engaged and spend an evening at a local amusement area to celebrate. Cartucho jealously watches Pedro dance with Dorita. Still believing that Pedro is guilty of Florita's death, he knifes Dorita in a crowd as Pedro goes off to buy some sweets for them. With Dorita now dead, Pedro has no other recourse than to practice medicine in the provinces and continue his cancer research elsewhere. Defeated in the city in all his aspirations, Pedro is once again totally alone, indifferent, condemned to silence in a society that has deprived him of all he wanted. He could not even cry out his rage. It was a time for silence, a time to settle in a small town, give prescriptions to the ailing, and play chess in the cafes.

COMMENTARY: Aranda's version of Luis Martin Santos classic novel is a wonderful, literal, artistic transposition to the screen. He has made some references to Pedro's "castration" and some allegorical references to the country (Spain) whose poor

Imanol Arias and Diana Penalver in *Tiempo de silencio.*

commit crimes and are unable to cope with their problems.

The film, unlike the novel, and despite the color and costumes, brings out the oppressive atmosphere of those post-Civil War years in Madrid, the years under Franco's dominance, when Madrillians were seeking enlightenment and freedom but were strangled in the vortex of darkness, ignorance and day-to-day survival.

Aranda, a careful observer, has portrayed the slum ambience with such naturalness and ferociousness that the cinematic reality imposes itself upon our consciousness. The film mesmerizes us, annihilates its viewers, casts us headlong into a world of despair from which there is no escape.

Although sex, death and alienation, the three major themes of the film, have been reiterated on the Spanish screen *ad nauseum,* Aranda adds a literary and philosophical (perhaps existentialist) dimension to the screenplay that leaves viewers distraught, off-balance, despairing. There is no let-up to the pessimism. Aranda's work is bleak, ugly, beautiful and unrelenting—truly a masterwork of Spanish cinema.

1986

EL AMOR BRUJO (BEWITCHED LOVE)

DIRECTOR: CARLOS SAURA

CREDITS: Screenplay & Choreography: Carlos Saura & Antonio Gades; Color Photography: Teo Escamilla; Producer: Emiliano Piedra; Music: Manuel de Falla's *El amor brujo,* performed by the National Orchestra of Spain under the direction of Jesus Lopez Cobos with songs sung by Rocio Jurado.

CAST: Antonio Gades (Carmelo), Cristina Hoyos (Candela), Laura del Sol (Lucia), Juan Antonio Jimenez (Jose), Emma Penella (the witch), Enrique Ortega (Jose's father), Diego Pantoja (Candela's father), Giovana (Rocio), Candy Roman (Chulo).

BACKGROUND: *El amor brujo* is the third and final artistic collaboration between Gades and Saura. The partnership began in 1981 with their dramatic flamenco rendition of Garcia Lorca's *Blood Wedding* (*Bodas de sangre,*) continued with Mérimée-Bizet's *Carmen* in 1983, and now ends with De Falla's *El amor brujo* (*Bewitched Love,* aka *Love, the Magician*) in 1985–86. Saura and Gades involve us in their passion for recreating Spanish myths through folklore and the dance. Their use of the flamenco is esthetic testimony to their recreation of a profound Spanish art.

This dance trilogy truly broadened Saura's directorial career, moving his thematic concerns from the boldly realistic films of the fifties and sixties, to his autobiographical-memory films of the seventies, onto his boldly aesthetic-folkloric collaborations with Gades into the eighties. (Saura will approach filming in the "epic" genre, another facet of his multifaceted career, with the making of *El Dorado* in 1988.)

PLOT: Candela (Cristina Hoyos) and Jose (Juan Antonio Jimenez) were promised to be wed, according to Gypsy custom, when they were children. However, Carmelo (Antonio Gades), another Gypsy lad, is secretly in love with Candela and silently watches the betrothal scene when they reach adulthood.

The wedding scene is finally celebrated but Jose is unfaithful to Candela, preferring his passion for Lucia (Laura del Sol) even on their wedding day. As Jose searches for Lucia, he leaves Candela on her own, secretly watched by Carmelo. Another group of Gypsies wanders into the traditional festivities, causing a fight over Lucia's affections. Jose is stabbed to death and Carmelo is mistakenly and unjustly taken to jail for his murder as well as for killing others in the rival gang.

At this point, the element of magic or sorcery enters the story. Candela, who refuses to accept Jose's death, goes out into a deserted field, desperately searching for the "ghost" of Jose, with whom she communes nightly. When Carmelo gets out of jail some years later, he does not believe the tales of sorcery and witchcraft attributed to Candela. He finally declares his love for her, but she is unable to respond since the ghost of Jose stands between them.

Carmelo, in desperation, consults with a local witch to exorcise the spirit of Jose in a ritual "Fire Dance" by moonlight. However, the magic fails and Carmelo learns that only by sacrificing Lucia will Candela be free of her ghostly husband. If Lucia was Jose's earthly lover, let her be so in death as well.

In the last scenes of the film, Lucia is convinced by Carmelo to meet the ghost of Jose. In a wonderful *pas de quatre,* to De Falla's glorious music, the lovers meet their proper destinies. Carmelo and Candela are reunited in life and Jose and Lucia are united in death.

COMMENTARY: *El amor brujo* is probably the most *beautiful* film in the Saura-Gades trilogy. From its opening shot, when the camera travels from the huge iron door banging shut, closing the entire sound stage (it was actually filmed at the old Bronston studios outside of Madrid) off from the public, we enter into the artificially created set of a Gypsy village in Andalucia, and are aware that the entire film is a contrivance for our imagination.

Once we enter this imaginary world, we are dazzled by the brilliance of Teo Escamilla's mobile camera from the opening tracking shot, by the superb score of de Falla, by the austere and brilliantly executed dancing of Gades, Hoyos, Jimenez and del Sol, and by the magic of the inspiration of Manuel de Falla's original story for his superb balletic masterpiece, originally performed in 1925 in Paris by Vicente Escudero.

Antonio Gades and Cristina Hoyos in *El amor brujo*.

We are amazed that some sixty years later, *El amor brujo* has resurfaced as a flamenco ballet through the medium of film, and that De Falla's music has retained its Spanishness—its expressivity for what is essentially a unique Spanish theme.

Antonio Gades, who owes much to Vicente Escudero as a dancer, has updated his flamenco style and given a new quality to something so traditionally Spanish. Because of Gades, the Gypsy world has become almost "universalized" for us, as well as spectacularly enriched with mythic qualities. These qualities perpetuate their own "Spanishness" and create an undeniable sense of continuity with the traditions of Spain's past artistic glories. Despite new trends in Spanish filmmaking, such as coproductions and the use of foreign capital (which sometimes transforms the Spanish film into a new "product," culturally devoid of its "Spanishness,") the collaboration of Gades and Saura has transcended this trendiness. They have transformed, modernized the old myths, and revivified the eternal, glorious images of Spain.

1987

LA CASA DE BERNARDA ALBA (THE HOUSE OF BERNARDA ALBA)

DIRECTOR: MARIO CAMUS

CREDITS: Screenplay: Antonio Larreta & Mario Camus, based upon the play of the same name by Federico Garcia Lorca; Color & CinemaScope Photography: Fernando Arribas; Producer: Ricardo Garcia Arrojo for Paraiso Productions; Music: Angel Alvarez; Songs: Fernanda de Utrera; Musical Groups: Salazar del Compas and Almirez.

CAST: Irene Gutierrez Caba (Bernarda), Ana Belen (Adela), Florinda Chico (Poncia), Enriqueta Carballeira (Angustias), Vicky Pena (Martirio), Aurora Pastor (Magdalena), Mercedes Lezcano (Amelia), Pilar Puchol (the maid), Rosario Garcia-Ortega (Maria Josefa), Ana Maria Ventura (Prudencia), Paula Borrell (Nina), Alvaro Quiroga (Pepe el Romano).

BACKGROUND: Fifty years after the death of Federico Garcia Lorca, *La casa de Bernarda Alba,* his most successful play, has been filmed for the first time in the actual locations of Ronda, Antequera and Zahara de la Sierra. This story of women without men is one of the most successful literary transpositions to the screen. Mario Camus has always taken care in his superb adaptations of other Spanish classics—novels such as *La colmena* by Camilo Jose Cela and *Los santos inocentes* by Miguel Delibes.

PLOT: After her husband's death, Bernarda forces her five daughters into a strict period of mourning that is to last eight years. It is so severe that they are not even allowed to leave the house, thus frustrating any amorous relationships the daughters of marriageable age may have entertained.

After forbidding Martirio to marry a local farmhand, Bernarda betroths Angustias to Pepe el Romano. Poncia, the servant, tries to warn Bernarda of the consequences of such rigid discipline, but Bernarda rejects this criticism because she wants to appear strong and will not accept advice from anyone within her employ.

Adela, the prettiest daughter, refuses to see Pepe el Romano, who has been her lover despite his supposed engagement to Angustias. Martirio watches the affair develop and stops Adela while she is on her way to meet Pepe in the stable. A loud argument ensues, bringing Poncia with a

Irene Gutierrez Caba in *La casa de Bernarda Alba.*

gun, Adela's sister and Bernarda. The latter sees someone jump out of a window, grabs the gun and fires two shots outside the door. When she returns, saying she had killed the intruder, Adela despairingly runs to her room, locks her door and commits suicide, hanging herself.

COMMENTARY: Mario Camus' film is a fascinating recreation of Garcia Lorca's trenchant drama, beautifully played by Ana Belen as Adela and Irene Gutierrez Caba as Bernarda. In fact, the entire cast of actresses is superb, as are the locations which are equally, thrillingly photographed.

Camus deftly captures the somber, oppressive mood of women living together in a 1920s repressive atmosphere. The sexual heat between Adela and Pepe el Romano is also adroitly portrayed, something never "seen" in the play, but mainly felt throughout. Although the film is set in the twenties, Lorca's tale of female repression is still timely in today's macho-oriented society.

Camus did something more than present a classic play on the Spanish screen. He comments upon women's rights, reminding us of a Spain under Franco's oppressive policies and their effect upon women's lives. He was the first to take on the challenge of filming this poetic tragedy with its Goya-like tones, de-emphasizing the use of Andalusian folkloric props in favor of concentrating on the passion, anxiety, and frustration of Lorca's characters, masterfully played by a cast of modern, emancipated actresses. This, the best, literal adaptation of this Lorca play to appear in any medium, is enhanced by a superb script, photography, direction and acting.

1987

DIVINAS PALABRAS (DIVINE WORDS)

DIRECTOR: JOSE LUIS GARCIA SANCHEZ

CREDITS: Screenplay: Enrique Llovet, Diego Santillan & Jose Luis Garcia Sanchez, based upon the play by Ramon del Valle-Inclan; Color Photography: Fernando Arribas; Producer: Victor Manuel San Jose Sanchez; Music: Milladoiro.

CAST: Ana Belen (Mari Gaila), Francisco Rabal (Pedro Gailo), Imanol Arias (Septimo Miau), Esperanza Roy (Rosa, "La Tatula"), Aurora Batista (Marcia del Reino), Juan Echanove (Miguelin, "El Padrones").

BACKGROUND: Another tale of Galician "grotesqueries" by the master of the "esperpento."

PLOT: The setting of the film is the province of Galicia, *circa* 1920, in the impoverished village of San Clemente. Since the village has no priest, ecclesiastic authority falls to Pedro Gailo, the sacristan, who has a young, beautiful wife, Mari Gaila. Greedy for any money that comes their way and eager to leave San Clemente and her husband, Mari cares for a hydrocephalous child and uses him to beg for alms. This misfortune of nature may be their source of wealth.

Settling the guardianship of the child with her sister-in-law Marica, Mari Gaila,

Ana Belen and Imanol Arias in *Divinas palabras.*

encouraged by another beggar woman, "La Tatula," decides to go to various fairs and festivals and there puts the hydrocephalic dwarf on display, to wheedle funds from good-natured, pitying, sympathetic people. Her husband, Pedro, the sacristan, is afraid that Mari's activities will ruin his reputation, but his lust for money overcomes his fear and pride. Mari Gaila sets out for the nearest city, confronting a world she never knew existed, full of music, cattle-trading fairs, picturesque people. She becomes the object of desire of other beggars, nomads like herself, especially shrewd tricksters like Septimo Miau.

Drawn sexually to this handsome outlaw, after a mild flirtation with him she leaves for home, loaded with money. The townspeople begin to gossip about her sudden wealth and freedom to leave the village at will. Mari Gaila meets up with Septimo again, teams up with him, using the hydrocephalic as a freak show, and decides to run off with him. While they are making love, the locals ply the hydrocephalic child with liquor at the local tavern, causing his death.

Septimo deserts Mari Gala, who becomes ill and returns to the sacristan, empty handed. But Pedro Gailo uses his nephew's corpse, showing off his gigantic member to families in other villages to make money. Later, Septimo returns and Rosa "La Tatula" acts as a go-between. The lovers meet in a forest, consummate their affair and are caught by the local, jealous neighbors of Mari Gaila.

Disgraced, desperate and poor, Mari Gaila is stripped nude, spat upon, mocked and stoned. The crowd ends its vengeance when Pedro, the sacristan, pronounces the "divine words" in Latin: "Let he who is free of sin throw the first stone." These words in the midst of such squalor are ironic yet miraculous, causing the crowd to disperse and look into their own motives. They are downtrodden peasants caught in a claustrophobic world, scheming, dirty people with nowhere to go.

After the crowd leaves, Pedro maintains a saintly pose, forgiving his adulterous wife. Mari Gaila (Ana Belen) seems too clean and noble to have groveled in this squalor and comes off almost saintly herself.

COMMENTARY: *Divinas palabras* is a bitter film displaying the greed and bitchery of provincial life in Galicia in the early part of the twentieth century. The display of excessive piety contrasted with the stultifying reality of survival by poor, poor peasants, struggling to eke out a livelihood in the face of grotesqueries and poverty, is as sad as it is ironic. One jarring note—Ana Belen's smooth, physical beauty seems too extraordinary in the context of the film, although her singing talent meshes well with the plot.

Francisco Rabal is just perfect as the cuckolded sacristan. There is an interesting scene in which he almost commits incest with his daughter, who also seems destined for a life of misery like the hydrocephalic child.

The director, Garcia Sanchez, deserves our praise for his accurate portrayal of this microcosm of Galician life, this savage, brutal, incestuous, avaricious world, beautifully shot in color and CinemaScope.

1987–1988

EL LUTE—CAMINA O REVIENTA (EL LUTE—RUN FOR YOUR LIFE) and *EL LUTE, II—MANANA SERE LIBRE (EL LUTE, PART II—TOMORROW I'LL BE FREE)*

DIRECTOR: VICENTE ARANDA

CREDITS: Screenplay: Joaquin Jorda, Vicente Aranda & Eleuterio Sanchez, based on the latter's autobiography; Color Photography: Jose Luis Alcaine; Producer: Isabel Mula and Jose Maria Cunilles for Multivideo Films; Music: Jose Nieto.

CAST: EL LUTE I: Imanol Arias (Eleuterio), Victoria Abril (Consuelo), Antonio Valero (Medrano), Carlos Tristancho (Agudo), Diana Penalver (Esperanza), Margarita Calahorra (Madre Consuelo), Raul Fraire (Civil Guard during first escape scene), Jose Cerro (brother-in-law), Rafael Hernandez (Civil Guard during second escape scene), Jose Manuel Cervino (Rufino).

EL LUTE II: Imanol Arias (Eleuterio), Angel Pardo (Lolo), Jorge Sanz (Toto), Pastora Vega (Esperanza), Blanca Apilanez (Maria), Silvia Rodriguez (Frasquita), Monserrat Tey (Emilia), Antonio Iranzo (Gypsy Chief), Margarita Calahorra (Consuelo's mother), Jose Cerro (Consuelo's father), and a cast of fifty.

BACKGROUND: During the last years of Franco's dictatorship, when it was clear that the regime had fallen into political and social decadence, the Civil Guard decides to make an example of a "chicken thief" whose talent is to escape from any prison in which he is incarcerated.

Based upon the diaries and published autobiography of Eleuterio Sanchez, the film and its sequel became instant box-office successes because the Spanish people admired the courage, boldness and

Imanol Arias in *El Lute*.

insubordination of this underdog, transmuting his heroism and ingenuity in eluding the Civil Guard into the form of a folkloric "outlaw-hero."

El Lute's struggle against injustice, and his harsh sentence for stealing some chickens, strike a parallel with Jean Valjean's theft of some loaves of bread in Victor Hugo's immortal nineteenth-century novel, *Les Miserables*. Both films deal with the creation of the romantic myth, that is, the entire story of El Lute's life, from teenager to middle age, from incarceration to freedom.

PLOT: In *El Lute—Camina o revienta,* Imanol Arias is a young Gypsy, in love with Victoria Abril. Making money as a vendor of tin lanterns, he marries and their first child is born. Needing more funds, he is unjustly accused of stealing a cash box with the proceeds from the lanterns and is brutally beaten and jailed. Escaping easily from the local prison, he begins running for his life with his family. Needing food, he steals six chickens, is caught and given the harsh, maximum jail sentence of eighteen months plus an additional six months at hard labor.

After he escapes again, the scene shifts to Madrid where El Lute, now known by this nickname because of his daring prison escapes as reported by the Spanish press, tries to become anonymous, and begins to build a house on the outskirts of the city. Ousted by a jealous neighbor, El Lute, to survive, commits a robbery in a local jewelry store.

Caught by the Civil Guard once again, he is brutally beaten in jail and given a death sentence which is later commuted to a thirty-year prison term. One of the benefits in prison is that El Lute learns to read and write. While being transported from one jail to a higher security prison, El Lute makes a daring escape from a railroad train. (Apparently, he had swallowed the key to his handcuffs and retrieved it while defecating on the train.) Caught once more, he is given an additional term of fifty years. Part I ends with the words, "However, it was not so. But that's another story."

Part II continues El Lute's plight through a series of robberies, after which he is caught and jailed. The centerpiece of this film is his second marriage (his first wife had died during his jail terms) to a gypsy virgin. The director is quite explicit regarding the "details" of their wedding day, and the gypsy marriage scene, complete with festivities, goes on for nearly twenty minutes. In this concluding part, Eleuterio's brother is killed—El Lute's family is traveling with him as he flees the Civil Guard. Caught again after donning many disguises, El Lute is finally given clemency after Franco's death.

COMMENTARY: Both films are well-made crimers, replete with naturalistic details that seem typically Spanish. For example, in Part I, we witness Victoria Abril washing her genitals in a local stream and El Lute becoming sexually excited as he watches. In Part II, the examination of the young Gypsy girl's hymen and the displaying of sheets to prove she is intact are gratuitous.

Imanol Arias gives a riveting performance in both parts. We watch him as an innocent, learning about make-up and disguises in order to elude the police. He even begins to change his Spanish accent, making transitions from Andalusian to Castillian.

The director, Vicente Aranda, tried to use the actual locales, the towns and prisons where the actual events and action took place. The films are the equal of anything made by Clint Eastwood in the "cops and robbers" phase of his career. The dramatic impact of *El Lute I* and *II* are the equal of any American crime film made in the eighties. Though Part I ends on a downbeat note, Part II is a faster moving sequel, and a large part of the torture scenes was eliminated in this section. What makes Part II difficult is the gypsy language used almost throughout.

Both films were tremendously popular

in Spain because Eleuterio Sanchez himself has become a kind of celebrity after his pardon. He lives quite comfortably in Spain and even participated in the writing and the promotion of the film at the 1988 Cannes Film Festival.

1988

EL DORADO

DIRECTOR: CARLOS SAURA

CREDITS: Screenplay: Carlos Saura; Color and Panavision with Dolby Sound; Photography: Teo Escamilla; Producer: Andres Vicente Gomez, with the collaboration of RTVE (Spanish Television) and RAI (Italian Televison); Original Music: Alejandro Masso; Songs sung by Amancio Prada; Lutes, Sanfonas and Vihuelas played by Arnaud Dumond.

CAST: Omero Antonutti (Lope de Aguirre), Lambert Wilson (Pedro de Ursua), Eusebio Poncela (Fernando de Guzman), Gabriela Roel (Dona Ines), Ines Sastre (Elvira), Jose Sancho (La Bandera), Patxi Bisquert (Pedrarias), Paco Algora (Llamoso), Feodor Atkine (Montoya), and a cast of hundreds.

BACKGROUND: Filming on *El Dorado* began in January, 1987 in Costa Rica at Tortuguero National Park, not far from where Christopher Columbus disembarked in 1502 on his last voyage. Most of the river sequences were shot in a canal which took the place of the Amazon and Maranon Rivers, a substitute for the actual Peruvian location of the Ursua expedition.

One of the greatest problems during production was the tropical climate. Amid torrential downpours and beset by medical problems, actors speaking a diversity of languages and sixty technicians spent ten months together with six hundred local extras to film this Spanish epic.

It was the most costly and lavish Spanish film ever made—eight million dollars for two hours and thirty-one minutes of screen time.

PLOT: Tales of gold and wealth circulated in European courts during the sixteenth century. The legend of *El Dorado,* a kingdom of gold, was one of them and attracted the Spaniard Pedro de Ursua, in 1560, to set out from Santa Cruz, Peru with some three hundred Spanish soldiers and three hundred native servants to find this "city of gold."

On January 1, 1561, Ursua was murdered by some of his own captains, among them, the bloodthirsty Lope de Aguirre, then aging and lame.

Aguirre proclaimed himself leader of the rebels in May of 1561, usurped Ursua's authority and denied his allegiance to the Spanish crown. Supported by a group of men known as "maranones," Aguirre abandoned the *El Dorado* expedition, believing it foolhardy and unprofitable. Instead, he set out to conquer Chile and other portions of Peru. After months of traveling, first in search of *El Dorado,* he was driven insane by his personal quest for final peace after being abandoned by all of his men, and died five months later in October, after killing his daughter Elvira by his own hands. This expedition was one of the greatest failures ever recorded by the Spaniards during their American conquests.

COMMENTARY: A wonderfully evocative film of the days of the Spaniard's Peruvian conquests, in which the director, Carlos Saura, utilized his Costa Rican locations to advantage.

Omero Antonutti in *El Dorado.*

Lambert Wilson played Pedro de Ursua with finesse, petulance, and an aristocratic air that conveyed his noble stature and faith to king and country in the quest for *El Dorado*. But Wilson is eclipsed physically by Omero Antonutti, who looks like an idealized version of Lope de Aguirre. Aguirre feels Ursua is a traitor to Spain, takes over his expedition out of selfish motives, and is doomed to die.

After watching two and one-half hours of "spectacle," in a voice-over we hear of Aguirre's demise. Omero Antonutti plays the part brilliantly, superbly. We watch Aguirre slowly lose his senses as heat, murder, betrayal and the difficulties of travel overtake him.

The sets and costumes in *El Dorado* are superb, as are the actresses who support the male leads, especially Gabriela Roel, who plays Dona Inez, a wily, gorgeous woman who meets her demise because of her adultery and treachery.

There are some beautiful panoramic sequences, spectacular graphic scenes of the slaughter of horses as food supplies disappear, gradual assassinations of leaders as the film plods to its conclusion.

This film will undoubtedly be compared to Werner Herzog's German epic, *Aguirre, the Wrath of God*. Although Herzog went to Peru and filmed in the actual locations, Klaus Kinski gives a mesmerizing performance as Aguirre, and the visuals are correct, the film is marred by a German soundtrack. And blue-eyed, hyper Kinski does not look right in the crucial emotional scenes of the film.

The great merit of Saura's production is that it recreates lovingly and with great detail in sets, costumes and music, Ursua's dramatic trajectory, his passion for discovery, his disillusion with conquest and love in a geographical setting that looks like the actual locale. Technically, it is a "great" film, but it skims lightly over the "real" cruelties the Spaniard's inflicted upon the native Indians and each other, probably because Spaniards don't want to be reminded of them as we approach the 500th anniversary of the discovery of America in 1992. Will *El Dorado* ever recoup its production costs? Perhaps by 1992. *El Dorado, redux!*

1990

AY, CARMELA!

DIRECTOR: CARLOS SAURA

CREDITS: Screenplay: Rafael Azcona, adapted from the play *Carmela* by Jose Sanchez Sinisterra; Color Photography: Jose Luis Alcaine; Producer: Andres Vicente Gomez; Music: Alejandro Masso; Producer: Andres Vicente Gomez.

CAST: Carmen Maura (Carmela), Andres Pajares (Paulino), Gabino Diego (Gustavete), Maurizio di Razza (Lt. Ripamonte), Miguel A. Rellan (Interrogating Lieutenant).

BACKGROUND: *Ay, Carmela!* is Carlos Saura's first film of the nineties, adding new luster to a career of film directing (mostly in Spain) spanning some forty years. After the notoriety caused by *El Dorado* (the most expensive film ever produced in Spain), Andres Vicente Gomez wisely had Saura scale down his production to a smaller story filmed in Iberia, with the internationally known star, Carmen Maura. The film dealt with, once again, the seminal and most traumatic event in Saura's life, the Spanish civil war. There are some artistic resonances which evoke memories of Ernst Lubitsch's great 1942 comedy, *To Be or Not To Be,* a film with which *Ay, Carmela* may well be compared artistically.

It should also be noted that Saura's 1989 Spanish film, *La noche oscura* (*Dark Night*), another smaller production effort dealing with a large theme—Spanish mysticism and the life of St. John of the Cross—but with a very tight budget, opened in Madrid in March of 1989 to less than enthusiastic reviews, and has not yet been seen internationally.

PLOT: *Ay, Carmela!* is set in the Republican Spain of 1938. Carmela and Paulino are entertainers who perform their vulgar music hall act for soldiers weary of the fighting. Along the way, they have picked up Gustavete, a mute who accompanies them playing solo guitar. Calling themselves "Tip-Top Variety," they are survivors, motivated not exactly by patriotism but by a desire for self-preservation.

After performing for the Republican soldiers, they steal their gasoline and are heading to Valencia when they run into the Fascists (Italians and Spaniards), who also desire their talents as entertainers. At first, the threesome is imprisoned with a group of Poles and other international soldiers from various brigades fighting against Franco's fascism. Carmela and Paulino are told that they must perform for the fascist soldiers and are assured of their safety. "Don't worry, Carmela—we who are innocent need not fear," says a fellow prisoner. Carmela remarks at one point as she dines on Italian spaghetti,: "If the Fascists always eat like this, we've lost the war."

When asked to perform an anti-Republican skit, Carmela rebels, displaying her true convictions as an anti-Fascist. She

Gabino Diego, Carmen Maura, and Andres Pajares in *Ay, Carmela!*

thinks of the blue-eyed Polish soldiers who have come to fight in Spain, a strange land whose name they cannot even pronounce. Carmela decides to abandon the skit, throwing the Fascist audience into a frenzy by displaying her breasts and intoning the Republican party-line. A demented Fascist soldier shoots her in the head and Carmela is covered by the Republican flag. Paulino and Gustavete visit her unconsecrated grave site to decorate it with flowers and the latter's chalk board, since Gustavete regained his voice when Carmela was shot.

COMMENTARY: Carlos Saura has once again made an intensely serious film about the Spanish civil war with biographical and comic overtones. Too much attention is paid to both actors' music hall performances. The simple plot-line (the film runs about 103 minutes) has obviously been padded. *Ay, Carmela!* could have been cut into a tight, dramatic drama about 90 minutes long. What troubles this critic is Saura's indecision over whether to make the film a broad farce or an intense drama. The performances of the actors, Carmen Maura and Andres Pajares, fall somewhere in between.

Carmen Maura gives the performance of her life as Carmela. Her coarseness and vulgarity soften as she realizes that she truly incarnates the Republican spirit of freedom and she gives up her life for this ideal. Andres Pajares is an excellent foil for her as Paulino: tender, sexy, vulgar, malleable, tragic as the husband who watches Carmela's real political awakening and suffers profoundly at her death.

Although there is much scatological humor, breaking of wind, burlesquing of homosexuals and mention of Carmela's menstrual problems, and other crude sex-

Carlos Saura directing on the set of *Ay, Carmela!*

uality in a song entitled "Doing the Uruguayan," there is also much more revelation about the grossness of the Spanish character. The murder of such poets as Federico Garcia Lorca, the slaughter of thousands of innocent foreign soldiers as well as fellow Spaniards who oppose Fascism—these are the real sins of the Franco regime. Saura does not spare the viewer at the film's conclusion from these harsh realities. And Carmen Maura gives such a finely tuned performance as the courageous Carmela that her death, played against Andres Pajares' buffoonery, resonates beyond the film's end titles.

Ay, Carmela! is certainly Spain's and Saura's first great film of the decade of the nineties. The refraction of events of the Spanish civil war as seen in two days in the life of this traveling vaudeville troupe is masterful. And the horror of these events will always stay with its spectators!

As Gary Giddens said in his *Village Voice* review of the film of February 12, 1991, "Its characters are so fastidiously primed between vaudeville comedy and tenable outrage, that . . . [*Ay, Carmela!*] . . . may be some kind of minor masterpiece." A minor masterpiece *Ay, Carmela!* certainly is, and Carmen Maura's terrific performance gives the film its affecting *longeurs* that will disturb many viewers.

V. CONCLUSION: THE NINETIES & BEYOND

What is there to say about Spanish cinema for the nineties and beyond? All one can do at this point is carefully analyze past patterns, diagnose the present trends and make some predictions.

With Spain now a member of the European Common Market, the Spanish people have been responsibly reexamining many social issues which have had an impact upon them since the death of dictator General Francisco Franco in 1975.

With a newly gained freedom of expression in all the arts, especially in cinema, many new themes were treated on the screen that had never been dealt with before: the use of illegal drugs, the problem of AIDS, the sexual revolution (for both sexes), equality for women in Spanish society. The Spanish cinema has discarded its earlier political and social preoccupations, its pro-Franco past, and a creative tide has taken hold of producers and directors in the film world.

Within the Iberian peninsula, Pedro Almodovar and his group of *La movida* artists and directors have instituted a great surge in the filmic arts. They are revolutionary, creating a cinema that is truly Spanish and devoid of Franco myths, a cinema without censorship, eschewing oblique political references and revisionism couched in an obfuscating style. Theirs is a direct cinema, re-creating its own myths, displaying its own individualism, rooted in its own pride and its own ideosyncrasies, displaying its Spanishness, its own particular identity.

Nearly every Spanish director who has worked during and after Franco's demise has flourished, especially the "younger" group. The Ministry of Culture, first under Pilar Miro's leadership, then Fernando Menendez-Leite's, and now under Jorge Semprun's, is providing much greater support for films. For example, Gutierrez Aragon received $300 million pesetas for his 1986 film, *La mitad del cielo* (*Half of Heaven*); Fernando Colomo received about the same amount for the 1985 production, *El caballero del dragon* (*The Knight of the Dragon*); Carlos Saura, about $250 million pesetas for *El amor brujo* (*Bewitched Love*), and Jose Luis Borau, about $150 million pesetas for *Tata, mia* (*Nanny, Dear*).

There is currently a great desire among Spanish filmmakers, producers and directors to sell their films abroad, with a special obsession to penetrate the American market. Is this an outrageous dream? Spanish films since the early eighties have been winning prizes at film festivals around the world. If the Spanish film industry could cash in on these kudos, it would give their industry more commercial clout than it now has.

All Spanish filmmakers today are working independently on "deals" of all sorts: pre-conditioning the sale of films before they are even produced, utilizing "packaging" strategies similar to those of the

American film industry (selling the film, the "novelization" of the film, the video rights, cassettes, promotional buttons, product marketing, recording rights, etc.).

To obtain a larger share of world profits, Spanish filmmakers have begun using foreign locales. For example, Bigas-Luna made *Angustias* (*Anguish*) (1987) in Los Angeles in English, Jose Luis Garci shot part of *Volver a empezar* (*To Begin Again*) (1982) in Berkeley, and Jose Luis Borau made *Rio abajo* (*On the Line*) (1984) in and around Houston. All of these films are now available on video in the United States, some in subtitled versions. Most of these films used international actors—David Carradine, Zelda Rubenstein and Michael Lerner, among others. Filming in English assures a production a wider market, and using easily identifiable international stars creates a broader attraction for the film.

By using international casts the directors are also trying to use more "universal" themes in Spanish films. And by using foreign locales, co-productions are sometimes facilitated more easily abroad. Sometimes, too, foreign money is invested in Spanish productions shot in Iberia, where labor is cheap, there is perpetual sunshine, and production efficiency rivals the best of so-called Hollywood technology.

Video in Spain has had a tremendous impact. There have been more than four million units sold as of June 1989, and the trend continues upward, accounting for a great loss of attendance at Spanish cinemas. (There is an on-going fight between private cable companies, connecting a diversity of channels into individual apartments, versus community viewing, the use of one system wired to an entire building, with everyone viewing a single video cassette.)

There are just over two thousand movie houses in operation in Spain, and in 1987 some four hundred closed because film attendance dropped. Yet because of such 1988 box-office successes as *El Lute, La ley del deseo* and *El bosque animado* (which won the "Goya"—the Spanish equivalent of the "Oscar"), films recaptured more than 1.6 million spectators compared to 1987 figures. From a global view, Spanish film marked up only 14.7% of the total world box office, which is a very, very tiny figure, particularly considering that American and English films have virtually cornered the box office in Spain, and that national films (films in Spanish) do poorly in comparison.

Despite its poor box-office share, Spanish film production has risen modestly and the runaway box-office champion is now Pedro Almodovar's 1988 film, *Women on the Edge of a Nervous Breakdown.*

To sum up the box-office leaders, I have adapted from *Variety's* Cannes Film Festival Issue (May 1989, page 439) a chart of the highest-grossing Spanish films to date, compiled by Peter Besas, with my own notes about certain films:

YEAR	POSITION	TITLE	BOX-OFFICE GROSS*	DIRECTOR
1988–89	#1	*Women on the Verge*	8.6 million	Almodovar
1984	#3	*Santos inocentes*	4.5	Camus
1981	#4	*Crimen de Cuenca*	4.0	Miro
1987	#5	*El Lute - I*	3.5	Aranda
1982	#8	*La colmena*	2.9	Camus
1984	#9	*Las bicicletas del verano*	2.7	Chavarri
1986	#11	*Muerte de Mikel*	2.4	Uribe
1975	#15	*Furtivos*	2.75	Borau

*In pesetas: 115 ptas. = $1.00

The following films have never been seen internationally, except at isolated film festivals, even though they are among the box-office leaders in Spain:

YEAR	POSITION	TITLE	BOX-OFFICE GROSS*	DIRECTOR
1985	#2	*La Vaquilla*	4.6 million	Berlanga
1972	#6	*La guerra de Papa*	3.1	Mercero
1985	#7	*Se infiel y no mires con quien*	3.0	Trueba
1982	#10	*Cristobal Colon, Descubridor*	2.5	Ozores
1966	#12	*La muerte tiene un precio*	2.4	Leone
1982	#13	*To er mundo e gueno*	2.4	Summers
1978	#14	*La escopeta nacional*	2.3	Berlanga

*In pesetas: 115 ptas. = $1.00

Despite this impressive list of all-time Spanish film champions, most Spanish films, despite government subsidies, continue to lose money. Almodovar's latest film, however, will be "the most lucrative film in Spanish cinema" if it continues to rake in national and international profits. Almodovar's film has far outpaced Carlos Saura's *El Dorado,* which probably will never make back its $8 million investment, the biggest budget of any Spanish film ever made. The fact that Saura's film won no prizes at Cannes and was compared unfavorably with Werner Herzog's *Aguirre, the Wrath of God* did not augur well for box-office success.

As of June 1989, the problem of financing Spanish films has not been resolved. Menendez-Leite has been vehemently criticized by lionized directors such as Luis Garcia Berlanga, former President of the Filmoteca Nacional, for favoring the film projects of "younger" directors, seventy per cent of which Berlanga found "execrable" and "unbearable." No alternative policy for funding or subsidizing Spanish films has been entertained.

Nevertheless, RTVE (Spanish Radio & Television) has become a willing investor and the second greatest co-producer of Spanish films, paying top dollar for broadcast rights to the industry product. It has also become the leading agency for foreign sales of top Spanish films.

One of the dangers of television's intrusion into the film industry is the use of film directors to mount TV series, blurring the line between theatrical film and television product, and paving the way for the nationalization of the film industry by the government. Pilar Miro, now the head of RTVE, has embarked upon several "mega-series," filming Cervantes' *Don Quixote* and all of Perez-Galdos' *National Episodes,* using "film" producers like Elias Querejeta, Emiliano Piedra, Jose Frade and Luis Megino, diverting their attention away from independent Spanish filmmaking and discouraging private initiative and profits.

Outside of Castile, independent filmmaking is alive and well in Catalonia and the Basque provinces. Although each industry is pitifully small, they remain autonomous and free from the pressures of Madrid. Catalonia's TV3, based in Barcelona, has purchased the rights of many interesting films, among them *El vent d'illa* (*Wind of the Island*), directed by Gerardo Gormezano (already seen at New York's Fourth Spanish Film Festival); *El complot des anells* (*The Plot of the Rings,* aka *The Ring Conspiracy*) by Francesc Bellmunt; and a biography of Salvador Dali entitled

Dali, by Antoni Ribas. With the opening of a Catalonian Film Office, the film industry there is trying to launch Barcelona as the second center for Spanish film production.

Up through the end of 1988, Catalan film production has greatly increased, providing one-quarter of the total national product for the Iberian peninsula. Several titles have already been listed in the 1989 section of the chronology provided in this volume. Some new and worthy selections follow, in no particular order:

1. *L'home de neo* (*The Neon Man*), directed by Alberto Abril, a futuristic thriller with Feodor Atkine and Assumpta Serna.
2. *El nen de la lluna* (*Moon Child*), directed by Agustin Villaronga, a fantasy story.
3. *Gaudi,* a biography of the Catalonian architect directed by Manuel Huerga for Catalan television.
4. *Estacio Central,* directed by J. A. Salgot, a murder mystery with Feodor Atkine.
5. *Si te dicen que cai . . .* (*If They Tell You I Fell . . .*), directed by Vicente Aranda, based upon Juan Marse's novel, about a cross-section of Barcelona society, *circa* 1950.
6. *Un negre amb un saxo* (*Black Man with a Sax*), an adaptation of an "urban" novel set in Valencia.
7. *Inisfree,* directed by Jose Luis Guerin, a film tribute to the Irish people and landscape, with Maureen O'Hara coming out of retirement to "star" in this production.
8. *Es quan dormo que hi veig clar* (*In Sleep I See Clearly*), presented at the Barcelona Film Festival in 1988.
9. *Dali,* the biography directed by Antoni Ribas.
10. *El complot dels anells* (*The Plot of the Rings,* aka *The Ring Conspiracy*), directed by Francsec Bellmunt, is probably the most fascinating film of this group. It is set in Barcelona in 1992. The President of the Province of Catalonia is murdered on the eve of the beginning of the Olympic Games. Bellmunt has made a spectacular fictional political film with the ironic twist that a civil war will break out between Catalonia and Castille within the context of the Olympic competition.

Film production in the Basque province has been going on since the mid-eighties, with two most memorable films by Montxo Armendariz: *Tasio* (1984), about the indomitable free spirit of a coal maker, and *27 Horas* (*27 Hours*) (1986), treating the problems of teenagers dealing and taking drugs in La Coruna. The latest Basque production to come from this remote area is *A los cuatro vientos* (*To the Four Winds*) (1988), directed by Jose Antonio Zorilla, which treats the tragic bombing of Guernica by the Nazis in 1937, during the Spanish Civil War.

The nineties can only bring in an era of radical change for the Spanish film industry. Since Franco's death in 1975 Spanish cinema has enjoyed a long-sought freedom from government censorship. The *apertura* has affected all of the directors mentioned in this book, who have had a real impact both in and outside of Spain, bringing Spanish cinema overdue recognition and a long-deserved international status. One cannot talk intelligently about international cinema without mention of Spain's contribution.

After reviewing forty of Spain's best films and thirty that did not quite make "pantheon" status, as we approach the nineties it is clear that many more Spanish films will be more accessible internationally, will no longer be art-house-oriented or elitist cinema but commercial successes, truly artistic films that show off their glorious national heritage. Spanish cinema for the world! Que viva Espana! Que viva el cine espanol!

N.B. Much of the factual information contained in this conclusion comes from conversations and correspondence with Peter Besas, the *Variety* film critic based in Madrid. His articles in the Cannes Film Festival Issue of May 1989 were especially helpful, as was Jose Luis Guarner's

"Spain" section in Peter Cowie's *1989 International Guide to Cinema*, published by Tantivy Press in London.

At press time, *Variety* reports, in its Cannes Film Festival issue of May 2, 1990 (p. 204), that Spanish film production is decidedly down (from 58 to 47 features) for the period 1989–1990.

Also at press time, in New York City, at the Festival Latino of Theatre and Film, presented by Joseph Papp in late August, 1990, Josefina Molina was named best director in an elaborate selection of Spanish-speaking films, including four from Spain ("Two Films Share Prize at Festival Latino," *New York Times*, August 31, 1990, late edition, p. C15). The films from Spain were Molina's 1988 historical drama, *Esquilache*, Rafael Moleon's *Baton Rouge* (1988), Vicente Aranda's *Si te dicen que cai* (*If They Tell You I Fell*) (1990), and Pedro Olea's *El cura de Bargota* (*The Priest from Bargota*) (1990). The films by Aranda, Molina and Olea received their first theatrical showing at this Festival Latino, while Moleon's crime melodrama, *Baton Rouge*, received earlier exposure at the last Spanish Film Festival in Manhattan in 1989.

Esquilache, far and away the best Spanish film shown in the festival, detailed the political intrigues of the famous Italian Marquis living at the court of Carlos III. Fernando Fernan Gomez played the doomed Marquis admirably and was capably assisted by Concha Velasquez as his wife, Angela Molina as his maid, and Adolfo Marsillach as his king. Produced by TVE (Spanish Television) in sumptuous color, photographed lovingly on actual locations by Juan Amoros, and supplied with a beautiful musical score by Jose Nieto, the film still falls surprisingly flat despite its literary source: Antonio Buero Vallejo's play, *Un sonador para un pueblo*

Fernando Fernan Gomez in *Esquilache*.

(*Dreamer for a People*). Its title, like its principal character, dooms its commercial success abroad. The film recounts, in a series of flashbacks, the entire life of the Marquis, his reforms and failures that were to affect the social system of Spain in the eighteenth century and after.

If *Esquilache* was the "best" film to represent Spain in New York City during 1990, the other features were certainly poorer by comparison. Moleon's *Baton Rouge* was a crime melodrama that starred Carmen Maura, Victoria Abril and Antonio Banderas. Although it may be considered a "torrid murder mystery reminiscent of Lawrence Kasdan's *Body Heat*" (as the Festival program notes mention), it had such improbable plot twists that its murkiness made it tiring to watch, and not a candidate for inclusion in any book on the best of Spanish cinema.

Olea's *The Legend of the Priest of Bargota,* about an intending priest who sells his soul to the devil for favors on earth, and Iborra's *Dance of the Duck* (both 1990 productions), which deals with the desperation of a modern Madrillian journalist living in the fast lane, tempted by sex and drugs, avoiding responsibility in his marriage—these films may reflect modern Spanish society but they are rather pallid efforts by younger film directors to resuscitate early nineties Spanish cinema from its present downward spiral.

In an exclusive interview I had with *Variety*'s Spanish correspondent in New York City on September 16, 1990, Peter Besas mentioned the forthcoming San Sebastian Film Festival and said that Spain's single new entry would be Basque director Montxo Armendariz's *Las cartas de Alou* (*Letters to Alou*), about an African immigrant's experiences while living in Barcelona. Spain's share of box-office revenues for its own films was only 7.3% of the national market for 1990 (7.69% in 1989). Besas considers the presentation of *Atame* (*Tie Me Up, Tie Me Down*) at the 1990 Montreal Film Festival as well as the showing of a Catalan film entitled *Boum, Boum* (its director was Rosa Verges) at Venice this year to be indicative of a downward trend in Spanish film quality and production. He feels that Spanish cinema is moving toward producing more comedies, rather than films that have always seemed to be rooted in "personal problems." The phenemonal success of Carlos Saura's *Ay, Carmela!* (about two itinerant actors during the Spanish Civil War, starring Carmen Maura and Andres Pajares, which is due for an April 1991 release here in the United States by Miramax Films) indicates that Spaniards may be tired of making films about the Spanish Civil War and are seeking relief through comedy.

According to Besas, "It does not even matter what Spanish film directors put on to celluloid thematically. Most of the older directors are burnt out and the younger ones do not expect to make any real money at the box office since all new productions receive subsidies from the Ministry of Culture or Spanish television and all 'financial deals' are negotiated in 'pre-sale' packages for television. Spanish films are even pre-sold to Latin America as well as other Spanish-language markets in distribution package deals even before any cameras turn."

In the September 24, 1990 issue of *Variety,* Besas devoted several articles to the current state of Spanish cinema. Herewith is a distillation of his views (many of which are shared by this writer) as this book goes to press. (Peter Besas has been the only Spanish film critic from *Variety* on the scene in Madrid for over thirty years and continues to write cogent, perceptive criticism of Spanish films and the Spanish film industry.)

Besas' 35-page "global" report from Spain covers all phases of television, film and home video. As Spain nears the celebration of Columbus' discovery of America 500 years ago, "Spanish television is busting out all over." A seven-part documentary, "Columbus & the Era of Discovery," costing some $6.5 million dollars, is in production and ready for 1992 release to RTVE and to cinemas.

Tracking the top Spanish films released to the United States over the past twenty years, Besas finds Pedro Almodovar and Carlos Saura to be the leading directors of Spanish-language features exported to our country, with a few Buñuel films also included among the top dozen shown here. *Women on the Verge . . . , Tie Me Up . . .* and *Carmen* are the three leaders in box-office receipts in the U.S.A.

Despite such successes abroad, Spanish film continues to lose the numbers battle to Spanish television. Film attendance in 1969 peaked at 400 million tickets sold, while in 1989 attendance dropped to 60 million. The Spanish home video business is also in a tailspin, and more than 40% of the country's rental outlets may go out of business by 1991. "The bloom is off the home video rose," says Besas, because of too much free television and too many pirated tapes. The price of pre-recorded video cassettes is too high and the sale of VCR's has peaked at 3.5 million (a relatively small figure).

Catalan and Basque filmmaking are industries apart. It is only a "rare" production in either of these languages that breaks through the national or international barrier and draws audiences in Spain or abroad. Also, as the number of cinemas continues to decline despite the increase of "multi-plexes" and stable ticket rates (about $5 for a first-run film), distribution of Spanish films continues to be problematic because Spain maintains a system of dubbing licenses, forcing foreign distributors into making Spanish-dubbed versions of their product. This obliges some countries either to produce some of their own films in Spain or to include a number of Spanish films among their releases. Also, "v.o. films" and cinemas that show films in original language versions with appropriate Spanish sub-titles are slowly disappearing in Spain. With the average Spanish film costing as little as $1 million and budgets sometimes escalating to $3 million, and despite excellent post-production facilities for lab work, editing, sound mixing, et al., film production has reached an all-time low, with only 47 features produced last year.

Independent directors are finding it difficult to "resist the siren enticements of the country's television explosion," says Besas. "The television drain has taken its toll on the film business." Besas reports that the top directors and producers have made deals for their future films as well as for their "libraries" for television showing. The successes of Almodovar and Saura are "isolated cases." They continue to make films that are privately financed and enjoy huge international profits.

As we move towards Spain's 500th centennial, Besas feel box-office results for 1990 Spanish films "have not been heartening," and "if there is any new talent in the wings, it hasn't evinced many signs of life." Directors like Villaronga, Moleon and Vega, who made spectacular debut films, seem to have run out of steam. Besas believes that co-production is the best way to cut down rising costs of film production to increase foreign sales of Spanish films. One of the most successful of late, *El mono loco* (*The Mad Monkey*), starred American actor Jeff Goldblum, was shot mainly in London and Paris, and was directed by Fernando Trueba. This true hybrid production opened to fairly successful reviews in New York City during September, 1990. Many Madrillians flocked recently to American releases of *Total Recall* and *Batman*, in English, a reversal of the declining original version trend. Madrid is just crazy about English. However, just as the *siesta*, that lovely afternoon nap after the main meal of the day, may disappear, so may the "art" of filmgoing in Madrid and Barcelona. As reserved seating rather than general admissions has caught the public fancy, cafe/bars are being replaced by popcorn and soda-vending machines. As ticket-takers in multiplexes have decreased, ushers expecting a small gratuity for taking you to your seat may also disappear in the near future. Although the days of the "movie palace" are limited, one earnestly hopes that the film product itself does not disappear from the Spanish silver screen by the 21st century.

The July 1, 1991 issue of *Cambio 16* (No. 998, pp. 59–61) includes an article by Ramiro Cristobal entitled *"El mejor cine en Espana, desconocido en el extranjero"* (*"The Best Films from Spain—Unknown Abroad"*), in which a group of about one hundred Spanish film critics and specialists select Spain's ten best films of the eighties as well as reflect upon the current state of Spanish cinema. For five months, beginning at the International Film Festival at Huelva, they argued, speculated and finally came up with the following list, which was highly controversial, even among themselves:

1. *El sur* (*The South*) by Victor Erice (1982).*
2. *Los santos inocentes* (*The Holy Innocents*) by Mario Camus (1983).*
3. *Tasio* by Montxo Armendariz (1984).*
4. *Mujeres al borde de un ataque de nervios* (*Women on the Verge of a Nervous Breakdown*) by Pedro Almodovar, 1988.* (Spain's biggest international money-making film as of 1991.)
5. *El viaje a ninguna parte* (*Journey to Nowhere*) by Fernando Fernan Gomez, 1986.
6. *Padre nuestro* (*Our Father*) by Francisco Regueiro, 1985.
7. *El bosque animado* (*The Animated Forest*) by Jose Luis Cuerda, 1987. (Spain's biggest box-office draw nationally as of 1991.)
8. *Bodas de sangre* (*Blood Wedding*) by Carlos Saura, 1980.*
9. *Que he hecho para merecer esto?* (*What Have I Done to Deserve This?*) by Pedro Almodovar, 1984.*
10. *Demonios en el jardin* (*Demons in the Garden*) by Manuel Gutierrez Aragon, 1982.*

The asterisks [*] denote Spanish films which I felt were worthy of discussion in the main body of this book, a surprising *seven* out of the ten chosen by Spanish critics as their "best films of the eighties."

Except for *Women on the Verge . . .*, none of these Spanish films has had a highly successful long run internationally and the Spanish film critics decry what they call "the colonization of North American cinema," the worst of American film products taking the place of good Spanish, Latin-American or even other European films in Spain's local cinemas. Clearly, it is up to European initiative to create a common audio-visual market with its own production and distribution systems in order to compete with the American film industry. The occasional Almodovar or Saura film is not enough to sustain the presence of the Spanish film industry. Co-productions should also be encouraged to increase competition with American film products. Then and only then will a true cultural panorama and diversity in international cinema be accomplished. One hopes that we shall see this development in the nineties.

APPENDIX

The preceding discussion of Spanish cinema can do no more than suggest the vastness and eminence of the nation's film heritage. Spanish cinema has had almost as long and fascinating a history as its neighbor France, although the latter country has exerted a profound world-wide influence, while Spanish cinema is just being discovered.

The problem of selection of the best of Spanish cinema was quite formidable. Exigencies of space and the prohibitive cost of reproducing many more stills were other factors in limiting the preceding sections to the truly "great" Spanish films. Nevertheless, I have tried to stress the work of directors whose films and influence have extended beyond the borders of Iberia.

In this Appendix are discussed other special Spanish films which are noteworthy (once again in chronological order), to show even more of the variety and achievements of Spanish cinema since the 1950s. These films are significant and their inclusion here will help provide a more inclusive view of Spanish cinema, although not by any means a definitive study of Spanish cinema.

1953

NOVIO A LA VISTA (BOYFRIEND IN SIGHT)

Jorge Vico and Josette Arno in *Novio a la vista.*

DIRECTOR: LUIS GARCIA BERLANGA

CREDITS: Screenplay: L. G. Berlanga, J. A. Bardem, Jose Luis Colina & Edgar Neville; Photography: C. Paniagua, A. Ampuero, S. Perera, A. L. Ballesteros & M. F. Mila; Producer: Benito Perojo for CEA Films; Music: Juan Quintero.

CAST: Josette Arno (Loli), Jorge Vico (Enrique), Jose Maria Rodero (Federico), Julio Caba Alba (Dona Dolores).

COMMENTARY: Set in a northern Spanish beach resort during the time of the First World War, *Novio* deals with a young man's "rite of passage," his first love, his adolescent friends, his rebelliousness against adult authority, his transition to adulthood.

Berlanga's film, ingenious for its time, satirized the mores and customs of this era. The film was originally censored because it was thought that some of the characters who were widely burlesqued in this period film degraded the military. [*Note:* When the film was originally released in 1953–54, it carried the name of Benito Perojo as director. The film has only recently been restored to the filmography of Berlanga since the death of Franco.]

1959

LOS GOLFOS (THE HOOLIGANS)

DIRECTOR: CARLOS SAURA

CREDITS: Screenplay: Mario Camus, Daniel Sueiro & Carlos Saura; Photography: Juan Julio Baena; Producer: Pedro Portabella for Films 59; Music: Ramirez Angel y Pagan.

CAST: Manolo Zarzo (Julian), Luis Marin (Ramon), Oscar Cruz (Juan), Maria Mayer (Visi), Juanjo Losada (El Chato).

Manolo Zarzo in *Los golfos*.

COMMENTARY: Carlos Saura's debut film, this is a harsh, realistic semi-documentary of the tragic lives of a group of five young men in their twenties, living in and around the slums of Madrid. The group plans to burgle a garage in order to finance a friend's bullfighting career which goes awry. They are caught by the police at the conclusion.

The film is pessimistic but honest in its hard-edged look at city life, much of it photographed with a hand-held camera. [Compare Jean Luc-Godard's portrait of a petty criminal on the streets of Paris, beautifully played by Jean Paul Belmondo in his debut film, *A Bout de Souffle* (*Breathless*)]. It deals with the misery, the disillusion, the boredom, the loneliness of these young men, and the solidarity of the gangs and gang life as the only alternative to complete societal alienation.

Saura was influenced by the Italian neo-realistic style of the period but also believed in improvisation to capture the spontaneity and graphic quality of the action on screen. Saura's film was inevitably compared to Luis Buñuel's Mexican epic about juvenile delinquency, *Los olvidados* (*The Young & the Damned*), a film Saura had never seen before he made *Los golfos*.

The film is violent, full of tension, completely absorbing. It ends with the capture of Juan, as he waits for the police to arrest him for his complicity in the robbery. The civil guards await the end of Juan's poor performance as a *torero* as the end title comes up on the screen. In reality, Saura utilized the services of a young Colombian matador who was an expert at killing bulls. Saura photographed his third, not so perfect performance, which coincided with the screenwriters' conclusion to the film.

With *Los golfos*, Saura's directorial career was launched. Although this film was shot on an extremely low budget with several non-professional actors, even illiterate actors, and the film was severely criticized for its depressing portrait of Madrid and its "black humor," it demonstrates Saura's talent, and his later film, *Deprisa, deprisa* (*Hurry, Hurry*), made in 1980, represents his fulfillment as a director of this kind of social cinema.

1961

PLACIDO

DIRECTOR: LUIS GARCIA BERLANGA

CREDITS: Screenplay: L. G. Berlanga, Rafael Azcona, Jose Luis Colina & Jose Luis Font; Photography: Francisco Sampere; Producer: Jose Manuel Miguel Herrero for Jet Films-Alfredo Matas.

CAST: Casto Sendra "Cassen" (Placido), Jose Luis Lopez Vasquez (Gabino Quintanilla), Elvira Quintilla (Emilia), Amelia de la Torre (Senora de Galan).

COMMENTARY: Tired of immaculately made studio films filled with vacuous grandiloquence, Spanish directors like Bardem, Berlanga and Buñuel finally brought realism to the Spanish screen. The search for their own identity of a new generation of young Spaniards was portrayed in the social problem films of the three "B's." Berlanga, long a practitioner of dark humor tinged with sarcasm and sardonic wit, was as irreverent in his own style as Buñuel was in the surreal, symbolic masterpiece, *Viridiana*, produced the same year. Whereas Buñuel left the country immediately, however, taking a print of his film to Paris, Berlanga stayed to suffer the indignities of Francoist censorship.

Originally based upon an earlier film, *Los jueves, milagro* (*Every Thursday, A Miracle*), *Siente un pobre a su mesa* (*Seat a Poor Man at Your Table*) was again heavily censored and was retitled *Placido*. The title role was played by a Catalan comedian, famous for his television and vaudeville appearances in the early sixties. Actually filmed on the streets of the town of Manresa, *Placido* tells the story of a poor family man, owner of a tricycle he uses to deliver fruit baskets for the local charity drive. In debt, he must pay his note on Christmas eve or lose his vehicle. At the same time, a group of provincial society women decide to organize a charity drive, using the slogan, "Take a beggar home to dinner!"

A multitude of confusing situations ensue, some of them extremely funny, others tragicomic. For example, when one

Elvira Quintilla and Casto Sendra in *Placido*.

of the hostesses realizes that her beggar guest, who is on the brink of death, is not married to a woman with whom he has been living for many years, she demands a priest to satisfy her egotism and sense of Christian propriety, disregarding the beggar's wishes. The aristocrats must maintain face, even if there is no "real" love behind their notion of Christian charity. Placido witnesses many of these situations in the course of running his errands, trying to earn money to pay his debt, which he succeeds in doing. As he is about to celebrate Christmas with a dinner he kept in one of the fruit baskets for his family, he is accused by a fruit vendor of stealing and he gives it up. Cold and hungry, Placido and his family have suffered at the hands of Christians, who provide "charity" for beggars to ease their own consciences but who have little interest in the human condition of their hardworking fellow villagers.

Berlanga expresses, through his use of farce and corrosive wit, the eternal paradox found within the Spanish character: the disparity between Christian theory and the practice of good intentions.

Although the film was nominated for the Academy Award for Best Foreign Film of 1961, it was eclipsed by the infamy of *Viridiana.* Although it remains one of Berlanga's finest films, its realism and sardonic humor have lost the bite and urgency the film had at the time of its initial release.

1965

NUEVE CARTAS A BERTA (NINE LETTERS TO BERTHA)

DIRECTOR: BASILIO MARTIN PATINO

CREDITS: Screenplay: B. M. Patino; Photography: Luis Enrique Toran; Producer: Eco Films/Transfisa.

CAST: Emilio Gutierrez Caba (Lorenzo), Elsa Baeza (his girlfriend), Antonio Casas (his father), Mary Carillo (his mother).

COMMENTARY: In this film, shot in black and white in the city of Salamanca (the birthplace of the director), Patino examines, in almost documentary fashion, the thoughts of his alter-ego, Lorenzo, through a series of letters to a girl, Bertha, the daughter of an exiled Spaniard he has just met and visited briefly in London. Although we never see Lorenzo in London, we follow him through his days at home, in his university classes, and through his relations with classmates and his hometown girlfriend.

In these voice-overs of letters to Bertha, we hear Lorenzo's observations about provincial life, his judgments and personal feelings about his friends and family, everything that touches him, his crises of conscience. Although Lorenzo will be-

Elsa Baeza and Emilio Gutierrez Caba in *Nueve cartas a Berta.*

come a lawyer, by the conclusion of the film he is resigned to accepting the mediocrity of his provincial life, his father's empty retired-Falangist-veteran status, his lack of love for family and friends.

Cartas explodes the vision of "romantic love" by detailing the overwhelming, restrictive atmosphere of Salamanca. Patino uses the "revolutionary" film techniques of freeze frames, slow motion shots and still photographs to emphasize the static nature of Salamantine life. Frustrated by the memories of Bertha, Lorenzo renounces the intellectual freedom of England for the grayness and monotony of provincial life. Despite a somewhat ambiguous ending, and a cold semi-documentary style, *Cartas* is an intimate film reflecting the dissatisfactions of a completely modern alienated Spanish youth.

1975

PIM, PAM, PUM, FUEGO! (READY, AIM, FIRE!)

DIRECTOR: PEDRO OLEA

CREDITS: Screenplay: Pedro Olea & Rafael Azcona; Color Photography: Fernando Arribas; Producer: Jose Frade: Music: Carmelo Bernaola.

CAST: Conchita Velasco (Paca), Jose Maria Flotats (Luis), Fernando Fernan Gomez (Julio), Jose Orjas (Ramos), Maria Goyanes (Manolita), Jose Calvo (Policeman).

Jose Maria Flotats and Conchita Velasco in *Pim . . . pam . . . pum . . . fuego!*

COMMENTARY: Although this film, despite its title, did not catch fire internationally, probably because of its topic—music hall life in Spain during the 1940s—its indelible portrait of life in Madrid during that era is precisely what makes it such an appealing film.

It tells of a young woman, a singer (Velasco), in love with two men: a young revolutionary she saves from death (Flotats), and an older man, her impresario (Fernan Gomez), who murders her out of jealousy because of the singer's idyllic love affair with the younger man. It is the old, old story of frustration and the eternal triangle of lovers.

What makes this courageous film so worthwhile is director Olea's portrait of the post-Civil War years, the hard times, bread lines, hunger, blackmarketeering, set against the reproduction of the great songs of the forties in Spanish music halls. There is desperation in the actions of the lead characters that precipitate the atrocities at the conclusion.

Olea is suggesting that Fernan Gomez' brutality (ordering the death of Flotats and killing Velasco himself, dumping her body out on a dirt road) is a direct result of the post-war conditions of deprivation and scarcity. Olea has captured on film, through splendid period reconstruction, the ruthlessness, brutality and defeatism of Madrid of the early 1940s.

1976

PASCUAL DUARTE

DIRECTOR: RICARDO FRANCO

CREDITS: Screenplay: Emilio Martinez Lazaro, Elias Querejeta & Ricardo Franco, based upon the novel of Camilo Jose Cela, *La familia de Pascual Duarte;* Color Photography: Luis Cuadrado; Producer: Elias Querejeta; Guitar Music: Luis de Pablo.

CAST: Jose Luis Gomez (Pascual), Paca Ojea (his mother), Hector Alterio (his father), Diana Perez de Guzman (Rosario, his sister), Eduardo Calvo (Conde), Jose Hinojosa (Estirao), Maribel Ferrero (Lola, his wife), Carlos Oller (the priest), Salvador Munoz Calvo (Pascual as a child).

COMMENTARY: The director, Ricardo Franco, reshaped the *tremendista* or horrific sentiments of Cela's anti-hero into an esthetically artful experience, providing a catharsis for the audience which is not present in the 1942 novel.

Set in a bleak section of rural Spain, Extremadura of the 1930s, the film reveals the life story of a brutal but sensitive young man, Pascual, who is a violent product of this destructive milieu which leads him to multiple crimes of murder, matricide and death by garroting. Poverty and ignorance are rife in this primitive world, where love cannot be distinguished from rape, where irrational acts prevail over rational behavior.

Pascual's story (or history) is set against the background of Spain's Civil War and Franco's emergence as dictator in 1937. The novel and film are a metaphor for national violence as the garrote is for the choking repressive reality that is Spain herself. Like *Furtivos, Pascual Duarte* is a brutal reminder of Spain's "black legend" of violence.

The director deliberately photographed the film in color, framing the violent actions of Pascual from afar, with an immobile camera that blended into the landscape. No fancy zoom shots or close-ups are used to try to justify the "inexplicable" reasons for Pascual's murderous actions. Only external actions, rather than internal motivations, are perceived. The viewer must do all the work to understand the reasons for the actions in this monu-

Poster art for *Pascual Duarte*.

mentally ambiguous film, fraught with meaning but without literal explanations.

Pascual Duarte is an indictment of the corruption of the Franco regime, the ignorance and brutality of Spanish peasantry, the violence and purposelessness of rural Spain, and of the garrote for capital punishment. It dramatically extends the revisionist thinking achieved the preceding year in a documentary by Basilio Martin Patino entitled *Queridisimos verdugos* (*My Dearest Executioners*), which was a bold attack on capital punishment. *Pascual Duarte* is equally bold, angry, violent, brutal, provocative cinema at its best.

1976

CRIA CUERVOS (RAISE RAVENS)

DIRECTOR: CARLOS SAURA

CREDITS: Screenplay: Carlos Saura; EastmanColour Photography: Teo Escamilla; Producer: Elias Querejeta; Source Music: Song "Por que te vas?" ("Why Are You Going Away?") sung by Jeanette, and "Hay, Maricruz!" sung by Imperio Argentina; Music: Mompou, Valverde, Quiroga, Leon y tema cantado por Jeanette.

CAST: Ana Torrent (Ana), Geraldine Chaplin (Ana's mother), Conchita Perez (Ana's sister Irene), Maite Sanchez Almendros (Ana's sister Maite), Monica Randall (Aunt Paulina), Hector Alterio (Anselmo, Ana's father), Josefina Diaz (Ana's grandmother), Mirta Miller (Amelia, Anselmo's mistress).

COMMENTARY: Another of Saura's "memory" films following the autobiographical *La prima Angelica* (*Cousin Angelica*), *Cria cuervos* deals with loss—the loss of parents, pets, loved ones—and the fate of women in Spain, women destined to follow in the footsteps of their predecessors, embracing a religious education that will not prepare them for maturity under the Franco dictatorship. It is narrated by a child, Ana, who is deserted by her father, mother and pet guinea pig and will probably grow up indoctrinated into fascism by a strangling religious education, never to protest, never to rebel against the regime.

Cria was made in the last months of the Franco government, but was released in January of 1976. Its full title, *Cria cuervos,* is based upon the Spanish proverb, "Raise ravens, and they'll pluck out your eyes!" indicating rebellious behavior. Ana has just cause since her father was a womanizer, and her mother lived a completely hypocritical life in his shadow. Flashbacks reveal the memories of Ana: the specter of death is ever-present, the frustration of defeat inevitable. Ana will submit to patterns of the past, winningly docile, with no chance for escape from her past.

The film stresses the disparity between Ana's inner world of private traumas and the outer world of political realities and fascism. Ana will cope with her guilt in both arenas.

Cria cuervos deservedly received the Cannes Film Festival Special Jury Prize because of young Ana Torrent's superlative performance.

Ana Torrent and Geraldine Chaplin in *Cria cuervos.*

1978

EL CORAZON DEL BOSQUE (HEART OF THE FOREST)

DIRECTOR: MANUEL GUTIERREZ ARAGON

CREDITS: Screenplay: Manuel Gutierrez Aragon & Luis Megino; Color Photography: Teo Escamilla; Producer: Luis Megino for Arandano Films.

CAST: Norman Briski (Juan), Angela Molina (Amparo), Luis Politti ("El Andarin"), Victor Valverde (Suso), Santiago Ramos (Atilano).

COMMENTARY: Set in the forests of Cantabria and Asturias in 1952, where the director spent his youth, the film deals with El Andarin, a Basque revolutionary, a separatist (or perhaps even a Communist) who refuses to surrender to the Nationalist government, and Juan, who searches for this rebel throughout the film.

Angela Molina in *El corazon del bosque.*

The plot is fairly simple. Amparo, in love with El Andarin, is now engaged to the local shoemaker. When her brother Juan returns to Cantabria, she discourages his search for her former lover. Juan refuses and Amparo frustrates him by hiding El Andarin in a local corn field. Juan finally catches up with the anarchist, but is mistakenly taken for El Andarin and almost shot to death by the local Civil Guards. El Andarin saves Juan, but Juan shoots him because he mistakenly believes El Andarin betrayed their separatist movement. Amparo and her new husband offer Juan shelter as the Civil Guard searches for him for El Andarin's murder. As El Andarin prophesied, "You cannot trust anybody!" Juan takes over El Andarin's role, becoming an "animal" in the forest, surrounded by the Civil Guard, continually on the run, living off the earth to survive.

The real star of this film is the countryside of Asturias. The mist is everywhere. It rolls in magically and endows the struggle of the hunter and the hunted with great natural beauty. Although the struggle to survive is the film's major theme, love and betrayal are other important thematic concerns.

The film's story is told simply, straightforwardly, without artifice, but with much artistic feeling for the countryside and its people. *El corazon del bosque* is a very sensual film, full of atmosphere, glorifying the geographical beauties of Northern Spain. Apparently it is based upon a real event of the 1930s when the Maquis had offered armed resistance to the Franco government, and a few "outlaws," hiding in the mountains, became mythical figures, folk heroes.

Although the director intended to film

one of the childhood myths he grew up with, his terse and sober screenplay points up the ongoing problems of provincial separatism and violence as its consequence. It is far and away apposite to the extremely symbolic, heavily-laden "message" films which seem to be Gutierrez Aragon's forte. *Heart of the Forest* is a refreshing breather from the overly intellectualized concerns of the director.

1978

UN HOMBRE LLAMADO "FLOR DE OTONO" (A MAN CALLED "AUTUMN FLOWER")

DIRECTOR: PEDRO OLEA

CREDITS: Screenplay: Pedro Olea & Rafael Azcona, based upon a story by Jose Maria Rodriguez Mendez; Color & CinemaScope Photography: Fernando Arribas; Producer: Jose Frade; Music: Source music of the period.

CAST: Jose Sacristan (Lluis), Paco Algora (Surroca), Carmen Carbonell (Dona Nuria), Roberto Carmardiel (Armengol), Antonio Corencia (La Coquinera), Felix Dafauca (Police Chief).

Jose Sacristan (*right*) in *Un hombre llamado "Flor de otono."*

COMMENTARY: Filmed in color and CinemaScope in Barcelona in 1977 and set in the early 1930s, this is Olea's attempt to portray homosexuality and transvestism on the screen with as much psychological penetration and comprehension of the motives of its protagonists as possible in the new era of freedom from censorship.

Flor de otono is the story of a wealthy aristocratic lawyer, Lluis de Serracant, who belongs to an illustrious Catalonian family. Lluis apparently leads a normal professional life by day, but by night he becomes "Flor de otono" ("Autumn Flower"), a transvestite homosexual performer in a rowdy and cheap local cabaret. His lover, a combination boxer-bodyguard, protects Lluis in his dangerous double life.

The screenplay contains many plot twists. Lluis is always fearful that his homosexuality will be discovered by his family, especially his mother. As a transvestite performer, he becomes involved in many sordid situations, including the murder of a fellow performer with whom he had argued the previous night. Believing that Lluis murdered his lover, Armengol, a drug pusher, kidnaps him, beats him brutally and dumps him, dressed "in drag," on his mother's doorstep—the final humiliation. His mother had suspected her son's sexual inclinations years before and pretends to ignore what she has seen.

Meanwhile, Lluis, lawyer by day, joins an anarchist group seeking to overthrow the dictatorial regime of Primo de Rivera. One evening, he and his "family" set out to dynamite a train carrying the leaders to Barcelona. The explosion fails, the insurgents are routed and Lluis is jailed by the Civil Guard.

Eventually, the killer of the transvestite is revealed as a local sailor. Lluis has already taken vengeance upon Armengol; he steals drugs from a local pharmacy and frames the drug dealer by hiding this cache in the billiard hall Armengol owns. Armengol is arrested and charged, but denies the theft; he accuses Lluis of "anarchist" activities.

It is, nevertheless, coincidental that the Civil Guard has Lluis under surveillance and discovers his attempt to blow up the train carrying Primo de Rivera. Shooting it out with the police, Lluis and his lover are captured and condemned to death before the firing squad. Before Lluis-Flor de otono's execution, his mother visits him. In an extremely emotional scene, sensitively played, she hands her son a compact and lipstick. Lluis makes himself ready for the firing squad, embraces his lover and dies with his/her anarchist compatriots.

A Man Called "Autumn Flower" truly captures the spirit of the gay Catalonian world *circa* 1930–31 and the director, Pedro Olea, elicits a beautifully modulated, sensitive performance from Jose Sacristan. The film is very entertaining and fascinating when the "show business" numbers featuring transvestites are on screen. The director carefully researched the songs, the details for decor and costuming in order to present this elegant, accurate and decadent view of this hidden aspect of Catalonian society.

Homosexuality was always a taboo subject under the Franco regime, but with the dictator's death, Olea was able to film this extremely sensitive story he co-authored with Rafael Azcona. *Flor de otono* is commercial cinema at its best, dealing realistically and nostalgically with the period of Spanish history heretofore unseen on the Spanish screens. Olea's talent and marvelous professionalism are confirmed in this re-creation of minor historical moments of Spain's ignoble past.

1981–1983

EL CRACK (THE CRASH); EL CRACK - II

DIRECTOR: JOSE LUIS GARCI

CREDITS: Screenplay: J. L. Garci & Horacio Valcarcel; Color Photography: Manuel Rojas, in Eastmancolor; Producers: Francisco Hueva & Carlos Duran for Lola/Nickel Odeon/Lima Films: Music: Jesus Gluck.

CAST: Alfredo Landa (German Areta, private detective), Maria Casanova (Carmen), Miguel Rellan (Cardenas), Jose Bodalo (Don Ricardo), Rafael de Penagos (Don Miguel), Arturo Fernandez (Don Gregorio), Manuel Lorenzo ("Rocky"), Jose Luis Merino ("Meri"), Jose Manual Cervino (Frutos), Maite Marchante (Merche).

COMMENTARY: *El Crack* and its sequel, the most exciting crime thrillers filmed in Spain, are based upon America's tradition of the *film noir* of the 1940s and 1950s. *El Crack* is Garci's most imitative, eclectic, "American"-styled film, made with a definite commercial bias.

A private eye, Alfredo Landa, is initially hired to find the daughter of a dying man. She turns out to be a prostitute working in a local massage parlor. The story becomes convoluted as the detective's personal affairs (he is dating a psychological therapist played by Maria Casanova while playing father to her seven-year-old daughter) become confused with the prostitute's problems.

The prostitute apparently doubles as a messenger used by a high-level crime

Alfredo Landa in *El Crack.*

organization whose headquarters are in New York City. When the therapist's daughter is killed by a bomb planted in the detective's car (an obvious homage to Fritz Lang's *The Big Heat* if we compare Jocelyn Brando's demise), Landa leaves for New York to take revenge. He murders the head of the Syndicate at an Italian restaurant on Manhattan's East side and tells the Spanish gunsel who planted the bomb that he has tied three pieces of ham, not explosives, to his chest, to keep the gunman out of harm's way. As the gunsel undoes the bandages, a terrific explosion is heard in the motel room adjacent to Kennedy Airport as Landa boards a flight for his return to Madrid.

At home for Christmas, the detective renews his affair with the therapist, who no longer blames him for her daughter's death.

Alfredo Landa is excellent in his macho "little-guy" role as the detective. His penetrating stare truly mesmerizes his victims. The film is a truly charming homage to noir directors of the forties and Garci also succeeds in capturing the charm of downtown Madrid at night. His panoramas, pans and fadeouts are all reminiscent of the great American cameramen of the 1940s crime films, and a nostalgic musical theme highlighting the thrill of New York and Madrid city skylines revives the romanticism of a lonely detective's life in the jungle of urban life.

The film and its sequel are perfectly orchestrated, contain well-defined characters and are deftly played by the performers.

Garci had planned a trilogy, tentatively calling his last film *Areta investigacion* (*Investigations by Areta*), but decided against it. *El Crack (II)* was not as successful at the box office as the first film, with Garci indulging himself in magnificent but pointless mood shots of Madrid's skyline, using Alfredo Landa again acting in the Hammett mold of Sam Spade, and adding a homosexual ambience to a shrill story devoid of irony or humor.

But the first film, *El Crack*, was a runaway commercial success. Garci realized earlier in his career that filming on location would be a boon to the slack Spanish film industry of the early eighties. He is also a "movie" director, a mass-oriented director in search of commercial success. *El Crack* is an excellent sample of a "commercial movie," providing entertainment and an escape for Spanish audiences, but little serious thought.

1982

VOLVER A EMPEZAR (TO BEGIN AGAIN, aka BEGIN THE BEGUINE)

DIRECTOR: JOSE LUIS GARCI

CREDITS: Screenplay: Jose Luis Garci & Angel Llorente: Color Photography: Manuel Rojas; Producer: Jose Esteban Alenda & Angel Llorente for Nickel Odeon Films; Music: Johann Pachabel & Cole Porter's "Begin the Beguine," with piano versions by Jesus Gluck.

CAST: Antonio Ferrandis (Antonio Miguel Albaraja), Encarna Paso (Elena), Jose Bodalo ("Roxu"), Agustin Gonzales (Gervasio Losada), Pablo Hoyo (Ernesto), Marta Fernandez Muro (Carolina), Pablo del Hoyo (Sabino).

COMMENTARY: Touted by many Spanish film critics as a top-notch film, one of the best made in Spain in the early eighties, it was an international success, winning the Best Foreign Film Oscar in the United States in 1983.

A commercial crowd pleaser, *Volver a empezar* is an extremely sentimental film about the Spanish youth of the 1930s who never got a chance to fulfill their romantic dreams because of the Civil War.

Dedicated to a group of Spaniards in Northern Spain and to lovers everywhere, the film is the story of a Spanish professor (capably played by Antonio Ferrandis) who returns to Gijon to visit an old friend, a doctor named Roxu, and his first love, Elena (brilliantly played by Encarna Paso), with whom he danced to Cole Porter's famous song "Begin the Beguine" in 1936. She was his "Ginger" (Rogers) and he was her "Fred" (Astaire).

During the war, Antonio left for America and vowed never to return until Franco left the seat of Spanish government. When Antonio returns to Gijon, the new king, Juan Carlos, telephones him at the small hotel in which he is staying, creating quite a stir. He meets Elena, his former teenage sweetheart, at the Art Gallery she runs and they spend many romantic moments together. Antonio is divorced and has two grown-up sons living in America. Elena admits that she married a man she did not love and was in love with another man who could not leave his wife.

Throughout the film, the college professor is taking some mysterious medication, probably pain killers. In one amusing exchange with Elena, he makes fun of Americans, saying, "Everyone there is on some kind of pill." He confides his illness to his boyhood doctor-friend Roxu, and the latter realizes that Antonio has terminal cancer and about six months left to live. That is why Antonio wanted to return to his roots. He dances with Elena to the Cole Porter theme that haunts nearly

Antonio Ferrandis in *Volver a empezar*.

every frame of this film, although there are some other musical references to Pachabel and other "sentimental" melodies. Having spent the night with Elena, he returns to Berkeley, awaiting the inevitable. Before he leaves, Elena gives him a package to open when he arrives at his apartment overlooking the Golden Gate Bridge. The package contains some nostalgic photos of Elena and Antonio *circa* 1936 and the 78 rpm. record of Artie Shaw's famous version of "Begin the Beguine."

Despite its predictable conclusion, *Volver a empezar* is a lovely film, astonishingly sentimental and dedicated to lovers over thirty. The film has some outstanding performances, a sensitive script and flawless direction, cinematography and editing. These virtues won it the Academy Award for Best Foreign Film of 1983. However, the story is maudlin, and the director's handling of the script teeters on the edge of the lachrymose. Nevertheless, it was a big commercial success in the United States and has enjoyed a first-run engagement in Madrid for nearly two years. It is also available on videocassette and retains its popularity with the mass audience.

1982

LA MUCHACHA CON BRAGAS DE ORO (THE GIRL WITH THE GOLDEN PANTIES)

DIRECTOR: VICENTE ARANDA

CREDITS: Screenplay: Vicente Aranda & Mauricio Walerstein based upon the novel by Juan Marse; Color and CinemaScope Photography: Jose Luis Alcaine; Producers: Juan Antonio Perez Giner & Carlos

Duran for Morgana/Prozesa & Proa Films; Music: Manuel Camps.

CAST: Victoria Abril (Mariana), Lautaro Murua (Forest), Perla Vonacek (Elmyr), Pep Munne (Forest as a young man), Consuelo de Nieva (Tecla), Isabel Mestres (Soledad).

COMMENTARY: *The Girl with the Golden Panties* is a film that exhibits a sexual frankness which was off-limits in Spanish films made before 1975.

Based upon a best-selling novel by Catalonian author Juan Marse, it tells the story of an aging writer who feels guilty because of his political past and lives in virtual isolation while writing his memoirs in the late 1970s. One day, his niece Mariana (dazzlingly played by Victoria Abril) pays him an unexpected visit. She is on drugs and has a lesbian lover. The relationship between uncle and niece begins slowly, but inevitably the girl insinuates herself into his life sexually. It is only afterwards that the uncle discovers the truth: Mariana is his daughter!

The film is beautifully made and there are some extraordinary scenes of frank and open sexuality. It is a long film, visually beautiful, high in style, but the denoument is worth the wait. Victoria Abril's performance is inspired; she is one of the two most popular actresses in Spain in the eighties (Angela Molina is the other) and is on her way to international stardom. This film, which will certainly launch her career, is another Aranda master work, demonstrating his ability to exploit the new freedoms won by Spanish film directors of the late seventies.

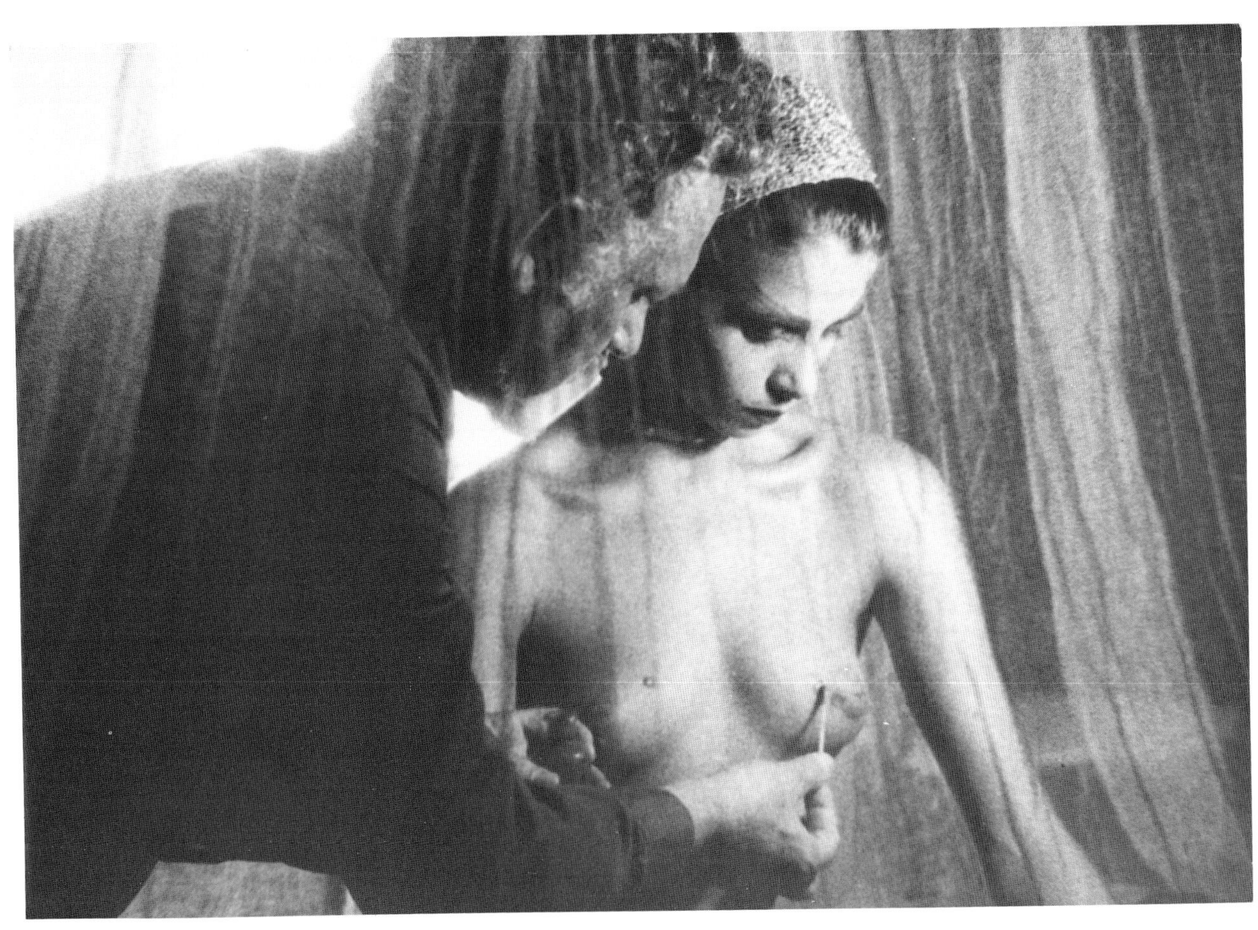

Victoria Abril and Lautaro Murua in *La muchacha con bragas de oro.*

1982

DEMONIOS EN EL JARDIN (DEMONS IN THE GARDEN)

DIRECTOR: MANUEL GUTIERREZ ARAGON

CREDITS: Screenplay: Manuel Gutierrez Aragon & Luis Megino; Color Photography: Jose Luis Alcaine; Producer: Luis Megino; Music: Javer Iturralde; Songs: "Coplas" by J. Mostazo and "Wenn dein Mutterlein" by G. Mahler.

CAST: Angela Molina (Angela), Ana Belen (Ana), Encarna Paso (Gloria), Imanol Arias (Juan), Eusebio Lazaro (Oscar), Alvaro Sanchez-Prieto (Juanito).

COMMENTARY: An atmospheric film set in the 1940s (and later, in 1952), *Demons in the Garden* is a traditionally romantic film, the story of a family and its seething sexuality, jealousies, dreams realized and shattered, hypocrisies. It stars Angela Molina and Ana Belen as the lovers of Juan (played by Imanol Arias) and his brother Oscar (Eusebio Lazaro), and the screenplay deals with a domineering mother's devotion (Gloria, the mother, is played by Encarna Paso) for her two sons.

Family portrait in *Demonios en el jardin* (*left to right, top row:* Eusebio Lazaro and Imanol Arias; *bottom row:* Ana Belen, Encarna Paso, Alvaro Sanchez Prieto, and Angela Molina).

The brothers, Juan and Oscar, have frequent violent disputes. Juan leaves the family store, called "El Jardin" ("The Garden") and run by his mother, and joins the Nationalist Army. Oscar and Ana marry but remain childless, and Angela is left pregnant by Juan. She gives birth to Juanito. As the years pass, he becomes ill while searching for his father.

Gloria takes her grandson Juanito into her store and pampers the boy; he is, incidentally, her only heir. Juanito, however, misses his mother and she returns to live with the family within "El Jardin." One day, Juanito hears that his father will pass with Franco's retinue; he finally meets him and discovers that he is only a waiter in the service of Franco's personal bodyguard.

The years move on and Juanito, no longer suffering from a rheumatic heart condition and totally disenchanted with his father, learns that his father is visiting Ana, Oscar's wife. Apparently, Juan and Ana had been lovers many years before. Because Juan now needs money, Ana steals one thousand pesetas from the family safe—profits from the black-marketeering the family practiced in order to survive during World War II. Juan has been cashiered out of the army and has run up many debts.

Gloria, Juan's mother, discovers the theft but blames it upon Angela, who is dragged off to jail by the local Civil Guards. Gloria discovers the truth and urges Juan to return home to marry

Angela so that the family will have a "legitimate" heir. Angela, however, refuses to marry the callow Juan, who is still in love with Ana.

Returning once more to "El Jardin," Juan again tries to seduce Ana, but she is so enraged by Juan's behavior that she shoots him in the shoulder with a hand gun. Oscar and Juan fight fiercely in their own sibling love-hate relationship, first over Ana, then Angela.

On the following day, Juanito's birthday is celebrated and the entire family is gathered by the local photographer for a family portrait in front of "El Jardin." The film ends in a "freeze-frame" of the photograph, offering no conclusions but exposing all the hidden hypocrisies within this petit-bourgeois family.

Demons in the Garden contains one lovely, nostalgic scene, when Juanito goes to a local movie house and watches Silvana Mangano do the mambo number from the Italian classic, *Anna,* arousing his own sexual stirrings and worries. *Demons* burns with a certain intensity and its director, Gutierrez Aragon, has achieved the prominence of a Buñuel or a Saura.

Demons has been applauded by many American critics and some feel it is one of the greatest films to come out of Spain in the early eighties. It does, indeed, blaze with star performances and is one of the best traditional realist films of its era. It is a serious, intelligent film, not given to over-intellectualizing, which is the director's usual penchant. *Demons* has had a respectable run abroad because it is a film of great beauty and sensitivity and is so typically "Spanish."

1983

LAS BICICLETAS SON PARA EL VERANO (BICYCLES ARE FOR SUMMER)

DIRECTOR: JAIME CHAVARRI

CREDITS: Screenplay: Fernando Fernan Gomez, based upon his own play; Color Photography: Miguel Angel Trujillo; Producer: Alfredo Matas for Incine-Jet Films; Music: Francisco Guerrero.

CAST: Amparo Soler Leal (Dolores), Agustin Gonzales (Luis), Victoria Abril (Manolita), Alicia Hermida (Antonia), Patricia Adriani (Maria), Marisa Paredes (Dona Maria Luisa), Carlos Tristancho (Julio), Gabino Diego (Luisito), Aurora Redondo (Marcela), Guillermo Marin (Don Simon), Emilio Gutierrez Caba (Anselmo), Laura del Sol (Dancer), Miguel Rellan (Basilio), Jorge de Juan (Pedro).

COMMENTARY: Based upon the successful play by that superlative Spanish actor-director-writer Fernando Fernan Gomez, *Bicycles* deals with the day-to-day experiences of a lower-middle-class family during the Civil War.

Set in Madrid during the summer of 1936, the story essentially concerns Luisito, who learns that he has flunked the

Gabino Diego, Amparo Soler Leal, and Victoria Abril in *Las bicicletas son para el verano.*

final physics exam. As a consequence, he will not receive a bicycle his parents promised to him if he passed the course. Luisito tries to change his father's mind, claiming that the professors were biased and, since his overall grade average is high, that he really deserves the bicycle. His father, who works in a local wine store, bends under Luisito's persuasion but the Civil War breaks out on July 18.

Everyone assumes the war will last only a matter of weeks, but it goes on for three years, affecting everybody's lives. Madrid is besieged, food and supplies run short, nightly bombings become ritualized.

Luisito's family is not spared any of its own tragedy. His sister Manolita, who works at a typing school and studies to be an actress, becomes pregnant. Needless to say, all hopes of Luisito getting a bicycle during this period are dashed. Manolita receives a marriage proposal from a neighbor's son who rescues her from further emotional stress. Luisito's thoughts wander far from bicycles as he is initiated into the mysteries of love by the family's attractive maid.

Filmed in glorious color, this film is well acted but is very predictable, parading all the cliches—sexual awareness of youth coming of age, wartime romances and the consequences of illegitimate children, friendships between teenage boys and girls. Not too much happens to this particular family headed by Agustin Gonzales and Amparo Soler Leal.

Madrid is the true star of the film as the director, Jaime Chavarri, sought to recapture the decor and the spirit of the 1930s. An earlier film by Chavarri, *The Long Vacation of '36* is superior to *Bicycles*, because it is less sentimental, more faithful to history and has great dramatic impact and urgency. *Bicycles* tends to be soap opera, nostalgic, sentimental. It does have some scenes of tasteful nudity.

Although it was not the real artistic success Chavarri expected, it was a commercial blockbuster. But it was totally devoid of any political thrust. Its recreation of the past and its set pieces, however, are worthy of the viewer's attention.

1983

LA LINEA DEL CIELO (SKYLINE)

DIRECTOR: FERNANDO COLOMO

CREDITS: Screenplay: Fernando Colomo; Color Photography: Angel Luis Fernandez; Producer: Antonio Isasi for La Salamandra Films; Music: Manzanitas.

CAST: Antonio Resines (Gustavo, the photographer), Beatriz Perez-Porro (Pat, the video student), Jaime Nos (Jaime, the psychiatrist), Roy Hoffman (Roy, the lecher), Irene Stillman (Irene, Pat's sister), Whit Stillman (Thornton, the agent), Patricia Cisarano (Elizabeth, owner of the Soho loft).

COMMENTARY: *Skyline* was presented in New York City in April 1984 as part of the Museum of Modern Art's New Directors/ New Films Series. It was the hit of the festival, and deservedly so. Although Colomo originally came to New York to take English classes and do research for another screenplay, he departed from his original plan after a few seminal New York experiences and decided to make a film in the city.

Skyline tells the story of Gustavo, a Spanish photographer who is looking for work in New York, taking classes in English and seeking female companionship. He strikes out on all three and decides to return to Madrid, leaving unan-

Antonio Resines in *La linea del cielo.*

swered a phone call from *Life* magazine that holds out the promise of a bright future for him in America.

The film is a low-keyed comedy, quite witty and very enjoyable. Filmed on a shoe-string budget, it is Colomo's return to intimate filmmaking with hand-held cameras à la Godard.

Colomo is a sharp observer of the American scene and a keen satirist. For example, he notes the futility of English-as-a-Second-Language classes which Gustavo attends at the New School, finding it difficult to communicate. On love, Colomo shows the futility of relationships if the girl lives uptown in the Bronx and Gustavo lives in Soho.

At a Soho get-together, where Gustavo can hardly understand the "Jackie O" story (Jacqueline Onassis), everyone is drinking excessively and discussing therapeutic sessions with their psychiatrist. Gustavo's best friend Jaime *is* a psychiatrist, who decided to stay in New York City precisely because of its "nutty," pathological atmosphere.

At one point, Gustavo misunderstands a telephone conversation with Elizabeth, the landlord. She suddenly returns, unexpectedly, from Arizona and Gustavo is forced to spend three nights on Jaime's professional couch. The exchange between Gustavo and Elizabeth is hilarious; neither speaks the other's language and they have to resort to sign language. Somewhat fatalistically, Gustavo is doomed to return to Madrid, prompted by Pat's earlier decision to fly to Barcelona.

Skyline does some interesting things with titles. When Spanish is being spoken, English titles appear on the screen, and vice-versa. This is especially interesting here in America, and comical, since the English titles are not needed, but their gratuitous presence makes them screamingly funny.

There were two jarring notes in this film: the score is by a Gypsy group, Manzanitas, which does not seem to belong to the soundtrack, and Gustavo's decision is a *deus ex machina* type of conclusion. It was as if Colomo had run out of story content, money, or both, and could not find a suitable ending.

Nevertheless, Colomo has a fantastic ear and a real knack for telling visual and aural jokes. Like Fernando Trueba before him, he has restored a sense of comedy to the Spanish screen. Some critics have called him the "Woody Allen" of Madrid. I call him an innovative young filmmaker, interested in commercial success inside and beyond Iberia. *Skyline* has had a successful run on videocassette here and abroad. Perhaps the Woody Allen "appellation" has some validity.

1984

FANNY PELOPAJA (TOWHAIRED FANNY aka FANNY STRAWHAIR)

Fanny Cottencon and Francisco Algora in *Fanny Pelopaja.*

DIRECTOR: VICENTE ARANDA

CREDITS: Screenplay: Vicente Aranda, based upon the novel *Protesis* by Andreu Martin; Color Photography: Juan Amoros; Producer: Carlos Duran for Lola/Morgana/Lima/Carlton Films; Music: Manuel Camp.

CAST: Fanny Cottencon (Fanny), Bruno Cremer (Andres), Francisco Algora (Julian), Berta Cabre (Nena), Ian Sera (Manuel), Paca Gabaldon (Sociologist), Eduardo MacGregor (Calvo), Joaquin Cardona (Pajaro), Roberto Asia (White Hair).

COMMENTARY: *Fanny Pelopaja* is a highly-charged, colorful crime film with lots of violence and a detailed armored-car robbery executed in the best traditions of such "heist" films as Jules Dassin's *Rififi* or Basil Dearden's *League of Gentlemen.*

Poor Fanny is the victim of a masochistic cop (Bruno Cremer) who kills her lover. Fanny seeks vengeance and realizes it, murdering her cop/lover in bed at the height of his orgasm, at his most vulnerable moment. However, Fanny does not get away scot-free. She is convicted of the crime and sent to a mental institution, living there in solitude the rest of her life.

There are some interesting revelations, showing how to conceal revolvers within the female anatomy, and some daring uses of guns as weapons for punishment both phallic and anal. Performances by the leads are terrific; the film really holds you. A fantastic crimer from Aranda.

1984

LA HORA BRUJA (THE BEWITCHING HOUR)

DIRECTOR: JAIME DE ARMINAN

CREDITS: Screenplay: Jaime de Arminan & Ramon de Diego; Color Photography: Teo Escamilla; Producer: Serva Films; Music: Alejandro Masso.

CAST: Francisco Rabal (Cesar), Conchita Velasco (Pilar/Esmeralda), Victoria Abril (Saga), Sancho Gracia (Ruben), Asuncion Balaguer (Nun).

COMMENTARY: A beautifully photographed and acted film, *La hora bruja* is a fairy tale in which magic weaves its spell among the events of everyday life.

Francisco Rabal and Conchita Velasco play a couple who travel throughout northern Spain, bringing films and their "magic" act to small villages. Rabal ("The Great Caesar") has the power to recall thousands of poems from their first line. Velasco is merely his mistress-assistant.

One day, they encounter Saga (Victoria Abril) on the road, a witch who transcends and transforms their lives. Saga makes a point of sleeping with both Cesar and Pilar, bringing them to the realization that they are deeply in love with each other.

Two very well-conceived scenes, "magical" in nature, raise the story above the usual tedium of this type of fantastic film.

First, Rabal and Velasco dine out in an elegant restaurant, whose decor and prices are unbelievably cheap—as they were one hundred years ago—while they celebrate and affirm their love. The next day, visiting the exact site of the restaurant, they discover a burnt-out building left in its place. Perhaps they dreamed the entire experience.

Francisco Rabal in *La hora bruja*.

The second interesting scene in the film takes place when the couple are showing the Richard Burton-Elizabeth Taylor version of *Cleopatra*. The sound system breaks down and Rabal and Velasco dub their own voices over the film, using a hand-held microphone. No one is the wiser since they know the dialogue by heart. Burton and Taylor take over the dialogue when the soundtrack is restored. But the couple have once again reaffirmed their love through the artifices of fantasy and nostalgia. With interesting "magical" touches like these, *La hora bruja* works its charm on us, giving Jaime de Arminan, its director, a minor but resounding success.

1985

EL CABALLERO DEL DRAGON (THE KNIGHT OF THE DRAGON)

DIRECTOR: FERNANDO COLOMO

CREDITS: Screenplay: Andreu Martin, Miguel Angel Nieto & Fernando Colomo; Color and CinemaScope Photography: Jose Luis Alcaine; Producer: Fernando Colomo for La Salamandra Films; Music: Jose Nieto.

CAST: Klaus Kinski (Boetius), Harvey Keitel (Clever), Fernando Rey (Friar Lupo), Maria Lamor (Alba), Julieta Serrano (Clothilde), Jose Vivo (The Count), Jose Maria Pou (The Green Knight), Carlos Tristancho (The Town Crier), Santiago Alvarez (The Tailor), and Miguel Bose ("IX").

COMMENTARY: With an amazing international cast and filmed in English, this

Maria Lamor, Miguel Bose, and Klaus Kinski in *El caballero del dragon.*

Fernando Colomo film is Spain's first equivalent of a "Star Wars"-type epic, complete with some thrilling (and quite costly) special effects and a terrific musical score by Jose Nieto that rivals John Williams' classic themes for America's innovative "Star Wars Trilogy."

The "plot" of this film is really convoluted, part Middle Ages knight-errant tale with appropriate love story involving a mute, but extraordinarily handsome, extraterrestrial played by Miguel Bose, in a "silent" role; part *Close Encounters of the Third Kind*-brand of science fiction, all revolving around the fight between the Knight and the dragon to save the princess, and the search for the philosopher's stone which gives eternal life. But, ultimately, the film is about the struggle between the forces of good and evil, with the inevitable happy ending. Bose marries the princess and the villains, Keitel and Rey, are lost in space, imprisoned eternally in a space ship that floats aimlessly around the universe.

The Knight of the Dragon has stunning production values, an excellent script that is as amusing as it is clever, but unfortunately it has not been shown outside of Europe. It deserves wider distribution. This first worthwhile sci-fi epic to come from Spain displays a new burst of creative energy in Spanish filmmaking.

1985

LOLA

DIRECTOR: JOSE JUAN BIGAS LUNA

CREDITS: Screenplay: Luis Herce, Jose Juan Bigas Luna & Enrique Viciano; Color and Panavision Photography: Jose Maria Civit; Producer: Enrique Viciano for Figaro Films; Music: Jose Manuel Pagan.

CAST: Angela Molina (Lola), Patrik Bauchau (Robert), Feodor Atkine (Mario), Assumpta Serna (Silvia), Angela Gutierrez (Ana), Constantino Romero (Alberto), Marian Rodes (Francoise), Pepa Lopez (Isabel), Maria Gonzales (Carmen).

COMMENTARY: Lola is a beautiful, uncultured girl who works in a shoe factory outside of Barcelona and has a tempestuous love affair with Mario, who constantly berates and sexually abuses her. Tired of being used by Mario, Lola leaves for Barcelona and meets Robert one evening in a local bar. They marry and the story continues five years later in Barcelona.

Lola is now living a comfortable bourgeois life and is the mother of a little girl, Ana. Meanwhile, Mario, who has been searching for his lover, meets Lola quite accidentally in the street, discovers her marriage, but wants to continue the affair, threatening to break up her family.

There is a unique and unexpected plot twist. It seems that Robert had been married in Paris and his ex-wife has hired Mario to pursue Lola and break-up the marriage. At one point, Mario enters Lola's apartment while her husband is on a business trip, tries to seduce her in the

Angela Molina and Feodor Atkine in *Lola*.

kitchen and accidentally stabs her to death in a fit of passion. Her husband unexpectedly returns the same evening and is accused of the murder, but Mario is caught when Robert's ex-wife meets with him to give him a cash pay-off for breaking up Robert's marriage.

At the conclusion, the young Ana, now a teenager, is swimming in a pool, attracting all the boys around her—a younger version of her mother, Lola—as her adoring father looks on. *Lola* is a fascinating film, filled with graphic sexual scenes, unexpected violence and disturbing psychological connotations. Lola, as played by Angela Molina, echoes the Marlene Dietrich vamp-siren of Von Sternberg's *The Blue Angel* of 1930, but without Dietrich's heartlessness.

Bigas Luna has made a well-paced, suspenseful thriller, imitative of some of his other films such as *Caniche* (*Poodle*), *Tatuaje* (*Tatoo*), *Reborn* and *Angustia* (*Anguish*), the last two made on location in Texas and California and filmed in English. Bigas Luna is searching for success outside of the Iberian peninsula and wants to be viewed as an "international director." While all his films border on the horror genre, *Lola* is the most Spanish and his most pathologically fascinating production.

1985

LUNA DE AGOSTO (AUGUST MOON)

DIRECTOR: JUAN MINON

CREDITS: Screenplay: Juan Minon; Color Photography: Miguel A. Trujillo; Producer: Juan Minon in collaboration with

Aiman Mechebal and Patricia Adriani in *Luna de agosto.*

RTVE (Spanish Television); Music: Juan C. Arranz.

CAST: Patricia Adriani (Ana), Aiman Mechebal (Gibran), Claudia Gravi (Yamila), Chema Munoz (Miguel), Maati Zaari (Abselan), Arraji Med Timod (a shepherd), Khalil Bel Aziz (a cousin), Savad Ferhati (mother), Jillali Ferhati (Ali), Rodolfo Poveda (the villain).

COMMENTARY: Beautifully filmed on location in the Moroccan cities of Marrakech, Tangiers, Ouzud, Todra and Onarzazate, *August Moon* is the story of a young Spanish woman, Ana, in search of her lover, Miguel, but also fond of exotic adventures.

Arriving during the month of Ramadan in Tangiers, she is greeted by Miguel's cosmopolitan co-worker Abselan, who tells of a letter pleading with Ana to meet Miguel in Marrakech. Miguel also left Ana instructions to pick up a "gift" he bought for her at a local antique shop. Put off by the entire situation, rather than returning to Spain by way of Gibraltar, Ana decides to continue her trip, picks up a silver amulet (Miguel's "gift") and begins her trek to Marrakech. Unbeknown to her, the amulet contains a supposedly valuable "jewel" and Ana is acting as Miguel's courier.

Since this is Ana's first visit to a third-world country, she travels quite inexpensively on local buses and meets a charming, wily thirteen-year-old boy, Gibran, who joins her on her journey. Many dangerous incidents take place on their way to Marrakech and Ana is distressed. When she finally meets Miguel, she discovers her unknown role as courier and hands over the "jewel," which turns out to be as worthless as Miguel, who had risked her life, exposing her to unknown dangers and possibly to death. Ana walks out on Miguel, grateful for her relationship with Gibran and with the realization they have developed a real friendship.

What makes *August Moon* so interesting is its locale: the desertscapes are beautiful to look at, and Patricia Adriani is sensitive and intelligent in an arduous role. Although the film suffers from being a bit overlong, and some of the arabic is not translated with titles, it is a very worthwhile feature from Juan Minon. This is only his second film, after making *Kargus* in 1981. *August Moon* may be a small mystery film, but its extensive use of foreign locations makes it an unusual experience.

1985

TRAS EL CRISTAL (IN A GLASS CAGE)

DIRECTOR: AGUSTIN VILLARONGA

CREDITS: Screenplay: Agustin Villaronga; Color Photography: Jaume Peracaula; Producer: Teresa Enrich for TEM Associates Productions; Music: Javier Navarrete.

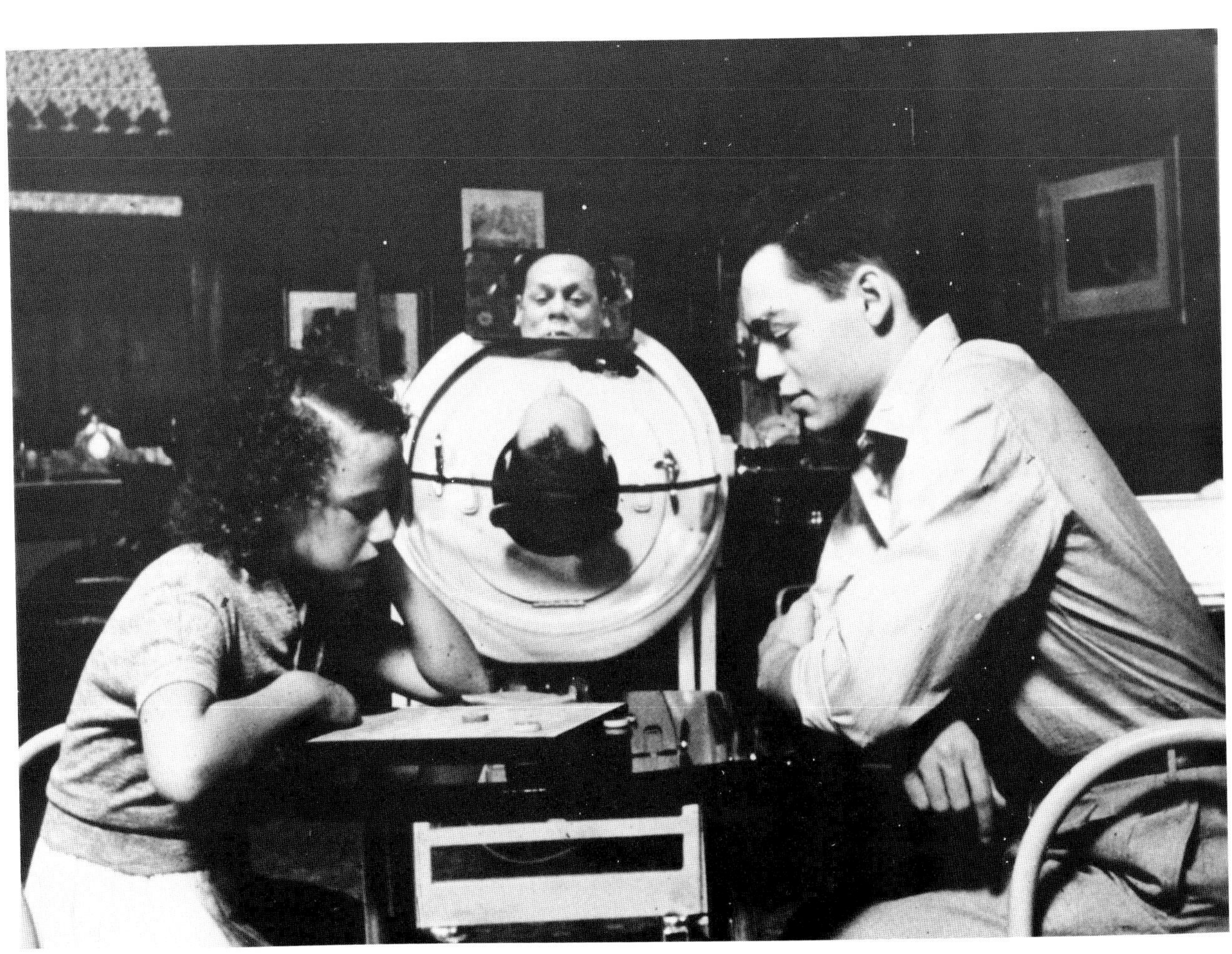

Gisela Echeverria, Gunter Meisner, and David Sust in *Tras el cristal.*

CAST: Gunter Meisner (Klaus), David Sust (Angel), Marisa Paredes (Griselda, Klaus' wife), Gisela Echeverria (Rena, their daughter).

COMMENTARY: Perhaps one of the most outrageous films ever made. Young Catalonian director and former set decorator Agustin Villaronga's debut, *Tras el cristal*, is really a wild, wild film.

The story concerns Klaus, a former Nazi medical officer who is now paralyzed and confined to an iron lung, living in exile in Barcelona with his wife and daughter. Klaus was involved with experiments carried out on children in concentration camps during World War II, "death" camps in reality, since Klaus performed his sadistic tortures on young boys who never survived the experiments. Klaus and his crimes against humanity are imprisoned within his "glass cage," his iron lung upon which his life depends.

A teenager named Angel enters the scene, deliberately coming to Klaus' home to take care of him, offering to serve as his nurse without pay. As the film progresses, we realize that Angel is one of the children who escaped from Klaus' tortures. Seeking vengeance, Angel first kills Klaus' wife in a very grisly and nasty scene, and later, two young boys (one by injecting fluid into the heart and another by slitting his throat). Angel has now become the "torturer," masturbating on Klaus to humiliate him and forcing him to commit fellatio. Wresting Klaus out of the respirator, Angel leaves him to die while finding his own suicidal resting place in the respirator.

The atmosphere in this film is claustrophobic, fierce, suspenseful, visceral. In a flashback at the conclusion, we learn that Angel was forced to perform fellatio on the doctor in the prison camp. The film is full of horror and its chilling conclusion is controversial. Villaronga's latest film, *Moon Boy* (1989), is another beautifully made, surrealistically-styled, visually fascinating work that is likely to provoke as much controversy as his debut film.

1986

TATA MIA (NURSEMAID MINE aka NANNY DEAR)

DIRECTOR: JOSE LUIS BORAU

CREDITS: Screenplay: Jose Luis Borau; Color Photography: Teo Escamilla; Producer: Jose Luis Borau for Profilmar/El Iman Films in collaboration with RTVE (Spanish Television); Music: Jacobo Duran-Lorgia.

CAST: Imperio Argentina (Tata), Alfredo Landa (Teo), Carmen Maura (Elvira), Xabier Elorriaga (Peter), Miguel Rellan (Alberto), Marisa Paredes (Paloma), Julieta Serrano (Magda).

COMMENTARY: A sentimental choice for one of the better films of the eighties, *Tata*

Imperio Argentina and Carmen Maura in *Tata mia.*

mia brings back to the screen the formidable singing star of the 1930s, Imperio Argentina, in a role tailor-made for her by director Jose Luis Borau.

In this feather-light comedy, the plot concerns the daughter (Maura) of a famous Spanish Civil War general; she has spent the last thirteen years in a convent and suddenly decides to come back into the world, convincing her nanny (lovingly played by Imperio Argentina) to accompany her back to Madrid.

There are several sub-plots, one involving an English historian (Elorriaga) who will do anything to obtain Maura's father's memoirs, another involving Maura's sexual yearnings for the historian and her final surrender to her brother/cousin/uncle (played by a restrained Alfredo Landa) in the film's final fadeout.

Borau is fond of taking pot-shots at the old "sacred" targets: Franco fascists, Maura's aristocratic family, the church, the military, the establishment. The film is beautifully mounted, some of it made on location in the province of Aragon. Imperio Argentina, looking remarkably well-preserved, sings only one song, a *jota,* but rekindles our memories of her greatest roles of the thirties in *Nobleza baturra* and *Morena clara*. When *Tata mia* played the Third Spanish Film Festival in New York in 1987, its genteel political critiques and mellifluous tone were warmly received. Although its director has not made a feature film in several years, he is currently working on some short documentaries dealing with Moorish influences in the art and architecture of Aragon, his home province.

1986

LA MITAD DEL CIELO (HALF OF HEAVEN)

DIRECTOR: MANUEL GUTIERREZ ARAGON

CREDITS: Screenplay: Manuel Gutierrez Aragon & Luis Megino; Color Photography: Jose Luis Alcaine; Producer: Luis Megino; Music: Milladoirio.

CAST: Angela Molina (Rosa), Margarita Lozano (Grandmother), Antonio V. Valero (Juan), Nacho Martinez (Delgado), Santiago Ramos (Antonio), Francisco Merino (Ramiro), Monica Molina (young Rosa), Carolina Silva (Don Pedro), Fernando Fernan Gomez (Don Pedro), Enriqueta Carballeria (Rosa's sister), and a cast of forty.

COMMENTARY: As the pressbook declares, "This is a story of working class ambition intertwined with old world mystery and superstition." *Half of Heaven* is an overlong tale about a girl from Santander, Rosa, who makes a success in Madrid, first as a wet-nurse, then as an owner of a stall, selling fish in a local market, then as a high-class restaurateur.

Her love life is equally interesting. In Santander she is plunged into an unfortunate love affair with a handsome *filadero* (knife-sharpener), who later dies in jail. Warned against this relationship by her grandmother, who has prophetic powers, Rosa takes her illegitimate daughter Olvido (who has magical psychic powers) to the big city of Madrid. Through her charms and guts, she rises from market vendor to be the proud owner of a respectable restaurant, helped along the way by Juan, a young student, and Don Pedro, a respected city politician and head of the Supermarket Division. The two men are also competitors for Rosa's love, but Rosa is determined to heed the call of ambition rather than romance. Juan marries, but keeps Rosa as his mistress, while she continues her long-standing affair with Don Pedro.

Antonio Valero, Angela Molina, and Fernando Fernan Gomez in *La mitad del cielo*.

The only jarring note in the film is the grandmother's tendency to prophesy and the continuation of this tradition with Rosa's daughter. Also, the grandmother re-appears during the film after her death, leaving viewers to speculate about the director's intentions in using this lyrical "ghostly" metaphor.

Nevertheless, the film is beautifully photographed and deserved its Academy Award nomination in the Best Foreign Language Film category of 1986. It had a fairly profitable run in New York City and is one of the few, very good Spanish films available on videocassette.

1986

MATADOR

DIRECTOR: PEDRO ALMODOVAR

CREDITS: Screenplay: Jesus Ferrero & Pedro Almodovar; Color Photography: Angel Luis Fernandez; Producer: Andres Vicente Gomez, with the collaboration of RTVE (Spanish Television) and the Ministry of Culture; Music: Bernardo Bonezzi.

CAST: Assumpta Serna (Maria, the lawyer), Antonio Banderas (Angel, her client), Nacho Martinez (Diego, the matador), Eva Cobo (Eva, his girlfriend), Julieta Serrano (Berta, Angel's mother), Chus Lampreave (Pilar, Eva's mother), Carmen Maura (Julia, the psychiatrist), Eusebio Poncela (the police detective), Bibi Andersen (the transvestite flower-seller), Jaime Chavarri (the priest), Agustin Almodovar (a TV announcer).

COMMENTARY: Even more outlandish than Villaronga's *Tras el cristal.* Almodovar has seized upon a quote by Yukio Mishima ("Violent death is always the ultimate beauty, especially when you die young") and created a screenplay which is zanier and more iconoclastic than his earlier films.

A fascinating and sensational piece of filmmaking, *Matador* opens with Assumpta Serna mounted on top of a Spanish stud, bringing him to orgasm as she takes a huge hairpin and plunges it into his neck, killing him instantly.

After this sensational opening scene the plot becomes somewhat convoluted. Serna (Maria) is a successful lawyer who is defending a supposed "serial" murderer in Madrid who just happens to kill his victims in the same manner she does. Maria discovers through her client's psychic powers that it is the former bullfighter Diego who is killing women this way.

She is attracted by this "matador," and they meet, fall in love and decide to share their ideal of death in orgasm by killing each other in a hide-a-way cabin outside of the city. (There is an amusing film-within-a-film scene, when Diego has followed Maria to a cinema in Madrid, and they stand watching the conclusion of *Duel in the Sun,* where Jennifer Jones and Gregory Peck shoot each other and then crawl

Nacho Martinez and Assumpta Serna in *Matador.*

miles over rocky terrain to finally die in each other's arms.)

Antonio Banderas, who plays Maria's client, is also, co-incidentally, Diego's student, enrolled in a bullfighting school Diego owns. He predicts the fatal tryst of the lovers. As the police race to prevent the double-suicide, Diego and Maria kill each other in orgasmic ecstasy, he with a knife, she with a revolver in her mouth.

Even with expressly heterosexual scenes, Almodovar still makes his "gay" sensibility felt. He always appears in his films, as either a television impresario or film director, critical of Spain and its mores. *Matador* is a total send-up of heterosexuality and the bullfight!

1986

EL ANO DE LAS LUCES (THE YEAR OF THE AWAKENING)

DIRECTOR: FERNANDO TRUEBA

CREDITS: Screenplay: Rafael Azcona & Fernando Trueba; Color & Cinemascope Photography: Juan Amoros; Producer: Andres Vicente Gomez; Music: Francisco Guerrero.

CAST: Jorge Sanz (Manolo), Maribel Verdu (Maria Jesus), Manuel Alexandre (Emilio), Rafaela Aparicio (Rafaela), Chus Lampreave (Transito), Veronica Forque (Irene), Lucas Martin (Jesus), Santiago Ramos (Pepe), Violeta Cela (Vicenta), Jose Sazatornil, "Saza" (Don Teodulo, the priest).

COMMENTARY: This film is an unexpected surprise from the director who began his career on a shoestring with *Opera prima* in 1980. *El ano de las luces* is a large-scale production, shot with panoramic lenses, in gorgeous color. It defi-

Maribel Verdu and Jorge Sanz in *El ano de las luces.*

nitely belongs in the category of "traditional" realist filmmaking, something I thought Trueba was incapable of. Gone is the effervescence and spontaneity of his early films, to be replaced by establishment production values.

The Year of the Awakening is a delightfully tame story about two brothers, sons of a "fallen" soldier in the Spanish Civil War, who are shipped off to a children's tuberculosis sanitarium situated on the Spanish-Portugese border in 1940. The "awakening" is that of Manolo's sexual awareness at age sixteen and his discovery of women through nightly peeping-tom adventures. Eventually some of his fantasies become realities and he truly falls in love with a young nurse, Maria Jesus. They have a short idyll until they are discovered and the girl is sent back home and Manolo is forced to return to Madrid.

The film is sensitive, well-acted, touching and nostalgic, in the same mold as *Summer of '42,* where sexual enlightenment and loss of innocence are the key experiences. There is some mocking humor of the sacred Spanish institutions—the church, marriage, the civil-service mentality, the army—but none of it is very memorable. If the film is slightly boring, it is because we know what stuff the director, Trueba, is made of; he could easily have transformed this tale, full of clichés into the tight, iconoclastic, outrageous film he is capable of producing. While a worthy successor to all those period films made in the seventies, like *Retrato de familia* by Gimenez Rico and *Tormento* by Pedro Olea, *El ano de las luces* seems like a beautifully-mounted anachronism for a truly hip director like Trueba in the eighties.

1987

LA LEY DEL DESEO (LAW OF DESIRE)

DIRECTOR: PEDRO ALMODOVAR

CREDITS: Screenplay: Pedro Almodovar; Color Photography: Angel Luis Fernandez; Producer: Miguel A. Perez Campos, for an El Deseo & Laurenfilm production; Music: Source music from Stravinsky, Ravel; Songs: "Lo dudo" (Los Panchos) and "Dejame recordar" (Bola de nieve), among several others.

CAST: Eusebio Poncela (Pablo Quintero, the film director), Carmen Maura (Tina, his transvestite sister), Antonio Banderas (Antonio, Pablo's jealous lover), Miguel Molina (Juan, another of Pablo's lovers), Manuela Velasco (Ada, Tina's adopted child), Bibi Andersen (Ada's real mother), Fernando Guillen (a police inspector), Nacho Martinez (a doctor), Helga Line (Antonio's mother).

COMMENTARY: This film could never have been made in Spain until after Franco's death, or as artfully, but for the pop, gay, audacious sensibility of its director, Pedro Almodovar. For Almodovar, the idea of Franco or censorship in films never existed. *Law of Desire* is one of the most uninhibited films depicting the swinging Madrid scene of 1987, where sniffing cocaine, homosexual couplings, transvestism, nudity and violence are rife. It is a pre-AIDS film.

The story concerns Pablo, a gay film director who is madly in love with Juan, a barkeeper working on the coast in Andalucia. Pablo, however, meets Antonio one night at a gay club and they become lovers. In one daring nude scene, depicting a lingering homosexual kiss, Pablo beds and fornicates with the uninitiated Antonio. The latter, after an evening's pleasure, inadvertently picks up a letter from Juan, Pablo's vacationing lover.

Extremely jealous of anyone who possesses Pablo, Antonio visits Juan one evening and murders him, throwing him off a cliff after plying him with a bottle of liquor. When Pablo discovers Juan's death, he is extremely upset and drives to see Antonio. Suspecting the truth behind Juan's death, Pablo is seriously injured as his car strikes a tree.

Meanwhile, the police suspect Pablo of Juan's murder. It is at this point that Pablo's sister announces she has a new boyfriend, who is attentive and really in love with her. Pablo innocently asks his name, and realizes this is the same "Antonio" who murdered Juan. Fearing that Tina's life is in danger, Pablo telephones and asks her to leave her apartment. But Antonio threatens to kill her unless he can spend one hour with Pablo before he gives himself up to the police. Pablo agrees and the two men make love in a final tryst before Antonio commits suicide. Pablo, overcome with grief, has come to love Juan's murderer, and has now lost two lovers tragically.

Antonio Banderas and Eusebio Poncela in *La ley del deseo.*

It is difficult to end a film with a scenario as daring as this in a satisfactory way. We see Pablo flinging his typewriter off Tina's balcony: it was Pablo's duplicity and misuse of the written word that precipitated the deaths of Pablo's two lovers.

The performances of all the men, especially Poncela, Banderas and Molina, are excellent. Carmen Maura lends some intelligence and comic relief to the difficult role of Pablo's transvestite sister, who was originally seduced by their father and whose life had been a great trauma ever since.

She has one uninhibited scene when she asks a sanitation worker to turn a huge hose of water on her (forgetting the phallic symbolism) as he cleans the streets, wetting her down completely on a sweltering evening in Madrid. Maura demonstrates her sensuality, her abandon, her freedom to enjoy the "pure" hedonistic moment.

Law of Desire is a very well-directed film, under Almodovar's expert control. Its portrait of post-Franco Madrid—gay sex and cocaine-sniffing in discos open till early morning—is as outrageous as it is accurate. And Almodovar, with his wonderful sense of humor, his campiness, his use of pop art and pastiche, makes it all work. He is, ultimately, an outrageous narcissist and *Law of Desire*, with all of it convolutions of style, is the ultimate fantasy, narcissism.

His 1990 production, *Atame* (*Tie Me Up, Tie Me Down*), promises more of the same, but this time in the realm of sado-masochism. Almodovar is the most uninhibited Spanish film director I have met; he stays clear of pornography, but deliciously enjoys his freedom.

1987

ASIGNATURA APROBADA (COURSE COMPLETED aka PASSING THE COURSE)

DIRECTOR: JOSE LUIS GARCI

CREDITS: Screenplay: Jose Luis Garci & Horacio Valcarcel; Color and Cinemascope Photography: Manuel Rojas; Producer: Jose Luis Garci for Nickel/Odeon/Dos Films; Music: Jesus Gluck.

CAST: Jesus Puente (Jose Manuel Alcantara, actor/playwright), Victoria Vera (Elena, his wife), Teresa Gimpera (Lola, his former girlfriend), Eduardo Hoyo (Edi, his son), Pastor Serrador, Manuel Lorenzo, Santiago Amon and others.

COMMENTARY: Filmed in Gijon, *Asignatura aprobada* tells the story of Jesus Puente, who leaves Madrid for Gijon, fed up with acting, playwriting and his wife of twenty-five years, Elena. Depressed and burnt-out because none of his new plays have had any success, Jesus returns to northern Spain, seeking happiness in the past.

However, he is not left alone to dwell in his reclusive state. A former girlfriend and actress, Lola, driving a new Porsche and with a twenty-one-year-old lover in tow,

Eduardo Hoyo and Jesus Puente in *Asignatura aprobada*.

asks his advice about her life-style. Depressed and abandoned, and unable to resolve her problems by seeking consolation from her former lover, she drives over a nearby cliff to her death.

Jesus' son, Edi, a rock singer-composer, turns up next, completely out of the blue and bringing his own problems. Edi has contracted AIDS. His father is sympathetic, as is his mother, who later visits Gijon to try to reconcile with Jesus. Edi's illness is handled off-screen, as is the "reconciliation" scene between Jesus and Elena after ten years of separation.

What makes *Asignatura aprobada* fascinating is its attempt to place the problem of AIDS victims on the screen, something which goes against the very grain (and *machismo*) of most Spaniards. *Asignatura* is Spain's first AIDS-problem film but, curiously, Spain's only Oscar award-winning director ducks confrontation with the problems involved and is content merely to show the emotional disenchantment, sorrow and pain the illness has brought upon the parents. The film turns nostalgic in its attempt to make despair and hopelessness viable qualities of life for the generation of men and women who reach the age of fifty and beyond. Whatever its failures as a film, philosophically speaking, *Asignatura aprobada* is beautifully photographed and acted, and presents an accurate, if somewhat downbeat portrait of contemporary Spanish society of the late eighties.

1988

BERLIN BLUES

DIRECTOR: RICARDO FRANCO

CREDITS: Screenplay: Ricardo Franco & Lawrence Dworet; Color Photography: Teo Escamilla; Producer: Emiliano Piedra; Music: Lalo Schifrin; Songs & Lyrics: Lalo Schifrin & Mark Mueller.

CAST: Julia Migenes (Lola), Keith Baxter (Prof. Hossler), Jose Coronado (David), Javier Gurruchaga (Micky), Gerardo Vera (Bauer), with Jesus Lopez Cobo, Mereia Ross, Jose Maria Pon & Maximiliano Reuthelein. Filmed on location in Berlin with an English soundtrack.

COMMENTARY: *Berlin Blues* is a romantic love story starring the extraordinary actress-opera singer Julia Migenes playing the role of Lola, a pop-music performer who works in the trendy club called Berlin Blues.

An American expatriate, Lola meets and falls in love with David Zimmerman, a young German concert pianist who defects from the Eastern zone while on a concert tour. The orchestra director, Professor Hossler, however, will not accept David's defection, but soon falls under Lola's spell.

Forcing David to return to East Germany, the professor himself decides to stay in the West because of the siren Lola. They move in together, and when Lola loses her job at "Berlin Blues" because an American serviceman is stabbed in a brawl, Hossler urges Lola into an operatic career. Hossler runs out of money and decides he must return to the Eastern zone despite Lola and her sexual enticements.

The film ends happily for all the protagonists, but also somewhat ruefully. Lola has become an opera star; David has cast aside his concert career to be a "rock" idol, and Hossler returns to the East after having known the charms of Lola. She claims she will always be faithful to him only.

Keith Baxter as Hossler gives a brilliant performance as an older man (aging conductor) whose flame burns brightly when kindled by the young siren Lola. There are

Julia Migenes and Keith Baxter in *Berlin Blues.*

echoes of Marlene Dietrich's *The Blue Angel* here in Julia Migenes' portrayal of Lola. Her Lola is a dynamic singer and a sexy presence on screen. Audiences may remember her in Francesco Rossi's version of Bizet's *Carmen,* where she literally chewed up the scenery and so thoroughly seduced Placido Domingo in the role of Don Jose that the poor man had no chance to escape his fate. Julia Migenes exhibits the same kind of raw emotional power and frank sexuality on the screen in Ricardo Franco's *Berlin Blues.*

It is a fascinating film, and with its English soundtrack, you would not recognize it as a Spanish production. As Spanish cinema moves into the decade of the nineties, international actors, co-productions and "universal" themes are becoming the rule.

1988

REMANDO AL VIENTO (ROWING WITH THE WIND)

DIRECTOR: GONZALO SUAREZ

CREDITS: Screenplay: Gonzalo Suarez; Color Photography: Carlos Suarez; Producer: Andres Vicente Gomez for Ditirambo/Viking Films (Norway); Music: Alejandro Masso, based upon themes of Vaughn-Williams. Filmed on location in Norway.

CAST: Hugh Grant (Lord Byron), Lizzy McInnerny (Mary Shelley), Valentine Pelka (Percy Bysshe Shelley), Elizabeth Hurley (Claire Clairmont), Jose Luis Gomez (Polidori), Virginia Mataix (Elisa), Ronan Vibert (Fletcher).

COMMENTARY: *Remando al viento* is a beautifully made film by a Spanish director, Gonzalo Suarez, transcending the boundaries of Iberia once again in order to bring to the screen a distinctly English subject—the lives and loves of Byron and Shelley. Beautifully photographed on Norwegian and Spanish locations, the film is excellently acted by the entire cast. It is also very frank in its depiction of male and female nudity.

The entire film is a flashback in the mind of Mary Shelley, who remembers her first meetings with her wild poet-lover-husband Percy, her elopement to Switzerland where they met Lord Byron and his unstable personal physician, Polidori, who made advances towards her and then committed suicide. But most of all, she remembers one historic night in November 1816 when, gathering around the fire, she told her most inspired story, the birth of the Frankenstein monster.

Frankenstein appears as a character within the film and at the film's conclusion is out of control. Mary Shelley feels he caused the death of her son (as well as Byron's daughter) and Byron urges her to courageously free herself from this creature and her own destiny by killing him off.

Poster art for *Remando al viento*.

Mary Shelley recalls all this: the orgies, the bon mots of Byron, the wry comments of Shelley, their extravagances, Shelley's inability to swim, Byron's intention to fight for Greek freedom, and her growing obsession that the Frankenstein monster had been causing all the tragedies in her life.

As her ship makes its way through the frozen wastes of the North Pole, Mary Shelley sets all this down on paper. The resultant film, *Rowing with the Wind,* is a wonderfully evocative literary creation of the tragic events in Mary Shelley's life. One of the best films to come from Spain, it was originally made in English and on foreign locations. It is another of those Spanish films that approaches "universal" themes and has international commercial possibilities because it is atypical, very different from the usual Spanish production.

1988

MUJERES AL BORDE DE UN ATAQUE DE NERVIOS (WOMEN ON THE EDGE OF A NERVOUS BREAKDOWN)

DIRECTOR: PEDRO ALMODOVAR

CREDITS: Screenplay: Pedro Almodovar; Color Photography: Jose Luis Alcaine; Producer: Agustin Almodovar for El Deseo/Lauren Films; Music: Bernardo Bonezzi; Songs: "Soy infeliz" sung by Lola Beltran, "Puro teatro" sung by La Lupe.

CAST: Carmen Maura (Pepa Marcos), Fernando Guillen (Ivan, her lover), Julieta Serrano (Lucia, Ivan's former mistress), Antonio Banderas (Carlos, Ivan & Lucia's illegitimate son), Maria Barranco (Can-

Antonio Banderas, Maria Barranco, and Carmen Maura (*partial face*) on the set of *Mujeres al borde de un ataque de nervios.*

dela, Pepa's friend), Rossi Von Donna (Marisa), Kitty Manver (Paulina), Loles Leon (Cristina), Chus Lampreave (janitress), Wili Montesinos (a "gay" cab driver), Jose Antonio Navarro (policeman), Agustin Almodovar (real estate officeholder), Imanol Uribe (messenger), and others.

COMMENTARY: If this film has any place in the history of Spanish cinema, it may well be as one of the most irreverent films ever made as well as the most lucrative at the Spanish box office. It is also Almodovar's most controlled film to date.

Its plot is somewhat convoluted but it reduces to this: Carmen Maura plays Pepa, pregnant and jilted by her lover, Ivan, for another woman, a mutual friend who happens to be a lawyer. Meanwhile, Ivan's former lover of twenty years, Lucia, who has spent most of her youth in a mental institution and has had an illegitimate son by him named Carlos, seeks revenge and shows up at Pepa's apartment. So does Carlos, who seeks to rent it. Pepa refuses to tell Lucia that Ivan is at Madrid's airport, but hurriedly takes a cab herself to warn Ivan of Lucia's threats. Lucia follows the "Mambo" cab, piloted by a "gay" taxi driver (one of the running sight gags throughout the film), and tries to kill Ivan, but she is stopped by Pepa who wrestles her to the ground with gun in hand. Ivan, now indebted to Pepa, decides to return to her, but Pepa realizes that life alone is better than life with him. The end.

The film boasts excellent performances and beautiful photography, but its sight gags and satirical jibes at the media are worth the price of admission alone. Pepa is a professional actress-dubber, as is Ivan. We watch them dub some terrific love scenes together although their tender emotions for each other are elsewhere.

There is also a hilarious ad for a new soap product in which Maura plays the mother of a psychopath son who has just bloodied his shirt after slaughtering several people. Maura pops the shirt into the washing machine with the new soap product as the police come by looking for evidence. Voila! A perfectly clean shirt, spotless, pops out of the washer—one of the many uproariously funny sight gags in the film.

Although the film does have some dull stretches, Maura's performance and those of Almodovar's "stock company" of actors make *Women on the Edge of a Nervous Breakdown* an international winner for 1988. It was nominated for Best Foreign Film at the 1989 Academy Awards but lost to Bille August's magnificently poignant drama, *Pelle, the Conqueror,* with a stunning performance by Max Von Sydow.

Women on the Edge of a Nervous Breakdown is now entering its second year at a Broadway cinema in New York City, a long (and well deserved) run for any foreign film.

SELECTED BIBLIOGRAPHY

Besas, Peter. *Behind the Spanish Lens. Spanish Cinema Under Fascism & Democracy*. Denver, CO: Arden Press, 1985.

Caparros-Lera, J. M. & Espana, Rafael de. *The Spanish Cinema: A Historical Approach*. Austin, TX: University of Texas Press, 1987.

Garcia Fernandez, Emilio C. *Historia Ilustrada del Cine Español*. Barcelona: Editorial Planeta, 1985.

Higginbotham, Virginia. *Spanish Film Under Franco*. Austin, TX: University of Texas Press, 1987.

Hopewell, John. *Out of the Past: Spanish Cinema after Franco*. London: British Film Institute, 1986.

Larraz, Emmanuel. *Le cinéma espagnol des origines à nos jours*. Paris: Editions du Cerf, 1986.

Luhr, William, ed. *World Cinema Since 1945*. New York: Frederick Ungar, 1987.

Menendez-Leite, Francisco, Jr. *Historia del Cine Español en 100 Películas*. Madrid: Guia del Ocio, 1986.

Saenz Plaza, Placido. *Retratos fotográficos de directores de cine*. Madrid: Ministry of Culture, 1988.

Sanchez, J. R. *50 anos de Cine Español*. Madrid: Ministerio de Cultura, 1985.

Schwartz, Ronald. *Spanish Film Directors (1950–1985): 21 Profiles*. Metuchen, NJ: Scarecrow Press, 1986.

INDEX

Note: Only major film titles and directors discussed in the main text and the appendix appear here. Italicized page numbers refer to photographs.

ABOUT THE AUTHOR

Ronald Schwartz (B.A. Brooklyn College; A.M., Ph.D., U. of Connecticut) is Professor of Romance Languages and Film at City University of New York (Kingsborough) and Lecturer at the New School for Social Research. He has published *Jose Maria Gironella* (1972), *Spain's New Wave Novelists* (1976), *Nomads, Exiles & Emigres* (1980), and *Spanish Film Directors* (1986); all but the first were published by Scarecrow Press. He received several PSC-CUNY Travel Grants for research on those volumes and is presently writing on Latin American cinema and *film noir*.

Dr. Schwartz teaches courses on Spanish, French, and Latin American cinema, as well as on Film Noir, and has conducted seminars on the films of Luis Buñuel. He is a member of both the CUNY Film Faculty and its Council on Foreign Language Study, where he has presented papers on the the use of film in the design and development of foreign-language courses at City University and elsewhere. He recently read a paper on Almodovar and Borau, two seminal film directors, at the first national Conference on Spanish Film at Clark University (Worcester, Massachusetts) in April 1991. He makes his home with his wife on Manhattan's Upper West Side.